Provocative Women's Filmmaking

Authorship and Art Cinema

Janice Loreck

EDINBURGH
University Press

Edinburgh University Press is one of the leading university presses in the UK. We publish academic books and journals in our selected subject areas across the humanities and social sciences, combining cutting-edge scholarship with high editorial and production values to produce academic works of lasting importance. For more information visit our website: edinburghuniversitypress.com

© Janice Loreck, 2023, 2024

Edinburgh University Press Ltd
13 Infirmary Street Edinburgh
EH1 1LT

First published in hardback by Edinburgh University Press 2023

Typeset in Monotype Ehrhardt by
Manila Typesetting Company
A CIP record for this book is available from the British Library

ISBN 978 1 4744 8349 0 (hardback)
ISBN 978 1 4744 8350 6 (paperback)
ISBN 978 1 4744 8351 3 (webready PDF)
ISBN 978 1 4744 8352 0 (epub)

The right of Janice Loreck to be identified as author of this work has been asserted in accordance with the Copyright, Designs and Patents Act 1988 and the Copyright and Related Rights Regulations 2003 (SI No. 2498).

Contents

List of Figures	iv
Acknowledgements	v
Introduction	1
1. Sexuality and Obscenity: From Catherine Breillat to Lisa Aschan	24
2. On Not Looking Away: Rape in the Films of Jennifer Kent and Isabella Eklöf	52
3. The Provocations of the Pretty: The Films of Lucile Hadžihalilović	79
4. Pursuing Transgression: Claire Denis's Taboo Intimacies	100
5. Posing as an Innocent: Irony, Sincerity and Anna Biller	121
6. Vaguely Disturbing: Humour in the Films of Athina Rachel Tsangari	143
Conclusion	166
Filmography	176
Bibliography	181
Index	197

Figures

All images are the author's own screenshots

1.1	The woman poses for the man in *Anatomy of Hell*	35
1.2	Sara admires her leopard-print bikini in *She Monkeys*	42
2.1	Michael responds aggressively to Sascha before assaulting her in *Holiday*	64
2.2	Clare sings for the local military detachment in *The Nightingale*	68
3.1	A painterly landscape in *Innocence*	87
3.2	The girls exchange coloured hair ribbons in *Innocence*	93
4.1	Monte cares for baby Willow in *High Life*	110
4.2	Monte's face in sensuous close-up in *High Life*	115
5.1	Barbi relaxes in her aqua-tiled bathroom in *Viva*	127
5.2	The depiction of Barbi's orgasm pays direct homage to *Camille 2000*	132
6.1	Marina and Bella kiss in the opening scene of *Attenberg*	149
6.2	The women dance to 'A Horse With No Name' in *The Capsule*	157

Acknowledgements

The ideas in this book developed over several years. I therefore have many people to thank for their stimulating conversation, enthusiasm and feedback. I am grateful to my colleagues at Curtin University who attended my first research presentation on this topic and who generously shared their knowledge with me on that occasion. I also extend my thanks to my colleagues at the University of Melbourne for their support in the years it took to write this book. I am grateful to the members of my writing group in Screen and Cultural Studies who provided me with encouragement and motivation in the final few months of writing.

I extend my warm thanks to Melanie Ashe for her extensive research assistance on this project. I am also very grateful to Belinda Glynn, not only for copyediting this manuscript, but for her advice and guidance. The team at Edinburgh University Press have also been most helpful in their professionalism, and I appreciate the useful and encouraging feedback from the anonymous reviewer who read the first draft of this book. I also extend my appreciation to the School of Culture and Communication at the University of Melbourne for providing financial support in preparing this manuscript for publication.

I am also indebted to several people who have encouraged this project through their friendship, support and solidarity. My warmest gratitude goes to Kirsten Stevens, Sian Mitchell, Whitney Monaghan and Joseph Walton. Lastly, I sincerely thank my family: Thomas, Lyn, Catherine, Daniel and Helen Loreck.

Introduction

Critics regularly use the term 'provocateur' and its cognates – rabble-rouser, incendiary, *enfant terrible*, mischief-maker – to describe directors working in narrative art cinema. Most individuals who attract this term are men. Luis Buñuel, Bernardo Bertolucci, Gaspar Noé, Lars von Trier and Michael Haneke, to list some of the more commonly cited names, far outnumber the women whom critics define in terms of their challenging, divisive auteurism. On one hand, this is not unexpected. Given that the discourses of film criticism ascribe the title of auteur far less frequently to women than to men, it makes sense that fewer women are labelled provocative auteurs.

On the other hand, it is, in fact, surprising. Women have a long and rich history of provocative art practice, and there are abundant examples of controversial work by women throughout the art world. In literature, the works of Valerie Solanas, Kathy Acker and Monique Wittig challenge readers with their incendiary, frank and radical writing. In the visual arts, Judy Chicago, Cindy Sherman, Carolee Schneemann and Tracey Emin all caused memorable stirs with their installation work and photography. Popular music has produced a heterogeneous variety of female provocateurs. A particularly striking and consequential example occurred in 2012, when Russian authorities arrested members of the punk group Pussy Riot and charged them with hooliganism following a performance in the Cathedral of Christ the Saviour in Moscow. Women artists are thus no strangers to controversy. It follows that women should be making provocative art films as well, and, indeed, auteurs from Věra Chytilová to Jennifer Kent, Liliana Cavani to Lucile Hadžihalilović, have produced transgressive narrative features that divide audiences and shock critics. Yet despite these clear examples of women who confront and challenge their recipients, the methods and meanings of women's filmic provocation has yet to be directly addressed.

Provocative auteurs have long been a feature of art cinema, beginning with the early avant-garde works by Luis Buñuel *An Andalusian Dog* (*Un chien andalou*, 1929) and *The Golden Age* (*L'Âge d'Or*, 1930), extending to the European art films of the 1970s and 1980s such as Pier Paolo Pasolini's *Salò, or the 120 Days of Sodom* (*Salò o le 120 giornate di Sodoma*, 1975) and Andrzej Żuławski's *On the Silver Globe* (*Na srebrnym globie*, 1988) to contemporary controversial films like Sandra Wollner's *The Trouble with Being Born* (2020). While never absent from cinema culture entirely, the provocateur has been particularly visible since the late 1990s in accordance with a distinct trend towards transgressive filmmaking in the European art cinema of the late twentieth and early twenty-first centuries.[1] This trend goes by many names, most infamously as the 'New Extremity' in line with James Quandt's renowned article on the topic.[2] The concepts *cinéma du corps*, *cinéma brut* and the cinema of sensation also refer to many of the same works. As Mattias Frey observes, this trend towards boundary-pushing cinema is in fact an intrinsic and longstanding part of art cinema as an institution.[3] Such transgressive filmmaking also links with the tendency for some art cinema directors to actively cultivate reputations as rabble-rousers. Filmmakers such as Noé, von Trier and Haneke 'continually project and confirm their identity as a boundary-breaking, radical artist in interviews and media performances'.[4] A notable example of this is von Trier's appearance at the 2014 Berlin International Film Festival wearing a T-shirt that read 'Persona Non Grata'. The stunt referenced his banning from the Cannes Film Festival in 2011 after he jokingly said that he sympathised with Adolf Hitler. Haneke has also publicly acknowledged and embraced the challenging nature of his filmmaking:

> I would like to be recognized for making an obscenity ... In my definition, anything that could be termed obscene departs from the bourgeois norm. Whether concerned with sexuality or violence or another taboo issue, anything that breaks with the norm is obscene. Insofar as truth is always obscene, I hope that all of my films have at least an element of obscenity.[5]

French 'art-porn provocateur' Catherine Breillat has also made comments that seemingly embrace the negative feelings she generates in audiences, stating: 'All true artists are hated ... Only conformists are ever adored.'[6] The provocateur is thus a longstanding feature of cinema that continues into the new millennium. It is a version of an auteur identity that both endures as a concept and also proves still useful for some directors.

Combined with the presence of provocative women artists in other fields, this persistence of the film provocateur raises an important question: how do women directors participate in the tradition of provocation in narrative art cinema? There are several reasons why this question is both necessary and important. In the domain of film scholarship, women auteurs have been the subject of ongoing interest to researchers for some decades.[7] This has also extended to broader public attention on women's filmmaking. Recent activist initiatives such as the 5050x2020 campaign, the Women's Production Group's establishment of the TIME'S UP Foundation, and the Women in Film and Television 'Sausage Party' protest movement have all highlighted the comparative lack of participation of women directors in the film industry. Such ongoing emphasis on women auteurs both allows and invites investigation into the female provocateur as a counterpart to the male rabble-rouser. Furthermore, an investigation into women's filmic provocations is needed to counteract an ongoing gendering of provocation as a hypermasculine author–recipient relationship. As this book shall address in detail, the discourses of philosophy and film criticism characterise provocation as an active and aggressive attack against a passive and therefore symbolically feminised spectator. To cite one example, Michael Haneke once famously said he is trying to 'rape the viewer into independence' through his confronting films.[8] While men, women and non-binary people can all commit and experience rape, the effect of such metaphoric language is clearly a masculinisation of provocation that symbolically excludes women.

A cursory look at film history also reveals that there are indeed many provocative women working as directors in cinema as well as numerous films by women that confront, generate negative emotions and spark debate. Although list-making is not a neutral activity – Elena Gorfinkel observes that lists always exclude and establish hierarchies[9] – a short and non-hierarchical list is illustrative here. Lois Weber's *Hypocrites* (1915) is an early example of a controversial text created by a woman. The film includes a depiction of female nudity performed by actor Margaret Edwards; she appears onscreen as the 'Naked Truth', an allegorical figure who literally holds a mirror to those she encounters. Though praised by many critics for its artistic merit, *Hypocrites* was also subject to censorship in several American jurisdictions for its depiction of female nakedness.[10] Věra Chytilová's film *Daisies* (*Sedmikrásky*, 1966) is another instructive example of a woman-authored provocation. A central work of the Czech New Wave, the film was banned by the Czechoslovak Socialist Republic (ČSSR) for wantonness and food wastage as well as the evident anti-authoritarian spirit embodied by its two anarchic protagonists, 'the Marias'. Liliana Cavani's *The Night Porter* (*Il portiere di note*, 1974) is also a film with challenging subject matter. It tells the story of a sexual relationship between a female concentration camp survivor and her former guard;

Annette Insdorf calls it 'a provocative and problematic film' that 'can be seen as an exercise in perversion and exploitation' but also 'a dark vision of compelling characters'.[11] Another case is Coralie Trinh Thi and Virginie Despentes's road movie *Baise-moi* (2000), which was banned and subject to cuts in several countries for using real sex to depict a rape. Although clearly showing the brutality of the assault it depicts, the British Board of Film Classification required that the scene be cut, claiming that it eroticised sexual violence.[12] There are other films by female directors that could be added to this list of provocations: *Born in Flames* (Lizzie Borden, 1983), *Head On* (Ana Kokkinos, 1998), *American Psycho* (Mary Harron, 2000), *In My Skin* (*Dans ma peau*, Marina de Van, 2002), *In the Cut* (Jane Campion, 2003), *We Need to Talk About Kevin* (Lynne Ramsay, 2011) and *Code Blue* (Urszula Antoniak, 2011), for instance. These examples make it clear that it is not only male auteurs who produce provocative works – women's filmmaking also challenges, scandalises, offends and divides.

Women's provocative cinema deserves and requires attention. There is an enticing and complex history of directors, women key amongst them, to be discovered by considering provocation as a relation between viewers, texts and their authors. The story of women's creativity in cinema cannot be complete without an investigation into the medium's most daring practitioners. Indeed, a fitting space has opened for such an enquiry in recent years. In the past two decades, film scholarship has seen an abundance of work on the transgressive cinema of the post-millennium, particularly the so-called New Extremity and associated trends within European art cinema. Women directors and their films have appeared in much of this work, particularly Catherine Breillat's oeuvre, Claire Denis's *film maudit Trouble Every Day* (2001) and her noir thriller *Bastards* (*Les salauds*, 2013), Marina de Van's confronting *In My Skin* and, to a lesser extent, Lucile Hadžihalilović's *Innocence* (2004) and Urszula Antoniak's *Code Blue*. This work on extreme cinema seems a likely arena within which scholars could examine women's provocation alongside questions of female authorship. Put another way, this pre-existing work creates an opportunity for a feminist, auteurist critical intervention into the provocative art cinema trend. Although this book does not attempt to see how women 'fit' into the New Extremity per se, it does concern itself with post-millennium cinema, examining art films released after the year 2000. It considers how the concepts of provocation and the provocateur can illuminate women's filmmaking, highlighting how female directors generate negative responses to their work. Foregrounding provocation as a distinct phenomenon not only allows for a closer focus on the author–recipient relationship that women create in their cinema. By investigating women's filmmaking, it is possible to achieve an expanded understanding of provocation itself and what it entails for the relationships among authors, texts and spectators.

Provocation, Cinema and the Avant-garde

Provocation describes an author–recipient relation: a spectator's reaction of negative emotions or affects in response to a perceived authorial action delivered via the text. It consists of two parts bound together: an incitement followed by a response. Whether shock, offence, discomfort, horror, disgust, boredom or irritation, there are many negative emotions and affects associated with provocation. What unites them is that they are the opposite of pleasure; feelings in counter distinction to the enjoyment derived from the consumption of conventional art or entertainment. Provocation also implies that these negative experiences are not sought out by the viewer, at least not for the most part. There are, of course, many examples of cinema spectators who experience pleasure in things that they find disgusting, horrifying or upsetting. For instance, Kier-La Janisse provides an eloquent and personal account of this in her hybrid memoir–analysis, *House of Psychotic Women*. In this work, Janisse points out the attraction of confronting cinema. She is drawn, she says, to films that 'devastate and unravel me completely', and her book acknowledges the power of challenging cinema to facilitate an exploration of the self, the human condition and the extremes of human experience.[13] Scholarly considerations of the value of negative feelings in the cinematic encounter exist too. Scholars such as Scott MacKenzie, Asbjørn Grønstad and Nikolaj Lübecker, to name a few, have considered the ways that negative viewing experiences may prompt critical thoughts and ethical considerations in the onlooker, inviting them to perceive and question their own acts of voyeurism or attraction to onscreen violence.[14] It is not difficult to imagine a spectator who seeks out such an experience in their encounter with cinema, unpleasant though it may be.[15] Recognising the complexity of emotional responses to cinema is important, as is acknowledging the varied responses of individual onlookers and how this may shift according to their own context, desires or inclinations. Provocation as it plays out for real-world audiences is highly contingent, frequently ambivalent and often ambiguous. Nevertheless, for the purposes of this analysis, provocation is a way of describing a spectatorial response – one defined by the experience of unwanted negative emotions or affects as a dominant part of the art encounter. These can be based on a variety of triggers: the shock of witnessing violent injuries onscreen, the discomfort of viewing explicit sexual content, the ethical troubles of seeing images that seem exploitative or the displeasure of perceiving ugliness.

The experience of provocation is also characterised by the saliency of the author–recipient relationship. Unlike the notion of transgression, provocation as a concept emphasises the art recipient's response to the author's act of boundary-crossing. This distinction is significant. Transgression describes what occurs in the text: its story, subject matter or aesthetic strategies. Provocation accounts for the onlooker's reaction to this transgression. As Grønstad observes of the extreme art cinema of the early twenty-first century: 'these films appear to be about the spectator' to the extent that the offensive content seems 'directed *at*' the audience rather than simply 'staged *for*' them.[16] The perception of authorial intentionality is thus an important component in provocation. Mette Hjort defines provocation as 'an intent to generate strong negative emotions on the part of specific individuals and groups'.[17] I would add a qualification by noting that true authorial intent is not actually required for a work to be experienced as provocative – only the impression of authorial intent is needed. It is entirely possible for an artist to unwittingly produce work that 'specific individuals or groups' find offensive and for those onlookers to believe it deliberate. This reveals that provocation is part of the author phenomenon. To use Dana Polan's notion of auteur desire, provocation is an extension of the tendency viewers have to seek out authorial agency in a film.[18] In the case of the provocateur, this tendency is not based in admiration for the director, but in a feeling of being directly addressed in a negative way: of being 'roused' as part of the 'rabble'. If successful, the spectator can blame the director (as author) for the unpleasantness of the art encounter. The feeling of provocation thus actively begets the provocateur insofar as the spectator senses the hand of the author, deliberately agitating.

Art historians typically trace provocation as an artistic strategy to Western avant-gardism in the arts and literary movements. As John A. Walker observes: 'Before 1800 European artists may have set out to astonish, impress and please their patrons and others who viewed their work but the idea of shocking and outraging them would not have crossed their minds.'[19] Peter Bürger agrees: 'In the historical avant-garde movement, shocking the recipient becomes the dominant principle of artistic intent.'[20] Anthony Julius quips: 'One could say, risking paradox, that the transgressive was hegemonic.'[21] The reasons for this shift have been widely speculated upon and assessed. Walker suggests that one reason was the development of the commercial art market. For art to be bought and sold among private collectors, works needed to have individuality and distinctiveness to increase their value. Moreover, 'avant-garde ideology' – the notion that artists should be 'ahead of public taste' – further encouraged distinctiveness through novelty, experiment and extremism of form and content.[22] Such novelty is not always well received. It can be experienced as ugly or offensive; the new has a propensity to shock. Art movements since the nineteenth century have repeatedly incorporated provocation, the incitement of negative emotions and affects, into their rationales. The call to *épater les bourgeois* – roughly, to scandalise the respectable middle classes and their conventional attitudes – is usually traced to the Decadent poets of the nineteenth century and attributed to French writer Charles Baudelaire, who declared 'Il faut épater les bourgeois' ('One must astonish the bourgeoise'). The phrase has since entered common parlance as a rallying cry to provocation. It is, according to some scholars, an organising thrust within surrealism.[23] Another key example from the Western avant-garde is Antonin Artaud's manifesto on the Theatre of Cruelty, which calls precisely for a provocation of the spectator via the 'cruelty' of his practice. Artaud states that the Theatre of Cruelty should awaken the 'heart and nerves' and inflict a 'tangible laceration, contained in all true feeling, on the heart and senses'.[24] The goal is to reconnect the recipient with their profound sensibilities and feelings – an ultimately liberating process, but one requiring agitation and stimulation.

Since the slicing of the ovine eye in *An Andalusian Dog*, provocation has had a place in art cinema. It appears in films throughout the twentieth and twenty-first centuries in works as diverse as *The Battle of Algiers* (*La battaglia di Algeri*, Gillo Pontecorvo, 1966), *A Clockwork Orange* (Stanley Kubrick, 1971), *The Idiots* (*Idioterne*, Lars von Trier, 1998) and *TERROR NULLIUS: A Political Revenge Fable in 3 Acts* (Soda_Jerk, 2018). The diversity of these films shows that there is a wide range of reasons why films might be experienced as provocative, condemned or banned; for example, because of their ostensive political stance on contentious issues, the fear they might corrupt impressionable viewers, their offensive depiction of individuals or groups, or the perceived indecency of their onscreen content. In the post-millennium era that is the focus of this book, it is provocative material in the form of gratuitous sexuality and violence that has featured heavily in the much-discussed extreme art cinema of Europe. There has been a helpful amount of theorising about the nature of these transgressions and, by extension, provocation in this cinema. Recent work is broadly grouped around two types of provocation: scopic offence or obscenity, and experiential provocation. Regarding the first type, Grønstad notes that one description of the 'unwatchable' in cinema is that it is a spectacle that is literally hard to look at.[25] This is the nature of the eye-slice in *An Andalusian Dog*, and such images appear frequently in New Extremity films. For example, it includes the lengthy rape scene in *Irréversible* (Gaspar Noé, 2002), the moment when the protagonist mutilates her genitals in *Antichrist* (Lars von Trier, 2009), and the scene where a young woman smashes her teeth in *Dogtooth* (*Kynodontas*, Yorgos Lanthimos, 2009). Grønstad describes this phenomenon in several ways, using terms such as 'visual transgression'[26] and 'transgressive visuality'.[27] It is a psychically, affectively painful spectacle. Such images can also provoke the spectator to walk out or turn away from the image.

The other form of provocation, described by Lübecker, is 'the feel-bad experience'.[28] Cinema of the feel-bad experience is not necessarily difficult to watch. Feel-bad films instead deny emotional satisfaction. As Lübecker writes, a feel-bad film produces 'spectatorial desire, but then blocks its satisfaction; *it creates, and then deadlocks, our desire for catharsis*'.[29] Examples that Lübecker lists include von Trier's *Dogville* (2003), Harmony Korine's *Trash Humpers* (2009) and Bruno Dumont's *Twentynine Palms* (2003). Although the methods may be different, both types of provocation – scopic offence and feel-bad cinema – have the same outcome, which is the incitement of negative feelings in the spectator. Using Grønstad's words, they involve 'the enactment of the refusal of pleasure as an aesthetic principle'.[30] One strategy consists of provoking via visual offence, whereas the other operates through the denial of emotional satisfaction via other means, including narrative and plot strategies. Lübecker's discussion of feel-bad cinema is an important acknowledgement that provocation is foremost an emotional response to film rather than a specific aesthetic property of the text itself (although, as the chapters in this book will demonstrate, there is a frequently assumed aesthetics of provocation too).

Debates about provocation repeatedly return to the question of why an artist would attempt to elicit negative emotions from the onlooker. Frey argues that filmic transgression, particularly the explicit depiction of sex and violence, is a normalised feature of art cinema as an institution. Within this milieu, the discourses of film criticism and marketing associate boundary-pushing with creative innovation, thus encouraging directors to make provocative works to distinguish themselves as artists and promote their films. As Frey remarks, 'institutions incentivize [such] routine behaviors to reproduce and persist'.[31] Following this, directors can cultivate the authorial persona of a 'provocateur' as a form of authorial branding and pre-promotion of their works. In the manner described by Timothy Corrigan in his work on the auteur as 'star' and 'brand-name', the provocateur is an authorial identity that has an observable commercial function.[32] Controversial star directors attract media attention and, by extension, publicity.

The purpose, function or ethics of offending the art recipient is also an ongoing concern in discussions of cinematic provocation. Some commentators express the positive view that provocative art can expand the cultural imaginary, challenge hegemonies and achieve progressive ends. As Maria San Filippo says in her analysis of sexual provocation in screen media, 'screen narrative and performance can bring us closer to understanding truths about erotic desire and intimacy', including those that otherwise may remain culturally repressed or unspoken.[33] Other critics routinely express scepticism about the motivations of provocateurs even as they acknowledge the value of *épater les bourgeois* in certain circumstances. As Hjort observes:

> While provocation may be taken up in order to pursue such properly artistic goals as formal innovation or the fostering of creative attitudes, it is clear that in many cases the strategy in question is linked to intentions that are far more pragmatic in their thrust. Provocation generates attention and discussion and thus has the potential to function as a highly effective publicity device.[34]

Here Hjort discusses what is broadly known as empty provocation, a catch-all term for art that provokes without an ideological, artistic or ethical purpose beyond scandal or sensationalism. Closely associated with empty provocation is empty transgression: art that positions itself as boundary breaking but does not actually transgress any meaningful cultural mores. In her analysis of Breillat's films, for example, Lisa Downing queries whether the aesthetic of pornography favoured by the director has been 'thoroughly dispossessed of its strategic political power', first because it is no longer a novel strategy, and second because much pornography upholds existing hegemonies.[35] Such concerns that provocation and transgression are outmoded recur often. Quandt ultimately decides on the view that the films of the New French Extremity 'bespeak a cultural crisis';[36] Hjort goes further in her analysis of von Trier's film *Manderlay* (2005), describing it as 'bullshit' because von Trier has little concern for the truth of what his film says about slavery and oppression.[37] Julius goes so far as to say that the transgressive tendency in art has become exhausted and dispossessed of its innovative and progressive power.[38] Concerns about the purpose and efficacy of provocation are important and, in many cases, well justified. Yet provocation is not a spent phenomenon. Filmmakers continue to make shocking, offensive and controversial art, and provocation, its means and ends, is an ongoing feature of cinema.

Gendering Provocation

Within the discourses that construct filmmakers and their authorial personae, the term 'provocateur' – and all it implies as an author–recipient relationship – is frequently gendered as masculine. It is no coincidence that women filmmakers are not named provocateurs as frequently as their male counterparts, nor is it accidental that provocation itself is symbolically characterised as a hypermasculine act. The provocateur is informed by ideas of creativity inherited from earlier centuries, long before the invention of cinema as a medium and Alexandre Astruc coined the concept of *caméra-stylo*.[39] Cultural critics and feminist art historians have argued that Western thought has gendered creativity as a male capacity for centuries. Christine Battersby observes this tendency in the words the European Romantics used to describe creative genius, which evoked qualities traditionally classed as feminine, such as heightened emotional sensibility, intuition or the power of generation: 'A man with genius was *like a woman* ... but was *not a woman*.'[40] In the nineteenth century, the qualities that philosopher-critics associated with the artist became even more overtly masculine. According to Andreas Huyssen, this trend began with Friedrich Nietzsche's idea of the free-thinker: 'the artist-philosopher-hero, the suffering loner who stands in irreconcilable opposition to modern democracy and its inauthentic culture'.[41] Huyssen evocatively terms this the 'male mystique in modernism' – the ideal of the wilful, solitary and misunderstood creative individual.[42] Such ideas surface in Karl Scheffler's treatise on women's non-creativity, *Women and Art: A Study* (*Die Frau und die Kunst: Eine Studie*, 1908), for example. An established German art critic, Scheffler extensively considers women's place in art and society, arguing that 'their work is never original' and can only imitate male-authored art.[43] He adds that women's creativity is 'only sufficient for the tonal, decorative, and ornamental; her taste is a child of sensitivity and not of critical aptitude'.[44] Notions of the masculinity of creativity also complement the advent of avant-gardism as the definitive creative principle. The artist's subversion – his readiness to shock and displease – is precisely what enables the production of novel works. Creativity is vitalised by the willingness to be disliked. The provocateur therefore epitomises avant-gardism because he flouts convention more profoundly, with less concern for his reputation in bourgeois society, than all others. If the notion of the auteur tends to imagine the artist as male, then the provocateur does so to an even greater degree.

This masculinisation of the transgressive artist is to this day consolidated by filmmakers and critics who characterise directorial provocation as a hypermasculine activity and a highly gendered author–recipient relationship. There is a broader masculinisation of provocation as a mode of address, expressed metaphorically in the language used by philosophers, critics and the artists themselves. For instance, Dominique Russell observes that violent metaphors are regularly used to describe Buñuel's surrealist shock tactics. It is no coincidence that the eye-slice of *An Andalusian Dog* consists of a male hand penetrating a female eye, a gendered relation that applies also to the director and his audience. The slice is a 'gleeful assertion of the director's power ... designed to shock the spectator out of ("feminine" and bourgeois) complacency'.[45] Echoing this, Haneke says his films *Benny's Video* (1992) and *Funny Games* (1997) were intended to be 'a slap in the face and a provocation', a description that positions the director as aggressor against a rather passive recipient.[46] Moreover, such directors encourage an accompanying mentality in their viewers – one that transforms the feminised, passive recipient of provocative assaults into a masculine spectator who accepts the director's challenge willingly, even proudly. Frey writes that Noé encourages a 'macho alternative-culture consumer identity' amongst his audience, insofar as those that can endure Noé's films feel a sense of accomplishment for making it through.[47] At the climax of *I Stand Alone*, for example, a title card directly addresses the audience, telling them that they have a thirty-second chance to leave the cinema: 'ATTENTION: VOUS AVEZ 30 SECONDES POUR ABANDONNER LA PROJECTION DE CE FILM.' Noé embraces this confrontational aspect of his work, writing in a column for the *Guardian*: 'I'm happy some people walk out during my film. It makes the ones who stay feel strong.'[48] Male directors' provocative stunts also receive willing media coverage at international film festivals, further reinforcing the association between male auteurism and provocation. Trier's 'Persona Non Grata' T-shirt is a case in point, as is a *Guardian* headline featuring a quote from Noé about his unusually well-received film *Climax* (2018): 'Six People Walked Out of Climax? No! I Usually Have 25%.'[49] This is not to say that women directors never attempt similar stunts. At the 2011 Cannes Film Festival, for example, a cryptic note was posted on the door to the screening of Antoniak's *Code Blue*: 'Attention. Some scenes of the film *Code Blue* ... may hurt the audience feelings [*sic*].' This provocation was not widely reported, however, and was eclipsed a few days later when von Trier jokingly described himself as a Nazi at a press conference, the very act for which he was declared 'persona non grata'. Provocation is thus not only an auteur identity inhabited predominately by men – it is a persona enthusiastically performed by some male directors and perpetuated by commentators who report on them in the press.

Alongside this gendering of male directors as provocateurs, the promotion and marketing of women's films encourages particular understandings of women's work as essentially non-provocative. In her account of women's world cinema, Patricia White observes that distributors frequently construct women's work as mature, intelligent and humanist. Her examples focus on cinema from the Global South, such as Deepa Mehta's *Water* (2005) and Marjane Satrapi and Vincent Paronnaud's *Persepolis* (2007), yet her observations apply to women's films the world over, including *Mustang* (Deniz Gamze Ergüven, 2015); *The Rider* and *Nomadland* (Chloé Zhao, 2017, 2020); *Certain Women* and *First Cow* (Kelly Reichardt, 2016, 2019); and *Tomboy* and *Girlhood* (Céline Sciamma, 2011, 2014). The marketing of women's art films, White argues, deploys 'the concepts of art and authorship in more accessible ways, branding themselves, and consequently their producers and audiences, as tasteful, serious, or brave – "artistic" in a middlebrow understanding of the term'.[50] This construction also brands women directors as 'guarantors of good taste'.[51] As always, there are exceptions: Breillat once more, as well as Antoniak. Yet compared to the macho language critics use to describe provocative male directors, film discourse and marketing practices more often align women auteurs with serious, adult humanism.

Provocation as an author–recipient relationship is discursively oriented toward masculinity. It is a way of thinking about creativity and creative genius that has long been associated with 'male' energy, aggression and anti-conformity. In contemporary art cinema, if women are ascribed author status it is similarly often gendered as anti-provocative, prosocial and affirming of values. These norms aside, it is clear that many women do possess a willingness to be disliked and absolutely intend their works to be challenging. There are many examples of women who push against expectations that their works should be humanist, for example, or uphold community values. For instance, after being asked about the absence of 'strong female leads' in her films, Claire Denis reportedly replied: 'What the fuck? I'm not a social worker.'[52] Swedish director Isabella Eklöf also exhibits similar defiance, stating: 'There's a part of me that really doesn't give a shit.'[53] Yet the need to respond in such a way in interviews, and the fact that such questions are even asked of them, is telling. It also begs an important question: how do women, and films directed by women, fit into the Western avant-garde practice of provocation?

Provocation in Women's Filmmaking: Authorship and Art Cinema

This book explores women's participation in the cinematic practice of provocation, considering how they construct provocative relations that elicit negative emotions and affects in the onlooker: from discomfort in stories of taboo acts, to offence at witnessing obscene imagery, to unease at ambiguous scenarios that may or may not have sinister implications. *Provocation in Women's Filmmaking* makes observations about the state of women's provocation via its case studies, which cover the work of Catherine Breillat, Lisa Aschan, Jennifer Kent, Isabella Eklöf, Lucile Hadžihalilović, Claire Denis, Anna Biller and Athina Rachel Tsangari. Some of these directors' films were highly controversial upon their release, prompting walkouts, jeering or debate in the broader public sphere. Others attracted more complex or mixed responses from critics and audiences: praise, qualified approval or ambivalence. By studying provocation through these filmmakers and their work, *Provocation in Women's Filmmaking* redresses a discourse of provocative auteurism that is still hypermasculine. It does so not only by examining the provocative films of women directors instead of those of men. It also theorises the aesthetics and strategies of provocation via analysis of these directors' works, considering how their approaches diverge from – and sometimes conform with – the masculinised aesthetics and strategies that have become so associated with filmic transgression, offence and feel-bad tactics. This book considers how some women directors provoke the recipient via stylistic approaches that have been as discursively feminised in the philosophy of aesthetics as the strategies of provocation have been masculinised. Examining women's filmmaking in this way expands definitions of cinematic provocation itself, yielding insight into cinema as a medium and vitalising provocation as a portable concept.

Insofar as it undertakes close readings of films by individual directors, this book is a feminist auteur study of contemporary art cinema and filmmakers. It considers directors' bodies of work and incorporates their authorial statements into an analysis of their provocative films. The notion of authorship has proved enduringly useful to feminist researchers, if not always uncontroversial. As White writes:

> Feminists have explored the work that has been made by women as an act of historical retrieval, a theoretical project of decoding biography and experience within film form and address, a site of identification and libidinal investment, and a practical matter of equity.[54]

Provocation in Women's Filmmaking is in part an act of historical retrieval as well as one of equity in its efforts to highlight the works of women directors and describe them alongside the films of acknowledged male provocateurs of the post-millennium. However, this book does not attempt a historical survey of women's provocative filmmaking since the invention of the medium. Instead of providing a study of controversial women directors throughout film history – from Germaine Dulac to Sandra Wollner by way of Chytilová, Cavani and Kokkinos – it focuses on the post-millennium moment. Moreover, this book treats the female auteur as what Katarzyna Paszkiewicz calls a 'hermeneutic key' – a way of framing films for analysis that offers new perspectives on the 'why' and 'how' of cinematic provocation, pushing the discussion of women's creative practice and provocative cinema forward.[55] There are, of course, well-established concerns about reclaiming the auteur concept for women, and these by implication extend to a study of women provocateurs. Particularly worrisome to some feminist scholars is that theorising the female auteur essentialises female subjectivity, implying that women make films in certain ways simply by virtue of shared sex or gender. Other objections are that auteur theory misrepresents the collaborative nature of filmmaking while also reinvigorating an intrinsically sexist notion of authorship that has long excluded women. I also add that a study of women filmmakers can be seen to reinforce a gender binary to the exclusion of those directors who do not identify with that binary. Studies of non-binary creators such as E. O. Gill, Jane Schoenbrun, Joey Soloway and Zena Igbe are yet to be written. However, this book emphasises the value in considering women's authorship as an illuminating critical lens. As Catherine Grant notes, it is valid to examine women's authorial influence on films, which she describes as their 'creative agency'. As Grant puts it, women 'have direct and reflexive, if obviously not completely "intentional" or determining relationships to the cultural products they help to produce, as well as to their reception'.[56] Such determining relationships are especially salient in art cinema, the domain within which the auteurs in this study produce and circulate their work. This milieu of film culture very much foregrounds the auteur in its discourses, spotlighting the director during screenings, festival runs and press junkets. This is further reason, therefore, to consider how films connected to the Western avant-garde tradition of provocation – those that circulate in an art cinema context of reception – court negative responses as an aesthetic strategy.

Provocation in Women's Filmmaking also asks these questions specifically in relation to contemporary Western art cinema made by women, although there are certainly examples of women-authored films that produce intensely negative responses outside of this designation; for example, those released in earlier decades, in non-Western contexts and in the domain of genre cinema and experimental film. To begin with, there are many important films from outside the Western context that could be examined in relation to provocation. Some of these are exactly the kind of 'tasteful' tales of the human spirit that White identifies – what reads as 'middlebrow' in a Western art cinema context may be genuinely incendiary in other environments. For example, Jocelyne Saab's film *Dunia* (2005) elicited death threats upon its release; Mehta's lesbian drama *Fire* (1996) was so controversial that far right groups vandalised cinemas in Delhi and Mumbai. These films' provocations are arguably far more profound and consequential for the filmmakers than the works of, say, Noé, Haneke and Lanthimos. This book, however, considers films connected to the Western avant-garde tradition of provocation and those that circulate in a Western art cinema context of reception. Experimental and genre cinema are also filled with creative, startling and challenging works by women. In fact, several of the case studies considered in this book could also be considered genre films: for example, Jennifer Kent's *The Nightingale* (2018) is arguably a rape-revenge work; Lucile Hadžihalilović's *Évolution* (2015) a horror film; Claire Denis's *High Life* (2018) a science-fiction movie; and Athina Rachel Tsangari's *The Capsule* (2012) a gothic tale. However, this book focuses on films that circulate within the domain of art cinema. They are produced outside major commercial industries, screened at leading international film festivals and are distributed through speciality channels. Art cinema is certainly an amorphous category and much debated in film criticism. As Carol J. Clover argues, 'the traffic between low and high is such that it is unnatural to separate them',[57] and Eleftheria Thanouli suggests retiring the term entirely.[58] Yet as I have argued elsewhere, art cinema remains meaningful as a discursive category that signifies aesthetic value, ambition and originality.[59] As Russell notes, art cinema connotes 'high culture, intelligence and prestige'.[60] In film criticism and marketing, it is also a mode that centres the director as the origin of the film's style and meaning. It is also positioned as an inheritor of the Western avant-garde ideology of innovation and creativity. Art cinema is therefore a fitting domain for an investigation into women's provocative cinema.

The choice of case studies in this book is motivated by all these delineations. An analysis of selected provocative works from eight filmmakers allows this book to undertake detailed textual analyses of each film and its critical reception, as well as making space to consider the voices and oeuvres of the directors themselves. The case studies also correspond to this book's objective of undertaking a contemporary study of post-millennium films that are aesthetically, discursively or industrially aligned with art cinema. Moreover, the case studies in this book enable me to consider provocation as a negative response that has several manifestations and triggers, from provocative depictions of sex, sexual violence and onscreen taboos, to the use of pretty aesthetics, subversive camp, utilisations of genre and black humour. I have included both established filmmakers, such as Claire Denis and Catherine Breillat, and less-studied directors. My goal is to frame these better-known filmmakers as provocateurs and place them alongside other directors and their works in illuminating ways. Due to these choices, some virtuosic filmmakers and their intriguingly uncomfortable films are not centred in this book. Examples include Jane Campion's important oeuvre, particularly her edgy depiction of sexuality in *In the Cut* (2003), Ana Kokkinos's film *The Book of Revelation* (2006) and the thrilling, oft-uncomfortable works of Lynne Ramsay. Timing is also an inescapable factor. During the writing of this book, several exciting and difficult works by women were released: Wollner's *The Trouble with Being Born*, Maïmouna Doucouré's controversial coming-of-age film *Cuties* (*Mignonnes*, 2020), Dasha Nekrasova's *The Scary of Sixty-First* (2021) and Julia Ducournau's *Titane* (2021), the last of which earned significant symbolic capital in art cinema milieus when it won the Palme d'Or. Indeed, Ducournau was only the second woman in history to win the prize (the first was Campion). The fact that these films were released during the writing of this book means that detailed textual analysis of them must be tabled for future scholarship. Yet these films' existence is, in fact, an overall positive for this book. New, exciting works by women confirm the need for an investigation into women-authored provocations. They show that provocation is not an exhausted aesthetic strategy, and women absolutely participate in it. There will also likely be more provocative films to come, and a framework for approaching these yet-to-be-made works and their challenge to spectators is required.

How to examine provocation as a relation between film and recipient? Such a project requires sustained attention to a film's textual construction but also investigation of its critical reception as a provocative work. Following this, the chapters in this book closely read the selected films' aesthetic strategies to understand how they position the onlooker to feel provoked: for instance, their use (or not) of explicit imagery, the duration and repetition of scenes, and the employment of pretty and ugly aesthetics, camp and black humour. I incorporate the directors' words throughout to investigate their films' objectives, as well as to reaffirm that women do indeed participate in the tradition of artistic provocation. However, in keeping with my contention that provocation does not require authorial intentionality – only the impression of it – my focus is on provocation as an effect of the texts these women create. I also draw primarily upon film critics' responses as a way of gauging the reactions these films generate. This is not to diminish the significance of individual moviegoers and their responses. Rather, I use film criticism because of the centrality this discourse has in positioning directors, and films, as provocative. Film critics hold the power to construct 'authorial signatures', identify directorial oeuvres, to deem films (or filmmakers) controversial and to report on boos, jeers or walkouts at film screenings. Where possible I place particular emphasis on reviews published immediately following premieres or film festival screenings for this reason. Doing so locates the films I analyse within a history of scandals in the Western avant-garde, with precedents like the reaction of attendees at the exhibition of Édouard Manet's *Olympia* (1863) at the Salon of Paris in 1865, the audience rioting following the first performance of Igor Stravinsky's *The Rite of Spring* in May 1913, and the violent right-wing protest staged during a screening of Buñuel's *The Golden Age* shortly after its opening in 1930. Festival screenings offer a contemporary equivalent of such debuts where the art object meets the public. Indeed, several films examined in this book – such as *Anatomy of Hell* (*Anatomie de l'enfer*, Catherine Breillat, 2004), *The Nightingale* and *Trouble Every Day* – were met with controversy upon their festival runs. Lastly, my analysis of the case studies in this book incorporates contextual and scholarly debates that illuminate these films and their strategies; for example, aesthetic theories of pornography, feminist debates regarding the representation of rape onscreen, notions of ironic camp and avant-garde traditions of black humour, to name a few.

Chapter 1 begins with a topic ubiquitously associated with provocation: sex. In literature and the visual arts, there are well-established traditions of female (and often feminist) intervention in the representation of women's bodies and sexuality. Chapter 1 investigates how women filmmakers engage provocatively with depictions of female sexuality and desire, examining Catherine Breillat's works *Anatomy of Hell* and *Fat Girl* (*À ma sœur!*, 2001), as well as Lisa Aschan's taut tale of sublimated envy, violence and queer desire *She Monkeys* (*Apflickorna*, 2011). Chapter 2 attends to another key topic in debates on provocation in cinema: the onscreen depiction of sexual violence. When Australian director Jennifer Kent's *The Nightingale* screened at the Sydney Film Festival in 2019, several audience members walked out during the film's rape sequences. Premiering the same year as Kent's film, Swedish director Isabella Eklöf's *Holiday* (2018) shocked festivalgoers with a lengthy sexual assault sequence filmed in one take. This chapter considers the depiction of rape in *The Nightingale* and *Holiday*, locating Kent and Eklöf's work within a tradition of feminist engagement with sexual violence.

Whereas Chapters 1 and 2 consider films that prompted onlookers to leave the cinema, Chapter 3 investigates the opposite spectatorial response: films that entice the spectator to look using the aesthetics of the pretty.

I examine this question through an analysis of the works of French director Lucile Hadžihalilović, considering how her films *Mimi* (*La bouche de Jean-Pierre*, 1996), *Innocence* (2004), *Évolution* (2015) and *Earwig* (2021) provoke using a visual style that Rosalind Galt calls 'the pretty'.[61] Chapter 4 turns its attention to one of the most admired filmmakers working in art cinema today, French director Claire Denis, considering how her work engages spectators in provocative relations. Throughout her career, Denis has cultivated a reputation as a sensitive, understated director interested in the subtleties of desire, family and inherited power structures. Denis's post-millennium work, however, poses a challenge to this understanding of her persona. Through an analysis of *Trouble Every Day*, *Bastards* and *High Life*, I consider how these films use the same stylistic approaches that have been seen as indicative of Denis's tasteful filmmaking style to implicate the spectator in transgressive onscreen scenarios: taboo acts, violence and perverse eroticism.

Chapter 5 investigates the work of American writer-director Anna Biller, a filmmaker whose subversively feminist films have been widely misinterpreted as camp provocations. A point of common critical admiration is that her films *A Visit from the Incubus* (2001), *Viva* (2007) and *The Love Witch* (2016) seem to ironically reference camp or lowbrow genres of yesteryear, such as occult horror, sexploitation and musical Westerns. However, I argue that the overall experience of watching Biller's films is not one of cinephilic joy but discomfiting seriousness. This chapter considers how Biller's aesthetics both disguise and intensify her accounts of sexual and emotional trauma in *A Visit from the Incubus*, *Viva* and *The Love Witch*, denying the ironic enjoyment that her aesthetics seem to promise. Lastly, Chapter 6 investigates the disturbing humour of Greek director Athina Rachel Tsangari, focusing on her short film *The Capsule* (2012) and second feature *Attenberg* (2010). Tsangari is associated with the so-called 'Greek weird wave', a spate of bizarre and alienating films that emerged somewhat contemporaneously to the 2009 Greek financial crisis. This chapter investigates *Attenberg* and *The Capsule* as films that provoke and unsettle their audience in ways that lead not to shock but to laughter: a reaction of amusement and discomfort. In *Attenberg* and *The Capsule*, Tsangari utilises vaguely disturbing humour to observe and critique life as a woman.

It is important to account for women's provocative filmmaking because, as I stated earlier, women's creativity in cinema cannot be fully understood without such an enquiry. There is also a feminist justification. Discourses of aesthetic philosophy and film criticism masculinise provocation even as women continue to disturb moviegoers with their transgressive filmmaking – an exclusionary act to be resisted. Yet looking closely at cinema that is, by definition, uncomfortable compels another justification – one that speaks to why artists and recipients make and consume art that disturbs them in the first place. In her account of another challenging director, the sexploitation filmmaker Doris Wishman, Tania Modleski offers an illuminating hypothesis regarding this issue. Intrigued and provoked by the longstanding feminist interest in Wishman's work, Modleski ponders the reasons why a female viewer might choose to watch the confronting images of violence against women that the director promulgated in her movies. To answer this, Modleski posits that some viewers may harbour a desire to look at such images precisely because they are upsetting. Modleski describes this as a 'counterphobic' impulse premised on a determination to not be terrorised or victimised by the image: 'to meet, to face down, and to survive [her] very worst fears'.[62] Modleski acknowledges her own impulse of this kind and, following her example, I admit to sharing this counterphobic desire to confront provocative images too, as both a film viewer and a scholar. Modleski is careful not to valorise this form of spectatorship over other types of engagement, noting that counterphobic viewing is 'only one possible form of refusing to be intimidated and terrified', and that refusing to look is another.[63] Nonetheless, counterphobic viewing remains an intriguing phenomenon and one explanation as to why viewers might seek out confronting art.

It is not difficult to imagine that this counterphobic impulse extends to female filmmakers and their work too – indeed it surely must. It is likewise not difficult to imagine women directors wanting to examine the darker aspects of human experience and aiming to challenge and shock in a variety of ways. *Provocation in Women's Filmmaking* considers the films that attempt such provocations, and it proceeds in the counterphobic spirit of turning towards provocative works. What emerges in the pages of this book is that there are no fixed aesthetics of these directors' approach, no shared target of their provocations and no single hegemony that is subverted. Films by women construct provocative modes of address via multiple stylistic strategies. Their provocations can be mixed with humour, eroticism, ambiguity and pleasure. They can also work towards various political ends: sometimes the goal is empathy with marginalised subjects, sometimes patriarchy is the target and sometimes it is the spectator's own ethics that are under interrogation. This diversity should be acknowledged and, indeed, celebrated. What these provocative filmmakers share is their willingness to engage with confronting images and subjects, and their invitation to us to do so as well.

Notes

1. For key entries in this area of scholarship, see James Quandt, 'Flesh & Blood: Sex and Violence in Recent French Cinema', *Artforum* 42, no. 6 (2004), 126–32; Tanya Horeck and Tina Kendall (eds), *The New Extremism in Cinema: From France to Europe* (Edinburgh: Edinburgh University Press, 2011); and Mattias Frey, *Extreme Cinema: The Transgressive Rhetoric of Today's Art Film Culture* (New Brunswick, NJ: Rutgers University Press, 2016).
2. Quandt, 'Flesh & Blood', 126–32. Quandt's article originally termed the trend the 'New French Extremity'. This corresponds with his observation that this extreme cinema seemed to appear in the work of French filmmakers, such as Bruno Dumont, François Ozon, Gaspar Noé, Catherine Breillat and Philippe Grandrieux. Except when referring to Quandt's original article, this book uses the term 'New Extremity' to acknowledge that the trend is observable in art cinema from many countries, including other European nations and countries in North America. My use of the term also corresponds with developments in the scholarship on extreme cinema. As Tanya Horeck and Tina Kendall note in the introduction to their edited collection *The New Extremism in Cinema*, extreme cinema is an increasingly global phenomenon. (Tanya Horeck and Tina Kendall, 'Introduction', in *The New Extremism in Cinema: From France to Europe*, eds Tanya Horeck and Tina Kendall [Edinburgh: Edinburgh University Press, 2011], 4.)
3. Frey, *Extreme Cinema*, 6–9.
4. Ibid., 20.
5. Christopher Sharrett, 'The World That is Known: Michael Haneke Interviewed', interview, *Kinoeye: New Perspectives on European Film* 4, no. 1 (2004), https://www.kinoeye.org/04/01/interview01.php.
6. Benjamin Secher, 'Catherine Breillat: "All True Artists Are Hated"', *Telegraph*, 5 April 2008, https://www.telegraph.co.uk/culture/film/starsandstories/3672302/Catherine-BreillatAll-true-artists-are-hated.html.
7. Recent publications include Sue Thornham's *What If I Had Been the Hero?: Investigating Women's Cinema* (London: BFI, 2012) and *Spaces of Women's Cinema: Space, Place and Genre in Contemporary Woman's Filmmaking* (London: BFI, 2019), Patricia White's *Women's Cinema, World Cinema* (Durham, NC: Duke University Press, 2015), Katarzyna Paszkiewicz's *Genre, Authorship and Contemporary Women Filmmakers* (Edinburgh: Edinburgh University Press, 2019), and edited collections including *Women Do Genre in Film and Television*, eds Mary Harrod and Katarzyna Paszkiewicz (London: Routledge, 2018) and *Women Make Horror: Filmmaking, Feminism, Genre*, ed. Alison Peirse (New Brunswick, NJ: Rutgers University Press, 2020).
8. John Wray, 'Minister of Fear', *New York Times Magazine*, 23 September 2007, https://nyti.ms/2rZn9VS.
9. Elena Gorfinkel, 'Against Lists', *Another Gaze*, 29 November 2019, https://www.anothergaze.com/elena-gorfinkel-manifesto-against-lists/.

10. Shelley Stamp, *Lois Weber in Early Hollywood* (Oakland: University of California Press, 2015), 60–1.
11. Annette Insdorf, 'The Night Porter', *Criterion*, 10 January 2000, https://www.criterion.com/current/posts/66-the-night-porter.
12. British Board of Film Classification, '*Baise-moi*', 26 February 2001, https://www.bbfc.co.uk/AFF165545/.
13. Kier-La Janisse, *House of Psychotic Women: An Autobiographical Topography of Female Neurosis in Horror and Exploitation Films* (Godalming: FAB Press, 2012), 7.
14. Scott MacKenzie, 'On Watching and Turning Away: Ono's *Rape*, *Cinéma Direct* Aesthetics, and the Genealogy of *Cinéma Brut*', in *Rape in Art Cinema*, ed. Dominique Russell (New York: Continuum, 2010); Asbjørn Grønstad, *Screening the Unwatchable: Spaces of Negation in Post-Millennial Art Cinema* (Basingstoke: Palgrave Macmillan, 2012); Nikolaj Lübecker, *The Feel-Bad Film* (Edinburgh: Edinburgh University Press, 2015).
15. As the author of this book, I admit to this complex fascination and interest in confronting cinema as well.
16. Grønstad, *Screening the Unwatchable*, 2; emphasis in original.
17. Mette Hjort, 'The Problem with Provocation: On Lars von Trier, Enfant Terrible of Danish Art Film', *Kinema: A Journal for Film and Audiovisual Media*, 36 (2011), 6.
18. Dana Polan, 'Auteur Desire', *Screening the Past*, upload date 1 March 2001, https://www.screeningthepast.com/2014/12/auteur-desire/.
19. John A. Walker, *Art and Outrage: Provocation, Controversy and the Visual Arts* (London: Pluto Press, 1999), 1.
20. Peter Bürger, *Theory of the Avant-Garde*, trans. Michael Shaw (Minneapolis: University of Minnesota Press, 1984), 18.
21. Anthony Julius, *Transgressions: The Offences of Art* (London: Thames & Hudson, 2002), 53.
22. Walker, *Art and Outrage*, 1.
23. There is some debate over the spirit of the surrealists' tendency to induce negative emotions and affective responses in the recipients of their work, which is unsurprising given the diversity and global spread of the movement as well as its incorporation of both literature and the visual arts. Some scholars directly refute the idea that the surrealists merely wished to *épater le bourgeois*, whereas others treat this as a given. For example, while Keith Aspley notes that the surrealists had a 'propensity to provoke, to shock and to challenge taboos of various kinds, generally to *épater le bourgeois*', J. H. Matthews rejects the notion, claiming *épater le bourgeois* is a superficial impulse compared to sincerity of the surrealist project. The surrealist's undertaking, Matthews writes, 'was serious and his effort sincere, judged by the surrealist mind to be necessities, not luxuries, and certainly not attempts to engage in the classic pursuit of French artists for a century and more: *épater le bourgeois*'. These debates, however, tend to centre not on whether the surrealists provoked their

audiences, but rather their goals for doing so. On both sides of the debate, there is an association to be explored between surrealism and *épater le bourgeois* as an avant-garde principle. (Keith Aspley, *Historical Dictionary of Surrealism* [Lanham: Scarecrow Press, 2010], 109; J. H. Matthews, *The Surrealist Mind* [Selinsgrove, PA: Susquehanna University Press, 1991], 105.)
24. Antonin Artaud, '"The Theatre and Its Double" (1931–7)', in *Artaud on Theatre*, eds Claude Schumacher and Brian Singleton (London: Methuen Drama, 1989), 120, 121.
25. Asbjørn Grønstad, 'The Two Unwatchables', in *Unwatchable*, eds Nicholas Baer, Maggie Hennefeld, Laura Horak and Gunnar Iversen (New Brunswick, NJ: Rutgers University Press, 2019), 151–4.
26. Ibid., 153.
27. Asbjørn Grønstad, 'On the Unwatchable', in *The New Extremism in Cinema: From France to Europe*, eds Tanya Horeck and Tina Kendall (Edinburgh: Edinburgh University Press, 2011), 194.
28. Lübecker, *The Feel-Bad Film*, 2.
29. Ibid., 2; emphasis in original.
30. Grønstad, 'The Two Unwatchables', 153.
31. Frey, *Extreme Cinema*, 20.
32. Timothy Corrigan, 'The Commerce of Auteurism: A Voice Without Authority', *New German Critique* 49 (1990), 45, 48.
33. Maria San Filippo, *Provocauteurs and Provocations: Screening Sex in 21st Century Media* (Bloomington: Indiana University Press, 2020), 5.
34. Hjort, 'The Problem with Provocation', 6.
35. Lisa Downing, 'French Cinema's New "Sexual Revolution": Postmodern Porn and Troubled Genre', *French Cultural Studies* 15, no. 3 (2004), 267.
36. Quandt, 'Flesh & Blood', 128.
37. Hjort, 'The Problem with Provocation', 22.
38. Julius, *Transgressions*.
39. Alexandre Astruc, 'The Birth of a New Avant Garde: *La caméra-stylo* (France, 1948)', in *Film Manifestos and Global Cinema Cultures: A Critical Anthology*, ed. Scott MacKenzie (Berkeley: University of California Press, 2014), 603–6.
40. Christine Battersby, *Gender and Genius: Towards a Feminist Aesthetics* (London: The Women's Press, 1989), 8; emphasis in original.
41. Andreas Huyssen, 'Mass Culture as Woman: Modernism's Other', in *After the Great Divide: Modernism, Mass Culture, Postmodernism* (London: Macmillan, 1986), 50.
42. Ibid., 50.
43. Karl Scheffler, *Women and Art: A Study* (*Die Frau und die Kunst: Eine Studie*) (Berlin: Julius Bard, 1908), 59.
44. Ibid., 59.
45. Dominique Russell, 'Buñuel: Storytelling, Desire and the Question of Rape', in *Rape in Art Cinema*, ed. Dominique Russell (New York: Continuum, 2010), 42.

46. Haneke, 'The World That is Known'.
47. Frey, *Extreme Cinema*, 25.
48. Gaspar Noé, 'I'm Happy Some People Walk Out During My Film. It Makes the Ones Who Stay Feel Strong', *Guardian*, 13 March 1999, https://www.theguardian.com/film/1999/mar/12/features3.
49. Xan Brooks, 'Gaspar Noé: "Six People Walked out of Climax? No! I Usually Have 25%"', *Guardian*, 22 May 2018, https://www.theguardian.com/film/2018/may/22/gaspar-noe-six-people-walked-out-of-climax-no-i-usually-have-25.
50. White, *Women's Cinema, World Cinema*, 68.
51. Ibid., 72.
52. Brooke Huseby, 'Claire Denis is in No Rush to Make Films for You – Or Anyone, Besides Herself', interview, *Interview Magazine*, 16 April 2019, https://www.interviewmagazine.com/film/claire-denis-is-in-no-rush-to-make-films-for-you-high-life.
53. Isabella Eklöf, 'In Conversation with Isabella Eklöf', *Another Gaze*, uploaded 5 August, 2019, video, 0:18, https://www.anothergaze.com/conversation-interview-isabella-eklof/.
54. White, *Women's Cinema, World Cinema*, 3.
55. Katarzyna Paszkiewicz, *Genre, Authorship and Contemporary Women Filmmakers* (Edinburgh: Edinburgh University Press, 2019), 37.
56. Catherine Grant, 'Secret Agents: Feminist Theories of Women's Film Authorship', *Feminist Theory* 2, no. 1 (2001), 124.
57. Carol J. Clover, *Men, Women, and Chainsaws: Gender in the Modern Horror Film* (London: BFI, 1992), 5.
58. Eleftheria Thanouli, '"Art Cinema" Narration: Breaking Down a Wayward Paradigm', *Scope: An Online Journal of Film and Television Studies*, 14 (2009), https://www.nottingham.ac.uk/scope/documents/2009/june-2009/thanouli.pdf.
59. Janice Loreck, *Violent Women in Contemporary Cinema* (Basingstoke: Palgrave, 2016).
60. Dominique Russell, 'Introduction: Why Rape?' in *Rape in Art Cinema*, ed. Dominique Russell (New York: Continuum, 2010), 3.
61. Rosalind Galt, *Pretty: Film and the Decorative Image* (New York: Columbia University Press, 2011).
62. Tania Modleski, 'Women's Cinema as Counterphobic Cinema: Doris Wishman as the Last Auteur', in *Sleaze Artists: Cinema at the Margins of Taste, Style, and Politics*, ed. Jeffrey Sconce (Durham, NC: Duke University Press, 2007), 62.
63. Ibid.

CHAPTER 1

Sexuality and Obscenity: From Catherine Breillat to Lisa Aschan

Art cinema has its share of controversial depictions of sexuality authored by women: Virginie Despentes and Coralie Trinh Thi's real-sex road movie, *Baise-moi* (2000), Ana Kokkinos's rape-revenge film, *The Book of Revelation* (2006) and Urszula Antoniak's transgressive *Code Blue* (2011), to name only a few from the post-millennium period. Sex, particularly women's sexuality, is a subject with rich potential for shocking critics and audiences alike. Indeed, the term 'provocation' is itself closely tethered to sex – while it broadly means 'to elicit a reaction', provocation can also describe an act that titillates and arouses. In keeping with this association, literature and the visual arts sustain well-established traditions of female, and often feminist, intervention in the representation of women's sexuality, from the experimental films of Carolee Schneemann, Barbara Rubin and Barbara Hammer to the photography of Nan Goldin and the fiction writing of Virginie Despentes and Kathy Acker. The question of how women filmmakers provoke through sex in their chosen medium is thus at the forefront of any investigation into filmic provocation.

In the space of narrative art cinema, the most notorious practitioner of sexual provocation is undoubtedly French filmmaker Catherine Breillat. Breillat is a multidisciplinary artist and has worked as a film director, screenwriter and novelist. Described sensationally as 'the auteur of porn' by scholars and the press alike,[1] her films are distinguished by their candid and explicit narratives about heterosexual women's experience. Although her film work is diverse and includes comedies and costume dramas, she is particularly renowned for her 'décalogue' of dramatic films about sexuality: *A Real Young Girl* (*Une vraie jeune fille*, 1976), *Nocturnal Uproar* (*Tapage nocturne*, 1979), *Virgin* (*36 fillette*, 1988), *Dirty Like an Angel* (*Sale comme un ange*, 1991), *Perfect Love* (*Parfait amour!*, 1996), *Romance* (1999), *Fat Girl* (*À ma sœur!*, 2001),[2] *Brief Crossing* (*Brève traversée*, 2001), *Sex Is Comedy* (2002) and *Anatomy of Hell* (*Anatomie de l'enfer*, 2004). These films are frank explorations of the sexual economy – as Brian Price succinctly puts it: 'The central preoccupation of Catherine Breillat's work is the sexuality of women.'[3] Breillat's oeuvre is also characterised by the graphicness of its onscreen sexual content, the frankness of its discussions of sexuality in the dialogue and its interest in the obscene: images that are meant to stay hidden. These qualities have been features of Breillat's work since the beginning of her film career. Her directorial debut *A Real Young Girl* went largely unseen for two decades due to its sexual content. Concerned that the film would be subject to a new tax on X-rated films in France, the producer of Breillat's debut withheld *A Real Young Girl* from release, and his company soon went bankrupt. The film was not released until 2000, over twenty years later.[4] Breillat's breakthrough work in English-speaking countries, *Romance*, was 'a minor *succès de scandale*',[5] gaining attention for its graphic sex scenes and discomfiting scenarios, such as a paid sexual encounter that becomes a rape.

Breillat is not the only practitioner interested in challenging audiences with women's sexual experience, however, and her favoured strategies are also not the only means to provoke an onlooker. A noteworthy counterpoint to Breillat is Swedish director Lisa Aschan, who impressed festival critics with her debut queer drama, *She Monkeys* (*Apflickorna*, 2011). Described as a 'disturbing, provocative work',[6] *She Monkeys* differs from Breillat's most famous films in a number of key aspects. Rather than showing sex acts or naked bodies onscreen or discussing sexuality openly in dialogue or voice-over, *She Monkeys* operates in the domain of the suggested and implied. It tells the story of two teenage girls' attraction to one another as they compete, often aggressively, for a position on the same athletics team. The film is defined by what it does not show and what does not occur. Instead of using explicitness, as Breillat does, the film opts instead for a tonal approach, constructing a tense atmosphere of eroticism and violence. It also deals with queer sexuality as opposed to the kind of heterosexual relationships that Breillat's films so closely scrutinise.

This chapter considers how Breillat and Aschan engage in provocative modes of address in relation to the onscreen depiction of sex and sexuality. I specifically consider the visual aesthetics of explicitness, or the conspicuous lack thereof, in these directors' films: the onscreen depiction of sexual acts and bodies as a strategy of provocation. To orient my investigation around visual explicitness, I draw upon the concept of 'the obscene' in my analysis, meaning the making visible of sights that are supposed to remain unseen. I compare Breillat's films *Anatomy of Hell* and *Fat Girl* with Aschan's more recent *She Monkeys* as a queer counterpoint to Breillat's work and a film that provokes its audience via deferral and not showing. This chapter also focuses on how the depiction of feminine sexuality occurs through the coming-of-age narratives of *Fat Girl* and *She Monkeys*, arguing that Aschan's work avoids the sexual overtness of Breillat's films in favour of unspoken and unsettling dynamics of power and queer desire. While distinct in their approach, both Breillat's and Aschan's provocations insert the spectator into the feminine sexual experience with a discomfiting vividness. This act is political, insofar as it redresses women's long history of representation as sexual objects rather than subjects. Both filmmakers challenge the visual economies of looking that for so long have determined women's depictions as sexual beings for a presumed heterosexual male onlooker.

Women, Sexuality and the Obscene

Before investigating how the films of Breillat and Aschan engage in sexual provocation, it is important to first offer a definition of obscenity as a concept, as well as to identify the norms of sexual representation that Breillat and Aschan engage with in their onscreen depictions. Feminists have long observed that women's bodies are subject to patriarchal and phallocentric construction in ways that frame the female body in accordance with a heterosexual male imaginary. This leads, so the argument goes, to a preponderance of depictions of women that are objectifying, pornographic and sometimes obscene. This idea is axiomatic in critiques of visual culture, including Laura Mulvey's important treatise on the male gaze in cinema, as well as John Berger's account of oil painting declaring that 'the "ideal" spectator is always assumed to be male'.[7] Breillat herself repeatedly demonstrates an awareness of this conundrum when discussing her filmmaking practice, observing: 'In our society pornography is written on every woman's body.'[8] Although Breillat's authorial focus is heterosexual women, her observation applies to queer women also. Representations of queer sexuality between women are also potentially subject to phallocentric regimes and ways of seeing – they can be depicted as either titillating spectacles for the presumed heterosexual male onlooker or else erased entirely from visual culture.[9] Queer or otherwise, women's representation as sexual beings is thus frequently determined by a heterosexual male imaginary. This means that the female body is constantly at risk of becoming obscene and pornographic, and expressions of female desire are elided in favour of the desire she elicits for the male spectator.

Disrupting this process is an important theme in women's sexual provocations in cinema, from art films to the experimental works of filmmakers such as Carolee Schneemann and Barbara Hammer. As Robin Blaetz's investigation of women's experimental cinema observes, the 'interrogation of the body's status as a cultural and linguistic sign' is a dominant theme, and this is true of women's narrative cinema too.[10] This disruption can take several forms – not all women who engage in sexual representation do so via explicit images of nudity or sex acts. Some, however, do choose to work precisely with this aspect of visual culture, utilising the kinds of sexual images found in pornography or erotic art. In the domain of experimental film, important works include Rubin's *Christmas on Earth* (1963), which depicts an orgy in an apartment in New York City, and Schneemann's *Fuses* (1964–6), which includes scenes of the artist having sex with her male partner as their cat, Kitch, looks on.

In narrative cinema, there are several instructive examples of women-directed films that use sexual explicitness to shock the viewer in ways that challenge women's objectification in visual culture. Coralie Trinh Thi and Virginie Despentes's notorious *Baise-moi* is an instructive example. The film uses the aesthetics of pornography, such as real intercourse, to authentically depict the sexual desires and drives of its female characters. The film tells the story of two women who go on a sex- and violence-filled road trip across France. As I have argued elsewhere, the film shows real sex onscreen as part of a rhetoric of authenticity, of 'speaking truthfully' about these women's lives by showing actual sex onscreen.[11] Indeed, real sex is just one of several strategies that *Baise-moi* uses to create an impression of authenticity, including shooting on digital video, *verité*-style handheld camerawork and the use of natural lighting. The film is also deeply anti-voyeuristic insofar as it uses real sex to depict a violent rape. The scene takes place in the first act of the film when one of the protagonists, Manu (Raffaëla Anderson), is abducted and assaulted by a group of men in an empty car park. While the assault is staged, the sex itself is real. The scene thus places the spectator in the uncomfortable position of witnessing a violent rape depicted with aesthetics that in a pornographic context usually work to titillate and arouse. Instead, the spectator is positioned to feel shame and self-consciousness at witnessing a rape performed with real sex. The strategy of *Baise-moi* is thus to take the conventions of pornography, reframe them within a different narrative context, and therefore construct a different relation between the image and the spectator: a relation that imagines the depicted female subject and her sexuality beyond the dehumanising strategies of the pornographic.

Although not usually 'hardcore' like Despentes and Trinh Thi's approach in *Baise-moi*, subversive appropriations of pornography can be found in works by other women screen creatives too. Maria San Filippo comments extensively on the engagement of Catherine Breillat and American writer-director Lena Dunham with pornography in their film and television work respectively. Although these directors hail from very different contexts, San Filippo brings Breillat and Dunham together to remark upon the shared characteristics of their work, particularly their subversive feminist challenge to pornographic visual culture through strategies of visual explicitness, narrative and characterisation. San Filippo argues that both Breillat and Dunham create representations of sex and sexuality that oppose phallocentric and objectifying depictions. Both directors use textual strategies that defetishise the female body and foreground authenticity and the 'realness' of women's sexual experience. Both directors also engage with women's abjection and coming of age, depicting the difficult processes of self-discovery, experimentation and shame – what San Filippo calls 'women's self-formation through sexual degradation'.[12] Observing the provocative explicitness of each director's output, such as sex scenes and frontal nudity, San Filippo suggests the term 'art porn' to describe the 'representationally revisionist critique' in Breillat and Dunham's work.[13] For San Filippo, the term 'art porn' is an appropriate descriptor because it builds on David Bordwell's conception of art cinema. In Bordwell's formulation, art cinema is characterised by both objective and subjective realism.[14] As such, for San Filippo, the term 'art porn' describes the capacity of Breillat and Dunham's work to convey objective and subjective verisimilitude. It speaks to their unvarnished, sometimes abject depiction of sex and bodies, but also to these directors' capacity to convey women's internal, subjective realities of sexuality, from pleasure to shame.

A concept in the provocative avant-garde that resembles San Filippo's notion of art porn is that of 'the obscene' as conceptualised by modernist scholar Allison Pease. Obscenity has several definitions; colloquially, it is often used simply to mean pornographic or explicit. However, the obscene more precisely denotes that which is meant to be hidden. As Linda Williams notes, 'In Latin, the accepted meaning of the term *obscene* is quite literally "off-stage", or that which should be kept "out of public view"'.[15] Obscenity and the depiction of the obscene thus describe a transgression of representation. According to Pease, experiments with the aesthetics of obscenity are a feature of the modernist avant-garde. Obscenity is especially important as a strategy in the works of literary modernism, such as those authored by James Joyce and D. H. Lawrence. Pease argues that these authors incorporated the pornographic into literature as a high art form and thus created an aesthetic of obscenity. For Pease, this aesthetic sought to initiate a new relation between art and its recipient, combining the sensory with the intellectual and demanding the reader engage with the artwork on both levels. In her words, the modernist aesthetics of obscenity aimed 'to bring the body and its senses more overtly into relation with the ethical and social realm' and positioned 'the sensual body as integral to forming aesthetic judgements'.[16] Importantly, Pease says that the obscene is an aesthetic because it demands the recipient reflect upon their sensual responses. Obscenity in the modernist arts is not a pornographic appeal to or arousal of the senses for its own sake, but rather makes the senses the object of intellectual contemplation. As she puts it, 'The aesthetic of the obscene continues to objectify and distance the senses, and in doing so it perpetuates the project of the aesthetic traditions'.[17] Pease's concept is not identical to San Filippo's notion of art porn – she explicates the obscene using very different case studies hailing from a different historical moment. Nevertheless, both the obscene and art porn share a strategy of redeploying the aesthetics of pornography for artistic, intellectual or aesthetic purposes beyond titillation. Such redeployment is the central strategy for Breillat in her films; as I explore in more detail below, her films take explicit imagery that would normally be associated with the pornographic and make it a subject of intellectual and aesthetic contemplation, as in the tradition of the obscene that Pease describes.

The way women challenge phallocentric codes of representation in relation to queer sex differs from the experiments around heterosexual women. Although contemporary art cinema offers an increasing number of conventionally staged sex scenes between women, strategies of obscenity or explicit visibility seem less common. There are, however, some noteworthy exceptions and practitioners that should be acknowledged, even though they do not fit the delimitations of this book's investigation. Working in experimental media rather than narrative art cinema, Barbara Hammer's work is remarkable for its close engagement with queer women's sexuality and its aesthetic strategy of explicitness. This extends from her early short film *Dyketactics* (1974) to her feature documentary *Nitrate Kisses* (1992), both of which contain scenes of queer women having sex. Other early works by Hammer, such as *Women I Love* (1976) and *Multiple Orgasm* (1976), contain additional types of explicit imagery. *Multiple Orgasm* shows an extreme close-up of fingers masturbating a vulva, superimposed over footage of textured rock formations and a woman's ecstatic face. *Women I Love* presents scenes of sex between women as well as shots of vulvas, limbs, used tampons and naked women juxtaposed with yonic fruits, flowers and vegetables. These short films from the 1970s are characterised by both their sexual explicitness and their imagery of natural environments, flowers, plants and insects. For Ronald Gregg, this aesthetic in Hammer's early work is one that conveys beauty and joy, bringing the viewer 'into a tactile, sensual encounter with queer women and space'.[18] Hammer's artistic practice – like those of other experimental artists such as Schneemann and Rubin – opts for a strategy of sexual explicitness to a degree not replicated in other film culture milieus.

Chantal Akerman's *Je tu il elle* (1974) is another important text to mention with regards to explicit depictions of sex between women. Unlike the experimental practitioners above, Akerman does fit the model of art cinema auteur – Michael Koresky calls her 'an art-film sensation'.[19] Her first narrative feature *Je tu il elle* focuses on the experiences of its young protagonist Julie, performed by Akerman herself, and the film ends with a sex scene between Julie and her lover (Claire Wauthion). Akerman's film is remarkable because it hides very little during the sex scene, opting for a strategy of visibility and frankness that remains distinct and unique in women-authored narrative art cinema. The scene is filmed in black and white, using long takes, medium shots and front-on framing. It shows the intimacy between the two women with directness: Tamara Tracz calls it 'both shocking and provoking', but also 'unsexual', 'not an erotic scene', and 'physical but formal'.[20] Tracz does not explain exactly how the scene is provocative. However, Akerman's achievement is precisely this directness of vision Tracz describes, combined with its avoidance of both pornographic titillation and obscenity: there are no close-ups of body parts presented for fetishistic contemplation. Akerman's aesthetic choices are thus neither exploitative nor do they evoke the shock of obscenity, of seeing private things that must be kept hidden.

Whether heterosexual or queer, sex is a rich terrain for women's provocative filmmaking. Sex is a frontier upon which women's representation in patriarchy can be addressed directly: a field where women can subvert the most overt manifestations of the male imaginary in visual culture. Provocative onscreen engagements with sexuality can offer opportunities too. As San Filippo mentions, such depictions can do more than just challenge hegemonic-looking relations and norms of representation. They can also expand a culture's sexual imaginary, prompting conversations and ideas about what it means to be a sexual subject: to '(re)shape our sexual imaginaries in productive (as well as pleasurable) ways'.[21] This point is well taken. Nevertheless, for filmmakers like Trinh Thi, Despentes and Breillat, negatively provoking the onlooker with explicit imagery is important work in itself. This process can be disturbing for the viewer, unsettling the visual aesthetics of obscenity and their dominant meanings.

Obscene Inoculations: *Anatomy of Hell*

It would be a considerable omission in a book on women and provocation to ignore the work of Catherine Breillat. As San Filippo says, 'The concept of provocation has been central to the discourse on Breillat from the beginning; one would be hard-pressed to find a discussion of her that does not at some point characterize her work as provocative'.[22] In interviews, Breillat frequently embraces her persona as a transgressive filmmaker, adding weight to her now widespread characterisation as a provocateur. While noting that her outsider status makes it difficult to finance films, she openly describes herself as 'the pariah of French cinema', adding: 'All true artists are hated ... Only conformists are ever adored.'[23] Breillat's persona as a provocateur has taken on an added dimension in recent years, however, for reasons not directly connected to the content of her films. In 2018, she attracted considerable controversy following comments she made about the Balance Ton Porc ('denounce your pig') and #MeToo movements on a podcast.[24] Amongst other remarks, Breillat said she was 'absolutely against' Balance Ton Porc, saying it was 'invented out of vengeance' and compared it to the history of anonymous denunciations of Jewish people in France.[25] In the same interview, Breillat also disputed Maria Schneider's claim that she was raped on the set of *Last Tango in Paris* (Bernardo Bertolucci, 1972) and stated that she did not believe Asia Argento's accusation of rape against Harvey Weinstein: 'If there's anyone I don't believe, it's Asia Argento.' Although Breillat acknowledged that 'there are real rapes and real violence ... women mustn't be afraid to speak out', her questioning of the accounts of professional actresses was widely reported in the media.[26] Argento also responded on Twitter by describing Breillat as 'the most sadistic and downright evil director I've ever worked with'.[27] Breillat therefore provokes not only via her films but also through her public statements.

The characterisation of Breillat as a filmmaker willing to challenge her audience is nowadays taken for granted in scholarly and critical circles. There are several reasons for this, not least of which is that references to her provocativeness frequently appear in scholarly publications about her.[28] Breillat's films are recognisable as provocations because they are about sex, and sex as a topic of art is closely associated with provocation as an artistic strategy. Breillat's decades-long interest in frank, explicit explorations of women's sexuality therefore align with the prevalent conflation of provocation with sexual provocation. Another reason Breillat is considered a provocateur *par excellence* is that her films transgressively integrate pornographic aesthetics into narrative art cinema: *Romance* and *Anatomy of Hell* show close-ups of vulvas, erect penises, semen, menstrual blood and sex acts like (simulated) fellatio and intercourse. Yet the provocativeness of Breillat's work – insofar as it can elicit sudden negative emotions of shock or feelings of discomfort – deserves further examination. Breillat's works are often funny, wry and heartfelt, yet the orchestration of negative emotion serves her purposes too. As I mention above, Breillat's work is an extension of the modernist project of obscenity: what Pease describes as 'a mode of sexual representation that, while potentially affecting the sensual interests of its readers, does not, as opposed to pornography, seek sexual arousal as its main purpose'.[29] Breillat confronts the spectator with obscenity as a way of undoing the phallocentric construction of women's bodies and sexuality as disgusting and taboo – a strategy that paradoxically requires spectators to experience and wrestle with disgust before they can overcome it. Breillat's body of work offers numerous case studies through which the viewer observes her mobilisation of the obscene; however, the film that embodies this strategy most overtly is *Anatomy of Hell*.

Based on Breillat's novel *Pornocracy* (*Pornocratie*, 2001), *Anatomy of Hell* tells the story of an unnamed woman (Amira Casar) who finds herself in a gay nightclub one evening. Clearly experiencing a devastation of some kind, she attempts to end her life in the bathroom but is stopped when a man (Rocco Siffredi) intervenes. The pair leave the nightclub together, and the woman invites the man to visit her over several nights to look at her body: 'Watch me where I'm unwatchable. No need to touch me. Just say what you see.' She promises she will pay him to do so. Because the man is gay, she reasons, he can look at her 'impartially' without desire. Over four evenings the man visits the woman in a house by the sea (it is never clear if this is the woman's home). The pair converse about desire and engage in numerous intimate and sexual acts: they have intercourse, the man paints the woman's anus with lipstick, and they drink the woman's menses together. The conversation turns repeatedly to men's revulsion against female bodies and sexuality. The woman insists that men do not understand women, that they despise their bodies and want to kill them; the man agrees with her assertions. The story of *Anatomy of Hell* ends ambiguously. Clearly affected by the intimacy he has shared with the woman, the man goes to a bar after their final meeting to drink himself into a stupor. A male companion consoles him: 'Forget it. She was a bitch. A slut like any other.' The man replies: 'Yes, but the queen of sluts.' In a final sequence that may or may not be fantasy, the man returns to the house. It is decaying and empty as if the woman had never been there. He finds her on a clifftop near the house and pushes her to her death into the sea.

Anatomy of Hell is a standout work in Breillat's oeuvre in its insistent presentation of the female body for observation and its direct (and literal) confrontation with the construction of women and their sexuality as disgusting and obscene. The film notably contains an explicit close-up of the woman's vulva, a shot made possible through the participation of a body double. As Breillat says:

> I wanted to confront this forbidden image, to present a closeup of the female sexual organ – that which can't be seen, which can't be watched – so as to ask if this is what sexuality is really all about. I created the terrifying emotional substrata exploring the nature of sex to allow me to transcend the usual, horrible images that form the basis of the porno films people take pleasure in watching.[30]

Reports of viewer reactions at the film's festival screenings indicate a rather negative reception to *Anatomy of Hell*. Gwendolyn Audrey Foster notes that numerous critics walked out of the film's screening at the 2004 Toronto International Film Festival, claiming that 'many reviewers despised and dismissed the film'.[31] Carina Chocano reports that audiences also laughed during the Toronto screening. When asked about it, Breillat describes this laughter as a reaction to the film's challenging premise, which is to confront the spectator with women's bodies and sexuality: 'I think it's the discomfort, like the little boys in the film who laugh at the little girl's body. Once we reach the age of reason – about 7 years old – we laugh at our discomfort about the body. But we are laughing at our own fear.'[32] At that point in her career, Breillat's reputation as a sexual provocateur was well established on the European and North American festival circuits. Several critics who evaluated the film negatively cited the supposed tediousness of the dialogue, the obviousness of the premise and a lack of originality from Breillat as reasons for their dislike.[33] Nevertheless, that there were both walkouts and laughter at the same screening suggest that *Anatomy of Hell* was experienced as provocative. Jonathan Romney observes that the film 'flouts taboos more confrontationally than any mainstream sex drama to date',[34] whereas Lisa Nesselson declares that the film's 'notoriety is assured'.[35]

While this reception suggests that the provocativeness of *Anatomy of Hell* is multifactorial – residing in its dialogue and its predictability as a 'Catherine Breillat' film – the film's chief strategy to shock and discomfit is its explicit depiction of what Breillat calls 'forbidden' images. *Anatomy of Hell* directly confronts the spectator with shots of genitals in aroused states, male and female nudity, sex acts and bodily fluids. It is not the first or only film of Breillat's to adopt such a manoeuvre. Her debut feature, *A Real Young Girl*, for example, contains a sequence in which the fourteen-year-old protagonist Alice (Charlotte Alexandra) imagines an earthworm draped across her vulva, a fantasy that the film literally and explicitly dramatises. *Romance* also shows its protagonist's vulva in extreme close-up after she engages in sadomasochistic role-play and also while she gives birth. However, *Anatomy of Hell* is notable for how reflexively the film shares, and enacts, the female protagonist's objective; just as the woman demands the man look at her, *Anatomy of Hell* insists the spectator look too. That said, while the woman's objective is to prove her hypothesis that men find women disgusting, Breillat has an additional goal. She explains that she wants to overcome the construction of women's bodies as obscene, a strategy that precisely involves showing these bodies: 'I wanted to show the most difficult thing to look at in order to inoculate the viewer, as if with a vaccine. It becomes impossible to say that something is obscene if we change the aesthetic codes.'[36] While it seems that Breillat is here referring to the shot of the woman's vulva, the premise also applies to the film's visual and narrative strategy as a whole. *Anatomy of Hell* shows the obscene to subvert it and drain it of its power to shock. In doing so, the film counters the cultural inscription of women's bodies as pornographic and taboo. Indeed, Breillat makes the point that it is through the cultural practice of hiding, veiling or obscuring that women's bodies become obscene.[37] The strategy to make it un-obscene must therefore be to unveil and to make visible the provocative image. This image will necessarily shock before it loses its power to do so; it must invite uncomfortable laughter first.

Breillat's strategy for subverting the obscene in *Anatomy of Hell* also involves what she describes as changing the aesthetic codes; that is to say, presenting imagery typically understood as obscene in ways that render them un-obscene, even beautiful. In *Anatomy of Hell*, this involves the referencing of visual art, including religious art, in the *mise en scène*. This imagery is intricately structured into the cinematography, production design and performance of the actors, presenting the woman's naked body in ways that resemble artworks legitimised by cultural authority. For example, Breillat explains that the shot of the woman's vulva directly references Gustave Courbet's *The Origin of the World* (*L'Origine du monde*, 1866).[38] Other scenes recall different oil paintings from West European art. On the first night in the house, the woman undresses and lies on her bed, adopting a reclining pose that resembles the many nudes of oil painting: Giorgione's *Sleeping Venus* (*Venere dormiente*, 1510), Titian's *Venus of Urbino* (*Venere di Urbino*, 1534) or Francisco Goya's *The Nude Maja* (*La maja desnuda*, 1797–1800) (Figure 1.1). Breillat also notes that Édouard Manet's *Olympia* (1863) is a key point of reference for the scenes in the house on the first night.[39] This choice is a curious one, suggesting a more complex signification than simply that of aestheticising the woman's body.

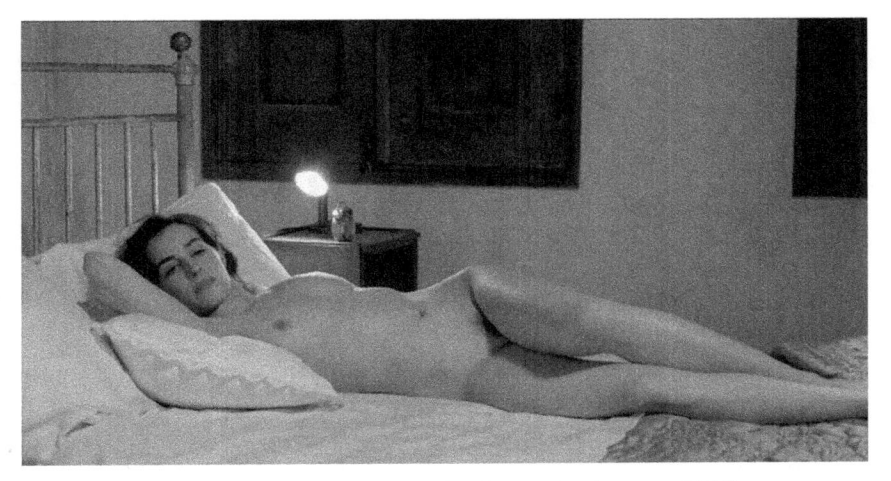

Figure 1.1 The woman poses for the man in *Anatomy of Hell*.

The painting produced a notorious scandal upon its exhibition at the Salon of Paris in 1865. As recounted by Charles Bernheimer, critics perceived the body in the painting as ugly and cadaverous, which Bernheimer considers the Parisian critics' sublimated way of communicating their feelings that the painting was pornographic, indecent and explicit.[40] Anne McCauley observes that some critics at the time compared the anatomical features of the model depicted in the painting to that of an ape.[41] Hence, it is paradoxical that Breillat should choose to reference a painting in her strategy to render the female body un-obscene that was itself considered a provocative obscenity. However, what Manet and Breillat share is the incorporation of preceding and culturally legitimated imagery – the nudes of Giorgione, Titian and Goya – thus integrating the familiar and acceptable into the graphic and pornographic.

Breillat also notes that she intended to draw on images of religious ecstasy as part of her strategy of reframing the female body in *Anatomy of Hell* (Breillat frequently discusses her strict Catholic upbringing and its negative impact upon her views about women's sexuality; as such, the strategy to enlist religious imagery operates in a direct response or corrective to this context). This begins early in the film; the very first sexual act between the protagonists of *Anatomy of Hell* occurs on the evening of their meeting, when the woman performs oral sex on the man in the street. The scene begins as the two walk home together through the empty city streets. The woman declares that the only reason the man found her in the toilets was because he must have been seeking an impersonal encounter: 'To get sucked, like all men.' The man slaps her angrily in response and she cries out, upset. Then, she does precisely what she accused, unzipping the man's trousers and fellating him. Once she finishes, the camera offers a lingering close-up of the woman's face and semen is clearly visible against her lips. While not a religious ecstatic pose – the woman appears ambivalent, defiant and still affected by her earlier suicide attempt – she is unashamed, and the beauty of her face remains intact. The moment invites a direct comparison with the conventions of contemporary pornography in which the close-up of a woman's semen-covered face is a spectacle of (and for) male pleasure. Instead of constructing the image in this way, Breillat suggests that the close-up performs a different function. She describes the woman's face as 'the face of a Madonna' – as performed by Casar, the woman indeed appears both calm and strangely radiant in a manner reminiscent of such artistic depictions. For Breillat, the scene thus takes the tenor of a spiritual encounter attempted through sexuality, a 'reuniting of the lowly and the sacred' via the combined imagery of both religious art and pornography.[42] This strategy also extends to the production design and *mise en scène* of *Anatomy of Hell*. The house in which the woman invites the man to visit her is a large Mediterranean-style building surrounded by aloe plants, cacti and yuccas. Her room is spartan and a crucifix hangs on the plastered wall. Such a setting allows the *mise en scène* to take on an ascetic appearance reminiscent of a monastery. Moreover, for the scenes in the bedroom, Breillat suggests that she wanted the woman to appear Christ-like on the bed, martyred and bleeding.[43]

As a director, Breillat is characteristically willing to explain her objectives as a provocateur and chronicler of heterosexual women's experiences. Amongst her many remarks, she frequently reiterates her desire to create something positive for women, intentions that often contrast with the pessimistic narrative outcomes for her protagonists, such as death in *Anatomy of Hell* and *Perfect Love!*, for example. She says her goal is to 'create a transcendent beauty out of things you've been told are purely ugly' – to make beauty out of obscenity and symbolically liberate women's bodies from patriarchal representational regimes.[44] Yet the route to beauty and liberation in Breillat's work is via negative emotions: it requires the onlooker to confront obscenity, to work through disgust and to experience shame precisely to overcome such responses. To paraphrase the protagonist of *Anatomy of Hell*, Breillat's films ask spectators to watch the woman where she is unwatchable. *Anatomy of Hell* involves a sting, a confrontation with obscenity that is necessary to inoculate against it. Provided, of course, that the spectator does not walk out of the cinema.

Queering Obscenity: *She Monkeys*

Given that the films of Catherine Breillat centre on heterosexual women, her work raises an important question: how has the sexuality of queer women been provocatively depicted in art cinema? Is there an art-porn provocateur of female queerness? After all, the history of art has its share of controversial queer moments and, as such, there is precedent for obscene female queerness in art cinema too. In 1907, an onstage kiss between Sidonie-Gabrielle Colette and her lover Mathilde de Morny provoked a riot at the Moulin Rouge. In 1928, Radclyffe Hall's *The Well of Loneliness* was subject to high-profile obscenity charges shortly following its publication. In 2017, Nat Randall, Anna Breckon and E. O. Gill's experimental short *Thrash-Her* – which depicts an all-female cast erotically brawling in a skate bowl – drew objections from some viewers upon its screening at the Melbourne Women in Film Festival.[45] However, a decade after the end of Breillat's décalogue of films about heterosexual women's sexuality, there appears to be no woman director on the narrative art cinema circuit who has taken up her project in relation to non-heterosexual characters – no director attempting to 'inoculate' the viewer with obscene imagery of female queerness.[46] Queer sex certainly appears in narrative art films by women, such as *The Watermelon Woman* (Cheryl Dunye, 1996), *The Monkey's Mask* (Samantha Lang, 2000) and *Portrait of a Lady on Fire* (*Portrait de la jeune fille en feu*, Céline Sciamma, 2019). Yet when filmmakers depict queer women's bodies and sexuality, provoking negative emotions of shock or disgust via the visual transgression of obscenity does not appear to be a favoured strategy. Provocation in relation to queerness occurs via another means.

One of the most intriguing queer films in post-millennium art cinema is notably inexplicit: Swedish filmmaker Lisa Aschan's debut *She Monkeys*, co-written with Josefine Adolfsson. The protagonist of the film is Emma (Mathilda Paradeiser), a teenager of fifteen who joins an equestrian vaulting group. She befriends Cassandra (Linda Molin), a beautiful and dominant girl who offers to help Emma train: 'I can teach anyone anything', she says. The two form a competitive friendship, as not all the girls who train will make the team for competition. The two hang out at the pool, drink alcohol and play pranks on a boy who is interested in Emma. Throughout this, Cassandra inflicts small and ambiguous acts of violence upon Emma. While visiting a local pool, Cassandra spins Emma around on the top of a high diving platform, from which Emma falls; she later humiliates the boy who is interested in Emma, demanding he undress himself, then stealing his clothes and wallet. Emma and Cassandra have no erotic contact apart from a kiss after a night of drinking – initiated by Cassandra;

Emma is too drunk, or perhaps simply unwilling, to reciprocate the kiss. Their relationship comes to a climax of sorts when Emma fails to make the vaulting team due, according to the coach, to her lack of charisma and showmanship. Shortly afterwards, Emma strikes Cassandra on the knee with a pitchfork, hurting her so badly that she can no longer compete at vaulting. Emma subsequently takes Cassandra's place on the team. When asked in interviews what inspired *She Monkeys*, Aschan cryptically replied that it was a series of images and associations: 'A copy of *Story Of The Eye* by George Bataille, an advert for ice cream with a little girl wearing a bikini, and Shirley Temple.'[47] Such an answer is itself provocative. Together, such images evoke sensuality and youthful femininity through the image of the bikini-clad girl, the performative innocence of Shirley Temple and the excessive, hallucinatory violence and sexuality connoted by Bataille's novella. They suggest a feminine coming of age undergirded by eroticism and violence.

The reception of *She Monkeys* on its festival run was mixed. Several critics observed that the film seemed highly charged and sexual even though it is notably inexplicit: it contains no nudity, no sex scenes, and only a handful of minor (albeit impactful) acts of interpersonal violence. Alissa Simon's review for *Variety* is indicative: 'Lisa Aschan thrillingly subverts the coming-of-age genre, political correctness, gender roles and (without ever becoming graphic) just about everything to do with the depiction of developing sexuality in the taboo-breaking "She Monkeys".'[48] Simon does not specify how the film is 'taboo-breaking', giving only her impression of its transgressiveness. Catherine Wheatley similarly gestures to the film's tone: 'Something sinister hovers in the air; we brace ourselves for horror, suspense, mystery. What we actually get is weirder, more slippery and somehow more dangerous.'[49] The film does contain a surfeit of suggestive imagery: horses that can trample and kick, guns, denim, boots (all signifiers of the Western, corresponding with Aschan's desire for every scene to be 'a duel'[50]). Not all critics appreciated the film's eschewal of the explicit. Andrew Pulver claims the film 'suffers a little from its resolute avoidance of titillation',[51] and Matthew Lee calls it '*Beautiful Crazy* [*Luan qing chun*, Chi-Yuarn Lee, 2008] without the male gaze and the shock tactics, and a good deal less interesting as a result'.[52] *She Monkeys* therefore occupies a thought-provoking position as a provocative film about queer desire and competitive friendship that resolutely avoids explicitness in favour of ambiguity. There are no shots of naked genitals or open discussions of sex. The rifle that Emma carries around with her – and provocatively points at her sibling, Cassandra, and sometimes the empty horizon – goes unfired. The film operates instead in the domain of the unsaid and unconfirmed.

Critical commentary on *She Monkeys* provides an important clue about the film's strategy, indicating that the film provokes tonally via imagery and allusion. Crucially, the film not only immerses the spectator in this imagery: it also draws them into sensuous identification with the protagonists' desire and aggression, communicating these affects via performance, gesture and onscreen movement. Katharina Lindner calls the process by which the film draws the spectator into a sensory identification with the bodies and images onscreen 'sensuous empathy'.[53] Given Aschan's desire for each scene between Cassandra and Emma to be 'a duel', these bodies are locked in battles that feel both transgressive and perilous. *She Monkeys* initiates the spectator into this sensory identification from its opening moments. In the pre-credits scene, Emma walks through the forest and obedience-trains her dog with a clicker while her sister, Sara (Isabella Lindquist), watches on. The animal behaves superbly but each time the dog obeys a command, its body tenses in anticipation of release from the compulsion to sit or stay. The scene ends on a cut to an image of a taut, trembling wire as the opening credits begin. The opening of *She Monkeys* therefore begins with no context and its significance is never made clear in the plot or referred to again in the narrative. It is instead a prologue foreshadowing the games of physical control and dominance that characterise Cassandra and Emma's relationship, expressed metaphorically through the obedience training Emma undertakes with her dog. Furthermore, the opening scene is constructed in a manner that sensuously identifies the spectator with the bodies onscreen, emphasising the tightness rippling through the canine's body, the tension as it waits and the piercing sound of the clicker that signifies release. Similar moments recur throughout *She Monkeys* that invite the spectator into a sensory, and at times unnerving, identification with the protagonists. On one occasion, Cassandra and Emma play a game in the shallow waters of the inlet near their homes. Emma wears a blindfold while Cassandra darts around her mischievously. Cassandra asks Emma to put her hands out. She then scoops a large jellyfish out from the shallow water and places it into Emma's hands. Rather than flinching or starting, Emma squeezes the creature – the scene cuts to a medium shot of the jelly coming apart and slipping between her fingers. A similar game occurs at the local swimming pool, when Cassandra leads Emma to the highest diving platform. She instructs Emma to close her eyes and spins her around until she becomes dizzy. It is not clear whether Cassandra pushes Emma, but Emma falls uncontrolled into the pool, bloodying her nose as she hits the water. In both scenes Cassandra inflicts a minor trick or cruelty upon Emma (albeit with a degree of Emma's consent in her participation in each instance). In both cases, the object is to dominate Emma by physically disorienting her and subjecting her to uncontrolled bodily sensations, whether it is the cold slime of the jellyfish or the sensation of falling through the air.

Through such scenes, *She Monkeys* constructs a vivid sensory world that positions the spectator to experience the erotic tension between Cassandra and Emma. While compelling, this empathy is also discomfiting. Eroticism in *She Monkeys* is enmeshed with hostility, aggression and anticipated pain. This imbrication lies at the centre of its provocative modality and address to the viewer. As Aschan herself says, 'I wanted to investigate how people behave together'.[54] The film's undercurrent of menace also corresponds with *Story of the Eye* (1928), a stated point of reference for Aschan. The erotic adventures of the protagonists in Bataille's novella are accompanied by gruesome violence: they decapitate a cyclist in a car accident, attend bull fights in Spain and murder a priest. While nowhere near the scale of these events in *Story of the Eye*, the small acts of aggression in *She Monkeys* are profound and jarring to experience.[55] As Lindner writes, it is 'the frequent clashing of corporeally affective registers – tenderness and sensuous proximity versus cold, detached violence and startling aggression – that shapes *She Monkeys*' sensuous trajectory'.[56] It is a film of understated but deeply felt cruelties.

The provocation of *She Monkeys* consists of this tonal indeterminacy – through what is conveyed through the sensuality of its images but remains offscreen and unspoken. The film provokes not by rewriting the obscene but refusing the clarity of visual or narrative confirmation. As Clara Bradbury-Rance writes, '*She Monkeys* provokes the frustration and even banality of closure's refusal'.[57] Indeed, for Lee it is this sense of the maintenance of the private, unrealised and unspoken between Emma and Cassandra that is precisely what feels discomfiting: 'The older girls' tentative overtures are sometimes unsettling, but more in that they can feel like a window onto something that's meant to be private.'[58] There are two implications of this tonal depiction of eroticism between the protagonists of *She Monkeys*. First, the exclusion of actual erotic elements evades the pitfalls of explicitness when it comes to depictions of lesbianism, avoiding representing queer desire (or indeed sex) as a titillating spectacle for a heterosexual male gaze. Instead, *She Monkeys* offers another way of experiencing sexuality beyond the visual – beyond 'heteronormative economies of looking'.[59] The film conveys teenage desire through the vividly experiential rather than the purely visual. It captures this desire's attraction, ambiguity and aggression; it is never clear whether Cassandra and Emma are lovers, competitors or both. *She Monkeys* thus allows their feelings to stay strategically, and queerly, undefined.

Girl Shame

Breillat's and Aschan's explorations of sexuality are not restricted to adult women and teenagers; both filmmakers confront girlhood too, particularly the painful experience of shame upon becoming a sexual being and inhabiting a body deemed obscene by cultural codes. This is central to their provocations: as Breillat has said, 'I want to describe female shame'.[60] Both she and Aschan provide vivid and at times excruciating depictions of life as a girl, particularly the constitution of the girl body under a social gaze. Breillat's *Fat Girl* – released five years prior to *Anatomy of Hell* – focuses precisely on the experiences of an overweight twelve-year-old, Anaïs (Anaïs Reboux), as she witnesses the sexual initiation of her older sister Elena (Roxane Mesquida). *She Monkeys* contains a secondary plot following Emma's sister Sara, a determined seven-year-old who decides she is ready for the world of adult femininity. *Fat Girl* and *She Monkeys* present what can productively be termed 'girl shame', a concept I coin in contradistinction to Lisa French's notion of 'girlshine'. French describes girlshine as 'the short and radiant period that young women experience when they become cognisant of themselves as powerful sexual beings', typically between sixteen and twenty-one years old.[61] This transitory phase is regularly depicted in women's cinema, for example, in films like *Holy Smoke!* (Jane Campion, 1999), *The Virgin Suicides* (Sofia Coppola, 1999), *Lost in Translation* (Sofia Coppola, 2003), *Marie Antoinette* (Sofia Coppola, 2006), *The Holy Girl* (*La niña santa*, Lucrecia Martel, 2004), *Water Lilies* (*Naissance des pieuvres*, Céline Sciamma, 2007), *Girlhood* (Céline Sciamma, 2014) and *Circumstance* (Maryam Keshavarz, 2011). Girlshine also describes the aura, both figurative and literal, that hangs over girls in such films. Young women are literally radiant in the *mise en scène* – ringed with light and colour – and are narratively empowered by their newfound grace, beauty and sensuality. Such a construction applies to the beautiful Elena in *Fat Girl* as well as to Cassandra and Emma in *She Monkeys*.[62] In contrast, Anaïs and Sara are girls who do not shine. Both inhabit bodies that other characters deem undesirable or that appear awkwardly juvenile in the *mise en scène*. *Fat Girl* and *She Monkeys* uncompromisingly depict this difficult girl corporeality, vividly positioning spectators to inhabit the girls' initiation into shame via the experience of their own bodies. Through the empathetic viewing experience they create, these films convey a female coming of age that is as characteristic as the girlshine moment but far more difficult to occupy as a spectator.

Although not the primary protagonist of *She Monkeys*, seven-year-old Sara's storyline is crucial to the film's exploration of female sexuality and bodily control. Round-faced and sporting a blunt fringe, Sara looks very much like a young girl barely out of toddlerhood. In an early scene, she snuggles with her father in bed on a summer evening and asks him to scratch her on her belly. She innocently asks about her handsome older cousin Sebastian; her dad replies: 'Sara, I don't think Sebastian fancies you the same way that you fancy him.' Sara's unselfconsciousness is short lived. During a swimming lesson at the pool, a lifeguard scolds Sara for going bare-chested without a bathing top. Sara is instantly mortified and covers herself with her arms. Although an older woman intervenes and insists that Sara should not feel ashamed, it is too late: she hides behind a potted plant, arms still crossed against her chest, and refuses to return to class. This incident sparks a change in Sara. Suddenly aware of her body's supposed obscenity, she experiences, as French describes, 'a self-awareness of what Mulvey described as "to-be-looked-at-ness"'.[63] Unlike in the girlshine moment French describes, however, this awareness comes too soon for seven-year-old Sara, insofar as she is clearly still a child and naive about adult sexuality. Following her initial shame, she chooses to embrace the supposed 'sexuality' that the lifeguard's words implied that she possesses. She demands her father buy her a leopard-print bikini and insists on wearing a fake tattoo on her arm (Figure 1.2). Sara clearly misinterprets the scolding she received at the pool; the lifeguard's chief concern is that paedophiles may be present. Yet in another sense, Sara has not misunderstood. The incident at the pool reveals that her bare chest is now socially and culturally considered to be obscene – something that must be kept out of view.

Sara's storyline culminates in her attempted 'seduction' of Sebastian, a sequence that can be experienced as both a funny and a discomfiting exploration of girlish desires and the potential for shame. One evening

Figure 1.2 Sara admires her leopard-print bikini in *She Monkeys*.

when Sebastian comes to her house to babysit, Sara puts on her leopard-print bikini and performs a dance for him. Wheatley describes it as 'a small child's version of a sexy dance routine, tugging pants from her wiggling bum'.[64] Such an account highlights the comedy of the moment, and the scene does not eroticise Sara's dance, cutting instead to Sebastian's bemused reaction throughout. Yet although blunted by comedy, the spectacle of Sara's 'wiggling bum' also contains the potential for provocation insofar as the moment positions the spectator into a discomfiting irony. There is a mismatch between Sara's self-image and how she is perceived by Sebastian. This has been a characteristic of their interactions from the beginning of the film. A few scenes prior to her dance routine, for instance, Sebastian arrives at Sara's house for an evening of babysitting; upon his arrival, Sara enthusiastically wraps her arms around Sebastian and refuses to let go. Such moments position the spectator to anticipate and, eventually, share Sara's humiliation at her failed seduction of her cousin. The dance scene also invokes the discomfiting taboo of the sexualised child body, the precise kind of spectacle that Sara was forced to cover at the pool. Although Lee argues that there is nothing exploitative about Sara's storyline in *She Monkeys*, the trajectory of the film's plot nonetheless raises the possibility that Sara's journey will lead somewhere catastrophic. It is therefore an uncomfortable plotline for the spectator to follow and anticipate before its eventual resolution. In addition, the fact that *She Monkeys* even acknowledges a child's attempt at sexuality contains the potential to unsettle. As Lee writes, 'Anyone offended by *Little Miss Sunshine* [Jonathan Dayton and Valerie Faris, 2006] pushing their buttons would most likely spontaneously combust at this'.[65] Sara takes the role of *enfant terrible* in *She Monkeys*, mortifying adults – and the spectator – with the naive and frank admissions of her desires and willingness to act upon them. She is also a figure for a discomforting, empathetic spectatorial experience of shame. As a girl, Sara's body is deemed too obscene to be unclothed at the pool but also too juvenile to seduce.

Breillat's *Fat Girl* shares with *She Monkeys* this thematic focus on girl shame and the obscene-yet-undesirable girl body. As the English-language title makes clear, *Fat Girl* is about the specific corporeal experience of an overweight girl defined by her fatness – a position that the film makes very clear is an abject one, and one that it demands the spectator occupy in their identification with the protagonist. The film centres on Anaïs and her fifteen-year-old sister Elena as they holiday together with their parents at a seaside town. Elena is a beautiful teenager with a willowy, slender appearance. She also carries herself with a confident self-awareness characteristic of the girlshine moment. To use French's words, Elena has a 'sense of power without the caution that age and experience impose'.[66] Anaïs, in contrast, is overweight and lacks her sister's graceful physicality. Whereas her sister possesses a narcissistic, and thus fragile, self-confidence and capacity for self-delusion, Anaïs exhibits a cynical self-awareness that gives her insight beyond her years. During their holiday, Elena meets an Italian university student named Fernando (Libero De Rienzo) and they begin a flirtation. Elena wants to lose her virginity to the handsome young man but is frightened to do so – she is afraid of the consequences, the physical pain of intercourse and the possibility that Fernando only pretends to care for her. Fernando eventually talks Elena into sex using a series of declarations and threats: that Elena is not like other girls, that he will propose marriage, and that Elena is wrong to doubt his intentions. Anaïs is present at almost every moment of their flirtation, including over two nights in which Fernando visits Elena in their shared bedroom and the pair engage in anal and vaginal intercourse. The girls' mother eventually discovers what has occurred and furiously cuts their holiday short. On the drive back to Paris, both Elena and her mother are randomly killed by a stranger while sleeping in their car at a highway rest stop. The man rapes Anaïs but leaves her alive.

Fat Girl invites a different relation between the spectator and Anaïs than that initiated by *She Monkeys*, although it is also a challenging one to inhabit, charged with negative affect. Anaïs is aware of her own supposed undesirability in a way that Sara has yet to discover; Anaïs is also older and, although inexperienced, possesses a cynical awareness about sex and sexual politics (she bluntly tells Elena as she cries about Fernando: 'Go to sleep. He's already forgotten you'). However, a key provocation of *Fat Girl* is its frank depiction of Anaïs's defining corporal experience as a fat girl. Repeated small humiliations and struggles over food and clothes define Anaïs's relationship with her mother and sister. Her mother regularly makes comments about her daughter's eating, such as pointedly asking, 'Are you still eating that?' as Anaïs snacks on some food. Moreover, the film places Anaïs in constant comparison with Elena in the frame (and, to a degree, their beautiful mother). Anaïs, however, responds with defiance to this shaming. She continues to eat; she expresses her desire by whispering to imaginary lovers while swimming in the pool; she wears the clothes she wants, even when Elena complains that Anaïs has selected the exact same dress to purchase as her sister. *Fat Girl* thus presents Anaïs's girlhood experience as a battle against near-constant humiliation. Anaïs's absolute resistance to being shamed is demonstrated with devastating clarity at the film's conclusion, in which she refuses to become the victim of the rape she experiences. The film ends abruptly as Anaïs, Elena and her mother are randomly attacked while sleeping in their car by the side of the highway. The assailant murders Elena and her mother but leaves Anaïs alive after sexually assaulting her in the nearby woodlands. During the attack, Anaïs struggles at first but then puts her arms around the rapist. Afterwards, she tells the police she has not been sexually assaulted, but cryptically adds: 'Don't believe me if you don't want to.' Such a statement suggests that Anaïs's resistance to shame is so strong that she even refuses to identify as a victim of violent assault, although she gives permission for others to take a different view. *Fat Girl* thus positions the spectator to bear witness to Anaïs's lived experience of shame and her refusal of humiliation in all its forms. The attempts to shame her and her resistance to these attempts are a defining aspect of Anaïs's girlhood that the film invites us to experience.

Far from an idealised moment, girlhood in *Fat Girl* and *She Monkeys* is marked by the experience of shame. Both Sara and Anaïs wish to claim their identities and bodies as autonomous participants in the sexual economy of desire and seduction. These girls learn an important lesson: their bodies are not their own to shape but are subjected to the gaze, judgement and shaming of others. Anaïs's refusal to identify herself as a victim, as well as Sara's determination to perform the sexual maturity she believes she possesses, can be read as acts of resistance against such disempowerment – as acts of self-determination in spite of others' subjectifying humiliations. Nevertheless, the lesson remains that Anaïs and Sara's bodies, and the sexual meanings associated with them, are largely not their own to make. Breillat and Aschan share this insight and explore it through their films. In keeping with San Filippo's thoughts, these filmmakers provoke because of their close interest in sexual humiliation and degradation as a formative aspect of women's subjectivity, and the result is discomfiting.[67] The youth of Breillat and Aschan's protagonists make for an even more poignant and disturbing viewing experience. Girlhood is not a utopian place that is free from the struggles of adult womanhood – quite the opposite. For Sara and Anaïs, the painful journey toward adult sexuality is already well underway.

Subversive Sex

The work of Breillat and Aschan shocks the onlooker via an aesthetics of obscenity, unsettles tonally with aggressive but unseen eroticism and disturbs via an engagement with girl shame. Yet not everyone is convinced of the subversive power of sex in cinema. For Lisa Downing, explicit sexuality is 'a territory that has apparently already been so thoroughly dispossessed of its strategic political power – in academic Cultural Theory circles at least'.[68] Ginette Vincendeau makes a comparable point in a somewhat mixed account of Breillat's oeuvre, questioning the political efficacy of the director's approach: 'The enthusiasm with which Breillat is championed by the French male critical establishment (not noted for its feminist awareness) would suggest that, like surrealism, hers is an art aimed at shocking rather than challenging.'[69] In the introduction to this chapter, I suggested that provocation via depictions of sex is the foremost issue in any investigation into cinematic provocation. Yet such comments from Downing and Vincendeau suggest that the foremost topic in provocation is now, consequentially, the most obvious. Following this, the only conclusion is that sex as a theme or spectacle is now the least incendiary of all strategies available to creators, the least political and the least capable of inducing negative emotions.

'Cultural theory circles' notwithstanding, Aschan's and Breillat's films demonstrate that sexual content still has the power to provoke an audience. What these directors clearly demonstrate is that women's sexuality – their desires, queerness, bodies and experiences of shame – are still confronting topics and spectacles. It is not an effortless process of unconscious spectatorial enjoyment to look upon vulvas, semen or menses in close-up, as in *Anatomy of Hell*, or to witness two teenage girls' hostile, ambiguous encounters in *She Monkeys*, or to inhabit burning juvenile shame in *Fat Girl* and *She Monkeys*. And indeed, *She Monkeys*, *Anatomy of Hell* and *Fat Girl* were not met with cool disinterest when they premiered on the festival circuit. Critics identified all these films as provocations, although individual viewers at festival screenings demonstrated a varying capacity to endure them, with some remaining in the cinema and others walking out. What is significant here is that provoking negative emotions of discomfort is precisely the point for Breillat and Aschan. Such a spectatorial response is both necessary and intrinsic to *She Monkeys*, *Anatomy of Hell* and *Fat Girl* and their commentary on female sexual subjectivity. These films deal with the interplay of sexuality both seen and hidden – of whose bodies are deemed obscene by whom and to whose empowerment or disempowerment. Breillat and Aschan show that the phallocentric visual codes that construct women's sexuality – particularly how women should be viewed, controlled and understood – are longstanding. The fact that challenging these codes is still an uncomfortable process attests to their enduring power. Sex, particularly women's sex, remains both personal and political.

Notes

1. Although regularly mentioning Breillat's nickname 'the auteur of porn', journalists, film critics and scholars routinely problematise the appellation too, considering how it misrepresents Breillat's body of work. (Cath Clarke, 'Catherine Breillat: "I Love Blood. It's in All My Films"', *Guardian*, 16 July 2010, https://www.theguardian.com/film/2010/jul/15/catherine-breillat-interview; Douglas Keesey, *Catherine Breillat* [Manchester: Manchester University Press, 2016], 1; Brian Price, 'Breillat, Catherine', *Senses of Cinema*, 23 [2002], https://www.sensesofcinema.com/2002/great-directors/breillat/; Maria San Filippo, *Provocauteurs and Provocations: Screening Sex in 21st Century Media* [Bloomington: Indiana University Press, 2020], 176.)
2. I refer to Breillat's film as *Fat Girl* throughout this book, although it has gone by other English-language titles. The most literal one is *For My Sister*, which is the name under which I first saw the film in Australia. *Fat Girl* is the film's North American title and is used by Criterion for worldwide release. Breillat herself has stated that *Fat Girl* was the film's original name, but that she changed it to avoid offending the young actress who portrayed Anaïs and, also, to not alienate a French-speaking audience with an English-language title. However, Breillat maintains 'Fat Girl' is the original title and that she considers it 'simpler, more basic, more real'. (Catherine Breillat, '*Fat Girl*: About the Title', *Criterion*, 3 May 2011, https://www.criterion.com/current/posts/1846-fat-girl-about-the-title.)
3. Price, 'Breillat, Catherine'.
4. San Filippo, *Provocauteurs and Provocations*, 176.
5. Saul Anton, 'Catherine Breillat Opens Up About "Romance", Sex and Censorship', interview, *Indiewire*, 23 September 1999, https://www.indiewire.com/1999/09/interview-catherine-breillat-opens-up-about-romance-sex-and-censorship-82059/.
6. Catherine Wheatley, 'She Monkeys', *Sight & Sound* 22, no. 6 (2012), 76.
7. Laura Mulvey, 'Visual Pleasure and Narrative Cinema', *Screen* 16, no. 3 (1975); John Berger, *Ways of Seeing* (London: Penguin, 2008), 64.
8. Geoffrey Macnab, 'Written on the Body', interview with Catherine Breillat, *Sight & Sound* 14, no. 12 (2004), 22.
9. Linda Williams discusses this possibility in her analysis of *Blue is the Warmest Colour* (*La vie d'Adèle*, Abdellatif Kechiche, 2013). Kechiche's film depicts queer women's sex onscreen in a series of explicit scenes between the two female protagonists, played by Léa Seydoux and Adèle Exarchopoulos. The film, adapted from Jul Maroh's graphic novel *Le bleu est une couleur chaude* (2010), caused a sensation upon its release and has since become a lightning rod for debates about the depiction of queer women's sex onscreen. In her discussion, Williams summarises and evaluates the concern some viewers have that the film represents sex between women in ways that appeal to the sexual interests of a heterosexual male onlooker. (Linda Williams, 'Cinema's Sex Acts', *Film Quarterly* 67, no. 4 [2014], 9–25.)

10. Robin Blaetz, 'Introduction', in *Women's Experimental Cinema: Critical Frameworks*, ed. Robin Blaetz (Durham, NC: Duke University Press, 2007), 12.
11. For a detailed discussion of this film, see Janice Loreck, *Violent Women in Contemporary Cinema* (Basingstoke: Palgrave, 2016), 54–74.
12. San Filippo, *Provocauteurs and Provocations*, 171.
13. Ibid., 174.
14. David Bordwell, 'The Art Cinema as a Mode of Film Practice', *Film Criticism* 4, no. 1 (1979), 57–9.
15. Linda Williams, 'Proliferating Pornographies On/Scene: An Introduction', in *Porn Studies*, ed. Linda Williams (Durham, NC: Duke University Press, 2004), 3; emphasis in original.
16. Allison Pease, *Modernism, Mass Culture, and the Aesthetics of Obscenity* (Cambridge: Cambridge University Press, 2000), 166.
17. Ibid., 35.
18. Ronald Gregg, 'The Documentaries of Barbara Hammer: Lesbian Creativity, Kinship, and Erotic Pleasure in the Historical Margins', *Camera Obscura: Feminism, Culture, and Media Studies* 36, no. 3 (2021), 106.
19. Michael Koresky, 'Eclipse Series 19: Chantal Akerman in the Seventies', *Criterion*, 9 January 2010, https://www.criterion.com/current/posts/1351-eclipse-series-19-chantal-akerman-in-the-seventies.
20. Tamara Tracz, '*Je tu il elle*', *Senses of Cinema* 67 (2013), https://www.sensesofcinema.com/2013/cteq/je-tu-il-elle/.
21. San Filippo, *Provocauteurs and Provocations*, 22.
22. Ibid., 166.
23. Benjamin Secher, 'Catherine Breillat: "All True Artists Are Hated"', *Telegraph*, 5 April 2008, https://www.telegraph.co.uk/culture/film/starsandstories/3672302/Catherine-BreillatAll-true-artists-are-hated.html.
24. The episode, which was broadcast on the Murmur podcast, has since been taken down from the Murmur network.
25. Michael Nordine, 'Catherine Breillat Says Asia Argento Is a "Traitor", Harvey Weinstein Isn't That Bad, and She's Against #MeToo', *IndieWire*, 29 March 2018, https://www.indiewire.com/2018/03/catherine-breillat-asia-argento-harvey-weinstein-jessica-chastain-me-too-1201945040/.
26. Ibid.
27. Shakiel Mahjouri, 'Asia Argento Accuses 'Sadistic and Downright Evil' Director Catherine Breillat of Abuse', *ET Canada*, 30 March 2018, https://etcanada.com/news/314343/asia-argento-accuses-sadistic-and-downright-evil-director-catherine-breillat-of-abuse/. Argento's tweets have since been deleted.
28. Examples include San Filippo, *Provocauteurs and Provocations*, 166; Mattias Frey, *Extreme Cinema: The Transgressive Rhetoric of Today's Art Film Culture* (New Brunswick, NJ: Rutgers University Press, 2016), 26–7; Keesey, *Catherine Breillat*, 1.

29. Pease, *Modernism*, 34.
30. Breillat in Mcnab, 'Written on the Body', 22.
31. Gwendolyn Audrey Foster, '*Anatomy of Hell*: A Feminist Fairy Tale', *Senses of Cinema* 80 (2016), https://www.sensesofcinema.com/2016/cteq/anatomy-hell/.
32. Carina Chocano, 'Anatomy of a Film Both Graphic, Abstract', interview, *Los Angeles Times*, 27 September 2004, https://www.latimes.com/archives/la-xpm-2004-sep-27-et-breillat27-story.html.
33. See the following reviews: Nathan Lee, 'Anatomy of Hell', *Film Comment* 40 no. 5 (2004), 72; Lisa Nesselson, 'Anatomy of Hell', *Variety*, 23 January 2004, https://variety.com/2004/film/reviews/anatomy-of-hell-1200536861/; Manohla Dargis, 'Four Nights of Sex and Zero Nights of Fun', *New York Times*, 15 October 2004, https://www.nytimes.com/2004/10/15/movies/four-nights-of-sex-and-zero-nights-of-fun.html; Roger Ebert, '"Anatomy of Hell" Just Disgusts', *RogerEbert.com*, 11 November 2004, https://www.rogerebert.com/reviews/anatomy-of-hell-2004.
34. Jonathan Romney, 'Anatomy of Hell (Anatomie de L'Enfer)', *Screen Daily*, 27 January 2004, https://www.screendaily.com/anatomy-of-hell-anatomie-de-lenfer/4017050.article.
35. Nesselson, 'Anatomy of Hell'.
36. Breillat, 'Anatomy of a Film'.
37. Ibid.
38. Keesey, *Catherine Breillat*, 142–3.
39. Ibid., 139.
40. Charles Bernheimer, 'Manet's Olympia: The Figuration of Scandal', *Poetics Today* 10, no. 2 (1989), 256.
41. Anne McCauley, 'Beauty or Beast? Manet's Olympia in the Age of Comparative Anatomy', *Art History* 43, no. 4 (2020), 743.
42. Keesey, *Catherine Breillat*, 138.
43. Ibid., 141.
44. Breillat in Mcnab, 'Written on the Body', 22.
45. This is a personal anecdote I include as one of the organisers of the Melbourne Women in Film Festival. Following the inaugural 2017 event, several members of the festival board raised concerns about the programming and screening of *Thrash-Her* owing to the apparent performance of sexual violence in the work. The board members voiced these concerns after attending the screening as part of the festival audience.
46. *Blue is the Warmest Colour* is one example of a narrative art film that contains lengthy and explicit simulated sex scenes between women. However, although Kechiche's film is derived from a queer non-binary person's source material, it is nevertheless a male-directed film. As such, while art film directors have attempted to depict queer women's sex onscreen, the most discussed attempt in post-millennium art cinema has been undertaken by a male director. There does not appear to be a directly equivalent 'auteur of porn' for queer women's sexuality, as Breillat is for heterosexual women.

47. Rosie Swash, 'She Monkeys Director Wanted Coming-of-Age Movie to Be "Like a Western"', *Guardian*, 28 April 2012, https://www.theguardian.com/film/2012/apr/28/she-monkeys-lisa-aschan-interview.
48. Alissa Simon, 'She Monkeys', *Variety*, 5 February 2011, https://variety.com/2011/film/reviews/she-monkeys-1117944506/.
49. Wheatley, 'She Monkeys', 76.
50. Swash, 'She Monkeys Director'.
51. Andrew Pulver, 'She Monkeys – Review', *Guardian*, 18 May 2012, https://www.theguardian.com/film/2012/may/17/she-monkeys-review.
52. Matthew Lee, 'LIFF 2011: SHE MONKEYS', *Screen Anarchy*, 27 November 2011, https://screenanarchy.com/2011/11/liff-2011-she-monkeys-review.html.
53. Katharina Lindner, 'Queer-ing Texture: Tactility, Spatiality, and Kinesthetic Empathy in She Monkeys', *Camera Obscura: Feminism, Culture, and Media Studies* 32, no. 3 (2017), 125.
54. Swash, 'She Monkeys Director'.
55. Given this suggestion of violence, there is a possibility that *She Monkeys* replicates a homophobic association between lesbianism and violence. As Lynda Hart explains, 'Lesbians in mainstream representations have almost always been depicted as predatory, dangerous, and pathological' (*Fatal Women: Lesbian Sexuality and the Mark of Aggression* [Princeton: Princeton University Press, 1994], vii.). However, such a characterisation does not ring true in the context of *She Monkeys*. The aggression between Cassandra and Emma is largely and obviously premised in envy and desire rather than an overwhelming 'perversion' that attributes their sexuality and violence to the same source, as is the case in the stereotype of the aggressive lesbian.
56. Lindner, 'Queer-ing Texture', 130.
57. Clara Bradbury-Rance, *Lesbian Cinema after Queer Theory* (Edinburgh: Edinburgh University Press, 2019), 95.
58. Lee, 'LIFF 2011: SHE MONKEYS'.
59. Lindner, 'Queer-ing Texture', 124.
60. Liz Constable, 'Unbecoming Sexual Desires for Women Becoming Sexual Subjects: Simone de Beauvoir (1949) and Catherine Breillat (1999)', *MLN* 119, no. 4 (2004), 672.
61. Lisa French, '*Centring the Female: The Articulation of Female Experience in the Films of Jane Campion*' (PhD thesis, RMIT University, 2007), 36.
62. The plot of *She Monkeys* makes clear that Emma is not as conventionally attractive as Cassandra. For example, Cassandra makes the vaulting team instead of Emma, and the coach euphemistically justifies the decision by stating that charisma is just as important as strength in the sport. Nevertheless, Emma is also experiencing a girlshine moment. She is youthful, strong limbed and self possessed, and these qualities clearly attract Cassandra.
63. French, *Centring the Female*, 181.
64. Wheatley, 'She Monkeys', 76.

65. Lee, 'LIFF 2011: SHE MONKEYS'.
66. French, *Centring the Female*, 183.
67. San Filippo, *Provocauteurs and Provocations*, 215.
68. Downing, 'French Cinema's New "Sexual Revolution"', 267.
69. Ginette Vincendeau, '*Fat Girl*: Sisters, Sex, and Sitcom', *Criterion*, 3 May 2011, https://www.criterion.com/current/posts/495-fat-girl-sisters-sex-and-sitcom.

CHAPTER 2

On Not Looking Away: Rape in the Films of Jennifer Kent and Isabella Eklöf

Art cinema abounds with images that shock, and scenes of rape are amongst the most controversial of these. As Tanya Horeck summarises, 'Visual images of rape have always been especially contentious' and singled out as 'objects of moral outrage'.[1] This is true for both popular culture images and those circulating in the domain of art film. Indeed, some of the most notoriously provocative (and celebrated) works in global art cinema concern acts of rape. It is an implied event in *Last Year at Marienbad* (*L'Année dernière à Marienbad*, Alain Resnais, 1961) and *Rashomon* (Akira Kurosawa, 1950), a relentlessly recurring act in *Salò, the 120 days of Sodom* (*Salò o le 120 giornate di Sodoma*, Pier Paolo Pasolini, 1975) and *Dogville* (Lars von Trier, 2003), and a graphically portrayed crime in *Twentynine Palms* (Bruno Dumont, 2003) and *Irréversible* (Gaspar Noé, 2002). Scenes of rape in art cinema are frequently so provocative that they prompt acts of spectatorial resistance such as walkouts and boycotts. *Irréversible*, with its lengthy and violent assault of the female protagonist, is an indicative case that reportedly prompted extensive walkouts at the 2002 Cannes and Sundance Film Festivals.[2] Scenes of violent cruelty in Trier's *Dogville* and Dumont's *Twentynine Palms* also allegedly provoked viewers to leave the screenings at the 2003 Cannes and Venice Film Festivals respectively.[3] Short of riots or threats against the director, such acts of spectatorial rejection are the most overt evidence of provocation available. They express outrage, offence, distress, upset and a moral and ethical objection to the text.

The issue of women-authored or feminist images of rape, whether in art cinema or popular film, is a complex one. Although men, women and non-binary people can commit and be victims of sexual assault, rape is often understood as a crime that men commit and women experience, both in the social world and in narrative cinema. Moreover, as Alexandra Heller-Nicholas notes, 'There is a mainstream assumption that women make certain types of films' and that 'ones with graphic violence – sexual or otherwise – do not fall into that terrain'.[4] Yet women directors have depicted rape onscreen many times, sometimes explicitly. In popular and genre cinema, examples of sexual violence in films directed by women include *Traps* (*Pasti, pasti, pastičky*, Věra Chytilová, 1998), *Boys Don't Cry* (Kimberly Peirce, 1999), *Monster* (Patty Jenkins, 2003), *Revenge* (Coralie Fargeat, 2017) and *Violation* (Madeleine Sims-Fewer and Dusty Mancinelli, 2020). Graphic and sometimes repeated rape scenes also appear in women-directed films exhibited for art cinema and festival audiences, such as *Baise-moi* (Coralie Trinh Thi and Virginie Despentes, 2000), *The Book of Revelation* (Ana Kokkinos, 2006) and *Code Blue* (Urszula Antoniak, 2011), to name only a few. Such examples show that women filmmakers have included images and scenarios of rape in their work in ways that are graphic, unsettling and controversial.

The issue of why and how women provoke via images of rape is brought into particularly urgent focus by two films that appeared on the international festival circuit in quick succession: Jennifer Kent's historical revenge drama *The Nightingale* (2018) and Isabella Eklöf's slow-burning thriller *Holiday* (2018). *The Nightingale* is set in colonial Australia and contains three instances of rape: two committed against the Irish convict protagonist and a third against an Indigenous woman. The film had a controversial premiere at the Venice Film Festival in 2018 when an Italian film critic was reportedly heard shouting misogynistic abuse as Kent's name appeared during the credits. Additionally, when *The Nightingale* screened at the Sydney Film Festival the following year, audience members reportedly walked out during one of the film's rape sequences.[5] Although Eklöf's *Holiday* did not generate such publicity, the film attracted significant commentary for its challenging extended and explicit sequence in which the protagonist is sexually assaulted by her boyfriend. Eric Kohn calls the moment 'a brutal, graphic rape scene more alarming than anything comparable in world cinema since "Irreversible"';[6] Heller-Nicholas describes the film as 'a deliberate provocation';[7] and Hannah McGill observes that *Holiday* is a 'stark, disciplined and genuinely confronting' provocation.[8] Both *The Nightingale* and *Holiday* thus contain depictions of rape that challenge and provoke audiences. Through duration or repetition, these films demand lengthy and intense witnessing from the spectator. Written and directed by women and circulating within art and festival cinema milieus, these films raise questions about how and why women directors engage with provocative and challenging images of rape, and how this might connect to broader art cinema strategies or feminist approaches in a post-millennium context.

This chapter examines how *The Nightingale* and *Holiday* provoke the spectator via their 'excessive' depictions of rape, connecting these films to the broader spectrum of women-authored depictions of sexual assault as well-established art cinema strategies for provoking the spectator. What does it mean to provoke via images of rape, and what does this tell us about women's engagement in the tradition of provocation? Both Kent and Eklöf's avowed desire for authenticity in their films locate their depictions of rape within a long-established feminist objective of representing rape from the woman's perspective as victim. I also consider the provocativeness of *The Nightingale* and *Holiday* in their representation of rape, locating their challenge to the spectator in an underpinning excess of representation – one that is linked to an ethics of authenticity and of witnessing. Both films show rape at length, with 'excessive' frequency, or with 'excessive' visibility. This connects them to an art cinema strategy of positioning the spectator in scenarios of endurance, generating intense emotions and forcing onlookers to uncomfortably reflect upon their own voyeurism. Given that debates in popular media regarding the depiction of sexual violence frequently centre on justifications for images of rape – whether they are 'necessary' or 'useful' – *The Nightingale* and *Holiday* challenge precisely because of this excess. Drawing both from the traditions of feminist art and *cinéma brut*, these films show rape unblinkingly, provoking through an ethics of enduring and not looking away.

Rape as Provocation

Rape has a persistent presence in art cinema and a significant connection to the tradition of provocation. Rape is itself a common metaphor for acts of filmic provocation. In an analysis of Luis Buñuel's work, Dominque Russell observes that filmmakers and critics frequently use rape to describe the author–recipient relation of provocation.[9] Michael Haneke's infamous statement that he is trying to 'rape the audience into independence' is a fitting example.[10] Rape metaphors like these convey the supposed passivity of the spectator as they sit, immobilised, in the darkened cinema. Rape metaphors also convey the director's power to deny enjoyment: to shock, to violate a spectatorial contract, or to defile viewers by forcing them to look at objectionable things. The infamous eye-slice of *An Andalusian Dog* (*Un chien andalou*, Luis Buñuel, 1929) is a case in point. Russell notes that this image has been interpreted as a symbolic assault of the spectator because of the visceral shock one can have upon witnessing such an injury. As she explains:

> The assault on the spectator is a gleeful assertion of the director's power, and the *frisson* in it the first of many times the spectator's pleasure is linked to illicit penetration and sexual violence in Buñuel's oeuvre. In this first work, as in *L'âge d'or* (France, 1932), the suggestions of sexual violence are designed to shock the spectator out of ('feminine' and bourgeois) complacency.[11]

The gendered implication is significant here. It is a male hand that slices a female eye in *An Andalusian Dog*. Moreover, as I describe in the introduction to this book, the symbolic language used to describe the director's provocations – violent and penetrating – are symbolically hypermasculine. The words used to describe the spectator, in contrast, feminise them as passive victims (although, as Russell points out, the intention of the 'assault' upon the spectator is precisely to awaken them out of this passivity).

Beyond just operating metaphorically, depictions of literal rape appear in art cinema too. Russell observes that, in addition to being an analogy for the relationship between the auteur and audience, rape is a concept through which some twentieth-century art films problematically investigate the topic of ambiguity and the elusiveness of truth. Key films *Last Year at Marienbad* and *Rashomon* both reject the narrative clarity of classical storytelling by offering multiple interpretations of the story events, which in both cases hinge on a question regarding whether a woman has been raped or not. In *Last Year at Marienbad*, these multiple interpretations centre upon whether the man (Giorgio Albertazzi) and the woman (Delphine Seyrig) had ever met each other before; he insists they had a love affair the previous summer, she insists it never happened. While the film never answers conclusively, one possibility is that the woman's forgetfulness is premised on her guilt over the affair; the other is that the man raped her and she has repressed the memory. *Rashomon* is also premised on multiple storylines that vary depending on whether a noblewoman was raped by a bandit, conspired with him, or both. In both films, rape becomes the issue through which the elusiveness of truth is explored. This set-up is problematic insofar as it frames rape as a phenomenon that is ambiguous and often unverifiable. This contradicts the efforts of activists who want to demystify rape and argue for its literal and concrete definition in a culture that so frequently doubts the testimony of women. As Lynn A. Higgins says, 'Rape can easily become a floating signifier, available for the elaboration of metaphor'.[12] In the post-millennium film context, rape again appears, this time as part of the explicit aesthetic strategies of European art cinema known as the New Extremity or *cinéma brut*. These include Alex's (Monica Bellucci) lengthy assault in *Irréversible*, the repeated rapes of Grace (Nicole Kidman) in *Dogville*, and the attack on David (David Wissak) that precipitates the violent conclusion of *Twentynine Palms*. Women filmmakers of this milieu have engaged with rape too. Catherine Breillat's films show rape onscreen: as discussed in the previous chapter, *Fat Girl* (2001) ends with Anaïs's violent rape, and the protagonist of *Romance* (1999) is also assaulted on a stairwell. In Urszula Antoniak's *Code Blue*, the protagonist witnesses a rape occurring on the grassy bank outside her apartment. As I discuss in Chapter 4, Claire Denis's *Bastards* (*Les salauds*, 2013) begins in the aftermath of a violent sexual assault; although the film does not show the event, *Bastards* commences as the teenage victim wanders naked down the streets of Paris, blood streaming down her legs.

Before investigating how women engage with confronting images of sexual violence in art cinema, it is important to first identify criticisms of depictions of rape both explicit and offscreen. Concerns that images of rape may encourage or perpetuate real-life sexual violence recur in debates on the topic. Russell notes that a broad cultural anxiety persists regarding 'how a rape scene might "teach" rape'.[13] The suggestion that films may endorse sexual violence by presenting it as titillating was the reason behind the censorship of Trinh Thi and Despentes's explicit road movie *Baise-moi* by the British Board of Film Classification (BBFC). Although the rape scene in the film very clearly shows the horrific and violent nature of sexual assault, the BBFC required that the scene be cut, explaining in its ruling that 'portrayals which eroticise sexual assault may be cut at any classification level'.[14] Feminist critics have also posited arguments against – or in criticism of – depictions of rape in cinema. Of chief concern is that images of rape are not mere representations but are discursive acts or enunciations that express misogyny in themselves. Horeck provides an account of this reasoning in her analysis of rape scenes in cinema, particularly *The Accused* (Jonathan Kaplan, 1988). Drawing upon Catherine MacKinnon's work, Horeck explains the concern that 'technologies of vision not only replay and repeat woman's original trauma, but produce a new dimension of pain'.[15] Even when fictional, depiction of rape is itself a form of violence. What follows, then, is the question of whether watching rape is in itself a form of participation in sexual violence. As Horeck explains, 'That we may be participating in a rape by "just looking" ... is the underlying anxiety'.[16] Sarah Projansky argues that images of rape can enact this symbolic participation even when they are ostensibly supposed to denounce rape. Projansky acknowledges the challenge here as a 'feminist paradox between a desire to *end* rape and a need to *represent* (and therefore perpetuate discursive) rape in order to challenge it'.[17] The argument here is that adding more depictions of rape to a culture that is already saturated with images of violence against women contributes to misogyny irrespective of the aims of creators. In other words, such images have the potential to not only retraumatise victims of real-world violence, they can also be seen as expressions of violence and hatred for women, even if they never lead to actual acts of rape. B. Ruby Rich articulates this while grappling with her thoughts on mainstream pornography, describing 'the seemingly unending exploitation of their/our images onscreen and real bodies offscreen'.[18] This conceptualisation of representation as discursive violence could apply not just to feminist films that denounce rape but also to films exhibited in an art cinema context. Art films generally benefit from the assumption that they have artistic goals beyond that of sensationalist entertainment. Nevertheless, the idea that a woman filmmaker would participate in the creation of images that supposedly hate her demands consideration, and women-authored images of rape are not automatically exempt from debates regarding the ethics of onscreen violence.

Rather than cutting away or simply refusing to address the topic, many women artists do indeed address sexual violence. Some also depict it graphically. The motives for doing so are numerous: as a means of coming to terms with rape, fostering empathy for victims, correcting misconceptions, reclaiming representations of rape from male authors,[19] or activating an ethical response of outrage in the spectator.[20] There are many examples from the art world that exhibit these impulses. One instructive case is Ana Mendieta's *Untitled* (*Rape Scene*) (1973), an important performance and visual art text. This photographic depiction of Mendieta's performance piece was one of a series conceived in response to the violent rape and murder of a nineteen-year-old student at the University of Iowa. Mendieta invited her friends to her apartment, where they found her posed across a dinner table, naked from the waist down and bloodied, with broken crockery scattered around. The pose was a recreation of the actual crime scene as reported in the press. It does not show the act of rape itself – an important distinction – but it does centre the brutalised victim, evoking a set of responses that can include empathy as well as a feeling of complicity and voyeurism. In the context of cinema, a landmark work concerning sexual violence is Trinh Thi and Despentes's *Baise-moi*, which films an assault scene using pornographic actors who performed real sex for the sequence.

Trinh Thi and Despentes insist that they were representing a violence that already exists in the world (and indeed, that they themselves had experienced). 'We didn't invent rape', Despentes stated. 'I've been raped and one of my actresses has been raped ... It's horrific, so I don't see why I shouldn't treat it that way.'[21] Another reason that women choose to show rape is to raise consciousness or reveal the injustice of sexual violence. Examples of this are numerous, and include Kokkinos's *Only the Brave* (1994), Pierce's *Boys Don't Cry* and Jenkins's *Monster*, to name some illustrative cases.[22] Such films call attention to and invite empathy for the victim and their suffering. They thus fall into the domain of what Rich labels 'conversion cinema', utilising negative emotions to change minds about rape and prompt real-world action. As Rich puts it, 'Gaze at the forbidden, react with your choice of anger or outrage or grief (or the male option: guilt), and leave a changed person ... A change in consciousness, a change of heart.'[23] In this formulation, the arousal of negative emotions – distress, rage, a sense of injustice – is necessary to spur the spectator into this kind of conversion. The degree to which this works, and whether it disqualifies arguments against depicting rape, is up for debate. Nonetheless, it remains one of several rationales that women creators draw upon for depicting sexual violence onscreen.

A third approach to the depiction of rape is one that provokes the onlooker – inducing shock and uncomfortable self-awareness – to invite the spectators' critical reflection on the ethics of watching rape as a representation. Such works are not only explorations of rape in the social world, but also concern the act of watching rape itself. To borrow Asbjørn Grønstad's words, they are 'about the spectator' and the ethics of looking.[24] Such artworks play on and even exploit the ethical anxieties the spectator might have about watching rape; about whether looking may constitute an endorsement of misogyny, or worries the spectator may have about feeling aroused by images of sexual violence. Scott MacKenzie offers an account of this process in his analysis of what he calls *cinéma brut*, a term that describes many of the extreme European art films of the post-millennium. Analysing *cinéma brut* films such as *Irréversible* and linking them to antecedents such as Yoko Ono and John Lennon's *Rape* (1969), MacKenzie argues that these films draw from the traditions of both Antonin Artaud's Theatre of Cruelty and Bertolt Brecht's epic theatre. Such films, he argues, are Artaudian because they force the spectator to endure a confronting, difficult-to-watch spectacle as a means of connecting them with strong emotions in the art encounter. These films are also Brechtian because they use aesthetic techniques to generate an awareness of the film as a construction. These techniques include *cinéma direct* approaches, such as the use of the long take and handheld cameras. MacKenzie writes:

> *Cinéma brut* and New French Extremist filmmakers introduce to the representation of sexual violence, and to rape in particular, a model of Brechtian distanciation that destabilizes traditional patterns of identification and voyeurism. Yet the relationship between spectator and image is more complex than this, as it is not pure distanciation that takes places, as moments of voyeurism still obtain – the spectator vacillates between voyeurism and alienation, paradoxically increasing the discomfiture because of the self-realization of one's own processes of desire and identification.[25]

For MacKenzie, the overall effect is an awareness of the cinematic apparatus and the constructed nature of the image but an inability to use this knowledge to ward off feelings of repulsion, horror or a sense of complicity that is generated through the act of watching. The subject matter of rape is ultimately too intense to disengage from emotionally and affectively, despite the estranging formalism of the films in question.

MacKenzie's analysis is valuable insofar as it explains the processes at play in *cinéma brut* representations of rape. It also accounts for the negative emotions that these films strategically elicit, describing their potential function in spectatorship. *Cinéma brut* offers a critique of cinema and representation itself, making spectatorship uncomfortable in ways that demand the onlooker think about film's potential to be an exploitative, sensationalist medium. Such films also demand the spectator reflect on their own ethics in watching brutal images. As MacKenzie writes, 'These new films profoundly question the complicity of the spectator in the acts of voyeurism and desire surrounding the representation of sexuality, violence and, a fortiori, rape on-screen'.[26] That said, MacKenzie argues that films like *Rape* and *Irréversible* do not actually resolve the problem that they uncomfortably position the spectator to consider. While these films' uncomfortableness may stimulate thought and critique, they do not seem to precisely advocate for or against showing rape, nor is it clear how much they condemn the spectator (or indeed the filmmaker) for their participation either. In short, such films raise the problem but do not offer a solution or stance.

Images of rape are highly implicated with the provocative author–recipient tradition of art cinema. They also have a long association with women's creative practice, insofar as women can and do choose to elicit negative reactions via depictions of rape. Kent and Eklöf's work can be understood in relation to both these contexts: as women-authored works and as art cinema provocations. Indeed, their noteworthy status as women-authored films about rape did not go unremarked upon by critics. As Guy Lodge observes of Eklöf, 'The club of contemporary cinematic provocateurs to whose brand of formalism "Holiday" is likeliest to prompt comparisons ... is an awfully male-dominated one',[27] whereas Heller-Nicholas observes that the surprised reaction to *The Nightingale* 'reveals assumptions about women's filmmaking more generally' and the type of subject matter that women typically address (or avoid).[28] Kent and Eklöf's work both illuminates provocation as a strategy used by women in art cinema and provides case studies for women's engagement with rape, showing how the two come together in important ways.

Unblinking Excess: *Holiday*

Isabella Eklöf is a director who is willing to be disliked: 'There's a part of me that really doesn't give a shit', she says. 'I don't automatically feel a need for approval.'[29] Originally from Sweden, Eklöf's provocative inclinations have shaped her career trajectory, from her study at the University of Gothenburg to a formative move to Denmark. Of Gothenburg, she notes, 'They thought my ideas were weird ... I think people thought I was a little bit yucky. There was too much sexuality [in my work], too much pushing boundaries.'[30] Her decision to pursue further study at Den Danske Filmskole, the National Film School of Denmark, was prompted, she says, by seeing a book by the director Jørgen Leth for sale in a Danish shop. Eklöf describes Leth as a 'great art house filmmaker but also a sexist pig'.[31] To Eklöf, the fact that Leth's book was available to purchase indicated that Denmark was a place where transgressive art could be made and where she would not be 'censored'. Eklöf has only made a few films thus far in her career, yet her body of work demonstrates a repeated interest in humanity's darker side. She worked as a location assistant on the vampire horror film *Let the Right One In* (*Låt den rätte komma in*, Tomas Alfredson, 2008) and co-wrote the screenplay for *Border* (*Gräns*, Ali Abbasi, 2018) with the director and John Ajvide Lindqvist, who is also the author of the short story and novels that *Border* and *Let the Right One In* are adapted from. In film school in Denmark, Eklöf wrote and directed *Willkommen in Barbaristan* (2009), a project about a dark-skinned exchange student living with a white German family.[32] Her final year film *Notes from Underground* (*Noter fra kælderen*, 2011) centres on a girl imprisoned in a suburban dungeon by a middle-aged paedophile. This film, Eklöf says, is about 'the dullness of evil' and was inspired by the memoirs of Sabine Dardenne, who in 1996 was kidnapped and abused for seventy-nine days by Marc Dutroux when she was twelve years old. What impacted Eklöf was Dardenne's account of the boredom of her imprisonment: 'How excruciatingly dull it was to be trapped like that with somebody evil.'[33]

This interest in the dullness of evil as well as the presence of sexual violence in mundane settings can also be found in Eklöf's feature debut *Holiday*. The story is loosely inspired by the novel *Louis liv* (2011) by Johanne Algren, who also has a co-writing credit on the film. It begins as a young woman arrives at a deserted airport. Her name is Sascha (Victoria Carmen Sonne) and she has travelled to Turkey to join her drug lord boyfriend Michael (Lai Yde) on a luxury holiday in Bodrum. Sascha seems new to Michael's world and uncertain of how to behave amongst the extended group of gangsters, girlfriends and their children. She spends much of her time in Bodrum enjoying the luxuries that her boyfriend's criminal life affords as well as testing the boundaries to see what she can get away with. She makes an early mistake when she borrows some drug money to buy a swimsuit, and Michael's henchman threatens to kill her. Michael himself subjects Sascha repeatedly to abusive behaviour. As I mentioned in the opening to this chapter and will discuss below, *Holiday* is notable for an extended scene in which Michael rapes Sascha, an incident that, despite its violence, appears a somewhat normalised part of their relationship. Once the rape occurs, it is never mentioned by any character or overtly referenced in the plot again. However, while Sascha is clearly a victim of Michael's abusive behaviour and aggression, she is not a moral character. She is, as McGill describes her, a 'hardened naif . . . childlike in her demeanour and appearance, but wily enough to select the most expensive earrings in the shop and turn up the TV when there's a beating going on in the next room'.[34] The film ends after Michael discovers a flirtation that Sascha has been having with a handsome Dutch man, Tomas (Thijs Römer), either to alleviate her boredom or once again test the boundaries. Michael threatens Tomas but leaves him unharmed. When Sascha visits Tomas to apologise, he turns on her and calls her a 'stupid cunt' and she bludgeons him to death in a sudden fit of rage. Michael covers up the evidence of Sascha's crime, thus aligning them permanently. As Eklöf explains, the story of *Holiday* is about a woman's decision to live in 'a golden cage'.[35] It is also told from the perspective of a gangster's girlfriend, a character who is ubiquitous but usually peripheral in the crime genre. *Holiday* received generally positive reactions on its international festival run. Several critics immediately identified the film as a provocation: as 'uncompromisingly tough and unforgiving'[36] and 'an audacious film that never flinches though it knows its audience may recoil'.[37]

The provocativeness of *Holiday* lies not just in the premise of the story and its violent ending but very much in the intensity and excess of the sexual assault scene. The entire scene is over six minutes long and the act of rape itself is presented using a three-and-a-half-minute unbroken take. The assault begins as a playful encounter in the villa where Michael and Sascha are holidaying. Sascha initiates contact by stroking Michael and smiles as he playfully pulls her down onto the loungeroom sofa in response. Things change, however, when Michael starts to handle Sascha roughly, grabbing and squeezing her throat. Although she resists, he eventually forces her into sex on the floor. The film cuts to a full shot at this moment, with Sascha and Michael just below eye level and fully in frame. The assault lasts for several more minutes; it is only when Michael finishes, gets up, puts his wristwatch back on and lies down on the sofa that the scene ends.

The scene's ability to provoke and incite a negative reaction depends on this extended duration. Several critics describe Eklöf's film as 'unblinking',[38] and this is a fitting metaphor to capture the film's visual demands upon the spectator. *Holiday* does not offer the relief of montage in its construction of the rape scene, never cutting away to another perspective or point of view. It instead represents the assault using a single long take, unfolding in real time. *Holiday* thus requires the onlooker to endure the spectacle of rape beyond what is strictly required for the plot (it is clear that Michael is a violent man – his potential to rape has already been established in an earlier scene where he drugs Sascha into unconsciousness as a sadistic prank.) As MacKenzie observes, this is a characteristic of *cinéma brut* films, which present intensely affecting scenes in ways that, via their formal construction, convey a directness of address. Such films, he argues, involve a 'synthesizing of *cinéma direct* aesthetics with the Artaudian concept of endurance (both in the sense of the length of the shot and in the sheer endurance, on the level of affect, needed to watch the images unfold)'.[39] The long take prolongs the spectator's immersion in the moment, from the beginning to the aftermath.

By positioning the spectator to endure this unblinking, minimally edited spectacle, *Holiday* operates in a tradition of provocative art that attempts to achieve a form of truthfulness in its depiction of rape. Discussing her stylistic choices, Eklöf argues that the refusal to cut is a way of restoring truth to cinema. Paraphrasing the director Roy Andersson, whom she cites as an inspiration, Eklöf says, 'Editing is cheating. Every time you edit you're actually bringing the spectator out of what is really happening and moving into a new place. And you can create emotions that way, but they will be fake.'[40] (Although the scene does contain two cuts in its six-minute runtime, this is a minimal amount of editing given the lengthiness of the takes and the scene overall.) The unfolding of Sascha's rape in real time, with such static, long takes, seems excessive compared to cinema that treats rape as a narrative event to be signified as a plot point. Although the scene explains much about the nature of Sascha's relationship with Michael, it has little obvious bearing on the events that follow. It is therefore possible to interpret the rape scene as surplus or needless provocation beyond the requirements of the plot. However, the duration of the scene enables *Holiday* to represent the experience of sexual assault with a degree of detailed realism: from its starting point as a consensual flirtation to the aftermath as Michael nonchalantly puts his expensive watch back on his wrist. The duration also allows for the scene to reveal that the rape has occurred within an established relationship, demonstrating how an initially playful interaction between partners descends into rape. Eklöf's own explanation for including the rape sequence (which is a frequent topic discussed in interviews and articles about the film) very clearly emphasises this goal of authenticity as a feminist impulse:

> I feel a need to show all aspects of life. Especially a woman's life. I feel like there is still a remnant of the whole thing where ... we don't want to see menstrual blood, we don't want to see rapes and all the other experiences that a woman can have because we're still ingrained in a patriarchal worldview where that shit is supposed to stay hidden.[41]

Eklöf also connects *Holiday* explicitly to the #MeToo movement, linking the depiction of rape to the frank and open discussions of women's experiences of sexual violence. The precise reason she portrayed rape so directly, she says, is precisely because 'things need to be spoken about in the open. The reason #MeToo has been so powerful is because there has been so much suppression of what you're allowed to talk about.'[42] Her words thus align the formal choices around the depiction of sexual violence in *Holiday* with the feminist strategy of speaking truth and exposing women's hidden realities. In this formulation, the refusal to cut is a provocative excess that is also a feminist and ethical strategy.

Other aspects of the scene's construction, particularly framing and lighting, also play a role in the rape scene in *Holiday*, working in close complementarity with the long take. *Holiday* does not offer the relief of montage, and the film's minimal edits during the assault means that the rape scene never offers any character's point of view on the events. The shot instead frames Sascha and Michael symmetrically, the full length of their bodies in view surrounded by luxury furnishings: a white sofa, a flat-screen television, a modern kitchen and a staircase to the upstairs living space.

This perspective is not identified with anyone in the scene: it is the camera's alone, and the film thus does not attempt to associate the act of witnessing the rape with anyone other than the spectator (Figure 2.1). (As I discuss in the next section, this differs considerably with the sexual assault scenes in *The Nightingale*, which almost exclusively use close-up.) Added to this, the scene is brightly lit, filled with daylight that streams through the windows. The shot therefore has a presentational quality, conspicuously framing the scene as a representation. By doing so, *Holiday* indicates the constructed nature of the film itself, a manoeuvre that can heighten the onlooker's discomfort. In keeping with MacKenzie's argument about the simultaneously affecting and estranging *cinéma brut*, *Holiday* returns spectators to their own consciousness, reminding them that they are onlookers and inviting them to consider whether they are engaging in exploitative voyeurism. By constructing the rape as a scene, *Holiday* positions spectators to acknowledge their voyeurism, which heightens the potential for discomfort. *Holiday* is thus not only exploring the truth of violence in mundane settings – it also concerns spectatorship, representation and what it means to be an onlooker. As Ana Fazekaš notes, when 'faced with a written narrative about rape, we do not identify as either the rapist or the raped, but we remain a bystander, Peeping Tom, ashamed but unable to withdraw'.[43] This is also the experience of watching *Holiday* and, indeed, midway through the assault, an unidentified character walks onscreen in the top right hand of the frame, hesitates and quickly leaves. Although the camera does not adopt that person's point of view, it is the perspective most aligned with that of the camera and, by extension, us. Although the film's formalism seems to contradict Eklöf's desire for truthfulness, *Holiday* nevertheless manages to accomplish two manoeuvres with respect to rape:

Figure 2.1 Michael responds aggressively to Sascha before assaulting her in *Holiday*.

showing it completely and without the relieving manipulation of editing, but also, via this strategy, exposing the artificiality of the cinema medium in ways that discomfit the onlooker. Indeed, this formalism exposes an extra-diegetic reality – that of the onlooker in the darkened cinema.

Although *Holiday* shows the circumstances of rape and how it can occur, Sascha's own consciousness as a victim remains somewhat mysterious in the film. *Holiday* does not show rape to reveal Sascha's subjectivity or prompt sympathetic identification. Although distressed in the immediate aftermath and clearly traumatised enough to lash out against Tomas, Sascha's behaviour otherwise does not change following Michael's assault, and she acts in the way she did before. As Eklöf explains, she is uninterested in Sascha's psychology: 'I'm not sure what Sascha is thinking to be honest. And I don't care.' Instead, Eklöf elaborates, 'I care what she does'.[44] And indeed, the choices Sascha makes are revealing in their own fashion. The film concludes by confirming Sascha's decision to accept a luxurious life with a violent criminal who rapes her: after bludgeoning Tomas, she returns to the villa and Michael sends his henchmen to dispose of Tomas's body, saving Sascha from the consequences of what she has done. Perhaps Sascha's trauma has made her volatile and violent, a misfit with limited options except to go back to Michael's criminal world. Perhaps her altercation with Tomas and his sexist slur makes her realise the world is full of misogyny, with Michael or without him, and she may as well maintain her existing arrangement. In any case, *Holiday* shows the provocation of rape to illuminate one woman's negotiation of the sexual violence in her life. It does so to expose acts that are otherwise hidden, both in the gangster genre and in women's lives more generally, rather than to generate impassioned empathy for the victim and her emotions. For that strategy, we can look to *The Nightingale*.

We Don't Need to See It Again: *The Nightingale*

Jennifer Kent's second feature *The Nightingale* prompted two widely publicised controversies during its international festival run, both reminiscent of the scandals that make up the history of provocative art. During its world premiere at the Venice Film Festival in 2018, an audience member was reportedly heard shouting abuse as Kent's name appeared during the end credits. The person, Italian film critic Sharif Meghdoud, stated in a social media post that his exact words were: 'Shame on you, whore, you're disgusting!'[45] He did not explain his reaction other than to say it was a spontaneous outburst. The following year when *The Nightingale* screened at the Sydney Film Festival, approximately fifty people walked out during the film's two sessions,[46] and one viewer was reportedly heard shouting: 'She's already been raped, we don't need to see it again.'[47] The shouter was allegedly responding to a scene in which the young Irish protagonist is brutalised for a second time by an English officer in the colony of Van Diemen's Land, now known as the Australian state of Tasmania and by its Aboriginal name *lutruwita*. The reception of *The Nightingale* in both Venice and Sydney made the news in Australia, Kent's homeland. However, Kent insists that her film was predominately well received during its festival run. Indeed, *The Nightingale* attracted plenty of praise. It was awarded the Special Jury Prize at the Venice Film Festival as well as the Marcello Mastroianni Award for Best Young Actor for Baykali Ganambarr, who plays an Indigenous man who assists the female protagonist. The Australian premiere of *The Nightingale* at the Adelaide Film Festival also generated no public scandal. Nevertheless, *The Nightingale* found its way into media articles querying the ethics of onscreen rape in cinema and pondering the impact, if any, of a female director upon such depictions.[48] As Heller-Nicholas aptly summarises, 'Perhaps unsurprisingly for a film whose central narrative action is sparked by the rape of a woman and the murder of her husband and baby, it in many ways feels almost inevitable that *The Nightingale* would infuriate and offend as much as demand reflection'.[49]

The controversy at the Venice and Sydney film festivals marks a noteworthy point in Kent's career, occurring at a moment when the director was enjoying a relatively newfound reputation as an important auteur in Australia. Kent initially trained as an actor at the National Institute for Dramatic Art in Sydney and after working for several years as a jobbing performer in film and television, she transitioned into directing. After seeing Lars von Trier's *Dancer in the Dark* (2000), Kent wrote to the director, who invited her onto a directing attachment for his film *Dogville* (2003). Kent went on to make a short film, *Monster* (2005), and some years later achieved fame with her debut feature *The Babadook* (2014), a horror film adapted from *Monster* about a struggling single mother haunted by an entity living in her house. The film's commercial performance was initially modest in Australia. *The Babadook* received a limited release when it debuted locally in May 2014, showing on thirteen screens at speciality and art house cinemas. The film's initial six-week run made $258,000 in Australian dollars at the domestic box office.[50] However, the film performed far better internationally, gaining attention at the 2014 Sundance Film Festival and Stanley Film Festival in the United States and at FrightFest 2014 in the United Kingdom. *The Babadook* also attracted an audience via online streaming platforms in Europe and North America. Additionally, Kent's film won endorsements from high-profile American horror writers and directors on social media. In November 2014, Stephen King tweeted: 'THE BABBADOOK [sic]: Deeply disturbing and highly recommended. You don't watch it so much as experience it',[51] and a few weeks later William Friedkin opined: 'Psycho, Alien, Diabolique, and now THE BABADOOK.'[52] Following the slow-burning success of Kent's debut feature, the Sydney Film Festival selected the director's much-anticipated second film *The Nightingale* for their 2019 showcase. The programming of the film at the Sydney event, a major domestic festival, was an important recognition of Kent as a key talent. The reaction was not an uncomplicated celebration of a national auteur, however. The negative response of some audience members at the Sydney Film Festival was prominently reported in the Australian media.[53] When asked to comment, however, festival director Nashen Moodley claimed the people who walked out of *The Nightingale* were in the minority.[54] The film's wider release a few months later also won many positive reviews from critics. Sarah Ward notes that both the film and the performance of lead actor Aisling Franciosi 'deserve and demand an audience'.[55] Sandra Hall calls *The Nightingale* 'one of the most powerful films yet seen about the country's colonial foundation'.[56] Although more measured, Keva York calls the film 'an affecting cinematic reckoning with the unremitting ugliness of Australia's colonial history'.[57]

As the audience reaction from SIFF suggests, the provocation of *The Nightingale* consists chiefly of its depiction of rape, particularly its repeated depiction of several assaults in the plot. Whereas *Holiday* shows rape at length, *The Nightingale* shows it several times over, containing three instances of sexual violence. The film centres on Clare (Aisling Franciosi), an Irish convict living in Van Diemen's Land in 1825 with her husband and infant daughter. She works at a tavern serving the local military detachment, and her beautiful singing voice earns her a regular role entertaining the soldiers (Figure 2.2). After performing one evening, she approaches the detachment leader, Lieutenant Hawkins (Sam Claflin), for a letter of recommendation that would free her from her term as a convict. The letter is three months overdue, but instead of providing it, Hawkins sexually assaults Clare. The scene unfolds in a way that suggests Hawkins has done this to Clare many times before. Hawkins's refusal to release Clare leads to an altercation between Clare's husband, Aidan (Michael Shaesby), and Hawkins and his officers. The soldiers murder both Aidan and the couple's infant daughter, raping Clare several more times and leaving her for dead. Clare, however, survives and employs an Indigenous man named Mangana or 'Billy' (Baykali Ganambarr) to help her track Hawkins across the island to take revenge. While on the journey, Hawkins and his men also capture, rape and murder Indigenous woman Lowanna (Magnolia

Figure 2.2 Clare sings for the local military detachment in *The Nightingale*.

Maymuru), adding a third scene of sexual assault to the film. The attack on Lowanna also intersects with the other key theme of *The Nightingale*, which is the genocidal violence inflicted upon the First Nations populations of Australia generally and Tasmania specifically. Colonisation is not just a backdrop for Clare's story but a parallel unfolding event that attributes Clare and Billy's suffering to the same source. *The Nightingale* is a story about Australia's colonial history and thus engages extensively with challenging subject matter – on top of both misogyny and racial violence, the film includes numerous scenes of brutality against both white and Indigenous children, for instance, as well as several violent confrontations among British settlers, Irish convicts and Indigenous people.

In its attempt to confront the ugliness of Australian history, *The Nightingale* encounters a conundrum regarding how much discomfort a film can elicit – and how much negative emotion it can arouse – before being deemed excessive, unjustified or gratuitous. The film's reception indicates that this issue centres very much on its repeated depiction of sexual violence. Like Eklöf, Kent's remarks in interviews insist that the rape scenes in *The Nightingale* support an organising goal of truthfulness. She stresses that her desire is to construct an honest depiction of life in colonial Australia, where rape was a systemic reality for convict women.[58]

The goal of truthfulness extends to the production of the film itself, which was shot sequentially where possible and on location in the deep Tasmanian forest. As Heller-Nicholas writes, 'Kent knew that to capture an emotional truth in *The Nightingale* it was vital to capture a physical one also'.[59] Truthfulness and accuracy are also intrinsic to the approach *The Nightingale* takes in its depiction of gender and racial injustice. In interviews, Kent notes that she enlisted a series of expert advisors while making the film:

> I felt an absolute responsibility to make as accurate as possible the details of the birth of white Australia. We enlisted 'Uncle' Jim Everett, a Tasmanian Aboriginal elder [and poet, playwright, and political activist], who could speak directly to the experience. We hired Australian historians, Irish cultural experts, language experts, and a clinical psychologist ... with detailed experience in the area of rape and sexual abuse. Rape crisis centers here gave the script their approval every step of the way.[60]

However, as the statement 'we don't need to see it again' suggests, a core provocation in *The Nightingale* has to do with the repetition of rape and the supposed excessiveness of showing it more than once. Implicit here is the notion that one rape would be 'enough' in narrative terms to establish Clare's oppressed status and communicate the sexual violence of nineteenth-century Van Diemen's Land. Pushing back against this is Kent's argument that sexual violence was widespread and common for women convicts in colonial Australia, and that to show rape as a one-off catastrophe would be misleading. In other words, Kent constructs repeated rape as realistic rather than excessive.

There is more to say about the sexual assault scenes in *The Nightingale* beyond the fact of their repetition, however. Like in *Holiday*, the visual and aural construction of the sexual violence positions the spectator into a specific relation with the image and the victim. Whereas *Holiday* opts for formal estrangement and the narrational occlusion of Sascha's interiority, *The Nightingale* opts for an anti-voyeuristic, empathetic positioning of the spectator through sound and image.[61] The rape scenes in *The Nightingale* predominately consist of close-ups of Clare's and Lowanna's faces, switching regularly to their point of view in a manner that starkly contrasts with Eklöf's distancing *mise en scène*. Even when Clare and Lowanna's bodies are in frame, they are never in a state of undress during the rape sequences or, indeed, at any point in the film. The use of aspect ratio is also important here. *Holiday* uses a widescreen format that encompasses the length of Sascha and Michael's bodies as well as their luxurious surroundings to intensify the felt voyeurism of the moment and create a sense of estrangement. In contrast, *The Nightingale* uses the 1.37:1 Academy aspect ratio to create portrait-like shots of Clare's and Lowanna's faces showing their pain, a strategy that invites identification and emphasises their experience. Furthermore, sound design is also a significant stylistic element in this process of identifying the spectator with Clare and Lowanna. When Hawkins and his men assault Lowanna, for instance, her anguished, unanswered cries ring out over the quiet Tasmanian forest. The aural dimension is particularly important in the films' second assault sequence in which Hawkins's gang murders Clare's husband and child. The dominant sound during the attack is Clare's baby, Brigid, screaming in distress. Distracted by the piercing noise, Hawkins demands that the baby be silenced. Ensign Jago (Harry Greenwood), the new recruit, obeys, bludgeoning the infant against the wall of the hut. As Kent notes, 'In the making of [this scene], I wanted to put the audience with the person experiencing it. So, rather than being voyeuristic, I think it's experiential.'[62] By making the scenes 'experiential', Kent demands an uncomfortable experience from the listener-onlooker – a form of endurance and shared powerlessness with the victim.

This construction of the *mise en scène* in *The Nightingale* invites an empathetic response in the spectator, directed towards Clare in particular as a historical subject but also Lowanna as an Indigenous victim of colonial violence. *The Nightingale* therefore operates within a longstanding feminist approach to depicting rape, which aspires to generate empathy for the victim and position onlookers to acknowledge her pain. This is what Angelique Szymanek calls the 'redemptive tropes surrounding the discourses of witnessing' and the 'ethically sound responses of empathy and revulsion' pertaining to the viewing of artistic renderings of sexual violence.[63] Shocking and inducing negative emotions in the onlooker is one means of generating empathy for the victim and condemning the violence of rape. Szymanek discusses this strategy in her account of the work of Mendieta, whose practice addressed themes of rape and murder. Mendieta's *Untitled (Rape Scene)*, a significant work I mention earlier, is a case in point. Szymanek argues that critics have understood Mendieta's famous work too simplistically, arguing that it elicits a more complex engagement of voyeurism as well as empathy for the victim. In other words, through her sensationalist use of blood and human figures, *Untitled (Rape Scene)* also prompts reflexive reflection on the spectator's desire to see gruesome things, evoking and highlighting the onlooker's voyeurism. Nevertheless, the idea of inviting empathy for the victim through graphic or confronting imagery is a powerful impulse. It appears frequently in the statements of those who create depictions of sexual assault, insisting on an ethics of not looking away. For example, the producer of the legal drama *The Accused*, Sherry Lansing, locates the film's ethics precisely in its graphicness. The film was controversial upon its release for a scene in which the protagonist (Jodie Foster) is raped by several men in the back room of a bar. The scene and narrative as a whole are inspired by a 1983 gang rape of a young woman in New Bedford, Massachusetts, and *The Accused* depicts the sexual assault scene at length for approximately six minutes.[64] It also includes stylistic elements that intensify the emotion and violence of the attack, such as close-ups of the victim's pained expression, emotive non-diegetic music and the explicit, misogynistic jeers of the attackers. Discussing the scene, Lansing states: 'We're hoping that no one seeing *The Accused* will ever again believe that rape is sexy or that any woman asks for it.'[65] Moreover, in the context of cinema, inviting the spectator's identification and empathy with the female victim of rape remains significant as a feminist corrective to earlier depictions of rape in film. Sexual violence against women in classical Hollywood cinema frequently serves a plot function to spur the male protagonist into violent action. In films such as *The Searchers* (John Ford, 1956), for example, identification with the female victim of rape is elided in favour of emphasis on the male protagonist: his subjectivity and his violent reaction to the rape. Understood in this context, the politics of confronting the spectacle of rape in *The Nightingale* becomes clear: its provocation consists of its demands on the spectator to identify with the victim as well as its ethics of witnessing and empathy.

It is important to acknowledge that *The Nightingale* has other qualities that can generate discussion, and potentially controversy, in addition to its scenes of sexual violence. While the rape scenes avoid fetishism by concealing Clare's and Lowanna's bodies (and also keeping the physical injuries of sexual trauma out of frame), the scenes of violent revenge unfold in graphic detail. The film therefore does not avoid voyeurism or sensationalism entirely. This is particularly evident during one scene in which Clare takes revenge against one of her attackers. Aided by Billy's guidance through the forest, Clare eventually catches up with Hawkins and his men, cornering and killing Ensign Jago, the murderer of her baby. The scene is prolonged and visceral. Clare shoots Jago in the leg and, after tense struggle, stabs him multiple times before bludgeoning his face repeatedly with the butt of her rifle. Unlike the rape, the scene does show the physical details of the violence: the bullet blasting a hole in Jago's thigh, the disfigurement of his face, and his final word, 'mother'. The scene is sonically graphic too. Clare's screams of rage and exertion ring out over the sound of crunching bone. These stylistic choices underscore the sickening physicality of murder, but they also heighten the spectator's sensory immersion in the violence itself. There is thus a disparity between the representational regimes of rape and revenge in *The Nightingale*. While the film conceals the physical injuries of Clare's and Lowanna's rapes as an anti-voyeuristic strategy, it represents Jago's murder in fetishistic detail. Jago's death also means that *The Nightingale* does in part fulfil the rape-revenge genre's remit of offering climactic and spectacular scenes of revenge. The film thus extends the possibility of affective pleasure in violence. This is despite Kent's strong resistance to categorising *The Nightingale* as a rape-revenge film: 'It has rape in it, it has revenge in it, but the whole construct of a rape-revenge film is about going into the violence and celebrating it.'[66] Another point of potential controversy is the film's suggestion of a kinship between Billy and Clare premised on shared suffering: Clare's oppression as a woman and Irish convict, and Billy's as an Indigenous man. In suggesting this bond, *The Nightingale* risks conflating very different injustices: on one hand, the injustice of being a transported Irish woman subjected to sexual violence and English oppression, and the other of being a First Nations man subjected to systematic genocide. *The Nightingale* ultimately creates this bond not by drawing equivalency between Clare's and Billy's suffering, but by attributing it to the same source – the catastrophe of colonialism. Nevertheless, *The Nightingale* walks a fine line in its attempt to address different injustices with different historical and social implications in the same film. Australia's history of wrongs is complex; the origins and complexities of one injustice are extensive enough for a single film to address, let alone two injustices.

The Ethics of Looking

Depictions of rape are amongst the most provocative spectacles available to filmmakers. It is therefore important to ask how women engage with them. *Holiday* and *The Nightingale* opt for an ethics of confrontation with the image – of not looking away – although the approach varies between the films. Both contain what can be experienced as an excessiveness around the depiction of rape: *Holiday* insofar as the duration of the rape scene is in supposed 'excess' of the plot requirements, and *The Nightingale* being similarly excessive in its depiction of multiple scenes of rape. Moreover, both directors emphasise truthfulness as part of their choice, connecting with a feminist impulse to challenge misconceptions and reveal realities about sexual violence. Eklöf says that she wants to expose all aspects of women's lives, whereas Kent says she wants her film to convey the systemic violence of colonial Australia. Beyond this, however, Kent's and Eklöf's strategies diverge. The ethics of looking in *The Nightingale* consist of experiencing empathy with the victim via witnessing. In lieu of graphicness or explicitness, the film uses close-ups of the face and repetition to draw out this empathy in the onlooker, painful though it is to inhabit. Although prompting walkouts, defenders of *The Nightingale* consider this approach fitting for the gravity of the subject matter. As Sheila O'Malley says, 'The film is appropriately difficult to watch',[67] whereas Heller-Nicholas says that Kent 'should be applauded' for her 'uncomfortable' and devastating film.[68] Eklöf's approach in *Holiday* does not allow for such emotional access to Sascha's pain. The *mise en scène* of the assault scene estranges the onlooker, keeping them at a distance, even as it devastates with the spectacle of violence. In its formalism, the scene in *Holiday* also positions spectators into an awareness of their own voyeurism. The moment is thus doubly provocative, forcing the spectator into a consideration of their own act of looking.

There is no question that there is already a tradition of women addressing rape in the arts more broadly and in cinema particularly – as Heller-Nicholas observes, women have been making depictions of rape in cinema since at least Ida Lupino's *Outrage* (1950), and indeed, sexual violence appears with regularity in the films this book addresses.[69] However, the controversies surrounding *The Nightingale* and *Holiday* reinvite consideration of the topic, particularly in relation to the tradition of provocation in film. The provocativeness of representing rape in *Holiday* and *The Nightingale* does not concern ambiguity or the elusiveness of truth, as Russell observes is characteristic of the metaphoric use of rape in twentieth-century art cinema like *Rashomon* and *Last Year at Marienbad*.[70] Although they still hold power to *épater la bourgeoisie* on the festival circuit, these films link to a broader impulse outside the domain of art cinema: a turning towards rape to represent it truthfully. The unpleasantness of the spectacle is the point, as is the demand for the spectator's witnessing. While some may describe this as a naive and ultimately ineffectual project, it is, nonetheless, the goal. In *Holiday* and *The Nightingale*, the ethics and the provocation consist of not looking away.

Notes

1. Tanya Horeck, *Public Rape: Representing Violation in Fiction and Film* (Routledge: Abingdon, 2004), 10.
2. Robert W. Welkos, '"Irreversible" Not For the Faint of Heart', *Los Angeles Times*, 3 March 2003, https://www.latimes.com/archives/la-xpm-2003-mar-03-et-itkirreversible3-story.html.
3. Roger Ebert, 'Audience Reacts with Confusion, Anger to Lars Von Trier Film', *RogerEbert.com*, 20 May 2003, https://www.rogerebert.com/festivals/audience-reacts-with-confusion-anger-to-lars-von-trier-film; Dennis Lim, 'DesertBlue', *Village Voice*, 9 September 2003, https://www.villagevoice.com/2003/09/09/desert-blue-2/.

4. Quoted in Harry Windsor, 'Tasmanian Torments: Jennifer Kent's "The Nightingale"', *The Monthly*, 1 September 2019, https://www.themonthly.com.au/issue/2019/september/1567260000/harry-windsor/tasmanian-torments-jennifer-kent-s-nightingale#mtr.
5. Sarah Thomas, 'Sydney Film Festival Controversy as Audiences Walk Out of The Nightingale', *Australian Broadcasting Corporation*, 11 June 2019, https://www.abc.net.au/news/2019-06-11/sydney-film-festival-the-nightingale-premiere-sparks-controversy/11198288.
6. Eric Kohn, '"Holiday" Review: Devastating Danish Drama Has the Most Unsettling Rape Scene Since "Irreversible" – Sundance 2018', *Indiewire*, 26 January 2018, https://www.indiewire.com/2018/01/holiday-review-isabella-eklof-rape-sundance-2018-1201921797/. Although it is not always helpful to find male-authored analogues to women-authored provocations, the comparison to Noé's *Irréversible* is productive to a degree and important to address simply because it is so often invoked in reviews of *Holiday*. The two scenes in *Irréversible* and *Holiday* are very different in multiple respects; however, what links them is the use of the long take to create a durational realism. Moreover, both show the rape from start to finish, from the instigating moments until the rape concludes, and then a little longer still. Both also include a moment when an unidentified person can be seen entering the scene, then leaving without intervening.
7. Alexandra Heller-Nicholas, 'What's Up Down Under?: HOLIDAY', *Alliance of Women Film Journalists*, 26 June 2018, https://awfj.org/blog/2018/06/26/holiday-review-by-alexandra-heller-nicholas/.
8. Hannah McGill, 'Holiday', *Sight & Sound* 29, no. 9 (2019), 65.
9. Dominique Russell, 'Buñuel: Storytelling, Desire and the Question of Rape', in *Rape in Art Cinema*, ed. Dominique Russell (New York: Continuum, 2010), 42.
10. Tom Shone, 'Michael Haneke Goes Cruelty-Free With *Amour*', *Vulture*, 9 December 2012, https://www.vulture.com/2012/12/michael-haneke-amour-at-nyff.html.
11. Russell, 'Buñuel: Storytelling, Desire and the Question of Rape', 42.
12. Lynn A. Higgins, 'Screen/Memory: Rape and Its Alibis in *Last Year at Marienbad*', in *Rape in Art Cinema*, ed. Dominique Russell (New York: Continuum, 2010), 24.
13. Dominique Russell, 'Introduction: Why Rape?' in *Rape in Art Cinema*, ed. Dominique Russell (New York: Continuum, 2010), 7.
14. British Board of Film Classification, '*Baise-moi*', 26 February 2001, www.bbfc.co.uk/AFF165545/.
15. Horeck, *Public Rape*, 83.
16. Ibid., 90.
17. Sarah Projansky, *Watching Rape: Film and Television in Postfeminist Culture* (New York: New York University Press, 2001), 95; emphasis in original.
18. B. Ruby Rich, 'Prologue: Sex, Gender, and Consumer Culture', in *Chick Flicks: Theories and Memories of the Feminist Film Movement* (Durham, NC: Duke University Press, 1998), 260.

19. As Russell notes, the prevalence of male directors depicting rape 'reinforces a hierarchy of masculine imagination over feminine body' ('Introduction', 6).
20. All of these motives can also apply to works that address rape in deeply confronting but not literal or explicit ways, such as Suzanne Lacy's *Three Weeks in May* (1977), Jenny Holzer's *Lustmord* (1993–4) and Naima Ramos-Chapman's *And Nothing Happened* (2016).
21. Linda Ruth Williams, 'The Limits of Sex: Sick Sisters', *Sight & Sound* 11, no. 7 (2001), 28–9.
22. Alongside Peirce's work, Ana Kokkinos's story of a man's rape in *The Book of Revelation* reveals that women also make films about sexual violence experienced by people who are not cisgendered women – another way of challenging hegemonic scripts and clichés about sexual violence as something that only happens to certain bodies for certain reasons.
23. B. Ruby Rich, 'Antiporn: Soft Issue, Hard World (*Not a Love Story*) (1982–83)', in *Chick Flicks: Theories and Memories of the Feminist Film Movement* (Durham, NC: Duke University Press, 1998), 263.
24. Asbjørn Grønstad, *Screening the Unwatchable: Spaces of Negation in Post-Millennial Art Cinema* (Basingstoke: Palgrave Macmillan, 2012), 2.
25. Scott MacKenzie, 'On Watching and Turning Away: Ono's *Rape*, *Cinéma Direct* Aesthetics, and the Genealogy of *Cinéma Brut*', in *Rape in Art Cinema*, ed. Dominique Russell (New York: Continuum, 2010), 160–1.
26. Ibid., 159.
27. Guy Lodge, 'Sundance Film Review: "Holiday"', *Variety*, 30 January 2018, https://variety.com/2018/film/reviews/holiday-review-1202681429/.
28. Windsor, 'Tasmanian Torments'.
29. Isabella Eklöf, 'In Conversation with Isabella Eklöf', *Another Gaze*, uploaded 5 August 2019, video, 0:18, https://www.anothergaze.com/conversation-interview-isabella-eklof/.
30. Isabella Eklöf, 'On *Holiday*', *Holiday* (Anti-Worlds, 2020), interview, 3:59, Blu-ray.
31. Ibid., 5:39.
32. Although the logline describes her as both 'a dark-skinned girl' and an 'exchange student', Eklöf's film never confirms the background of the teenage protagonist.
33. Eklöf, 'On *Holiday*', 7:11.
34. McGill, 'Holiday', 64.
35. Isabella Eklöf and Victoria Carmen Sonne, 'LEGION M Sundance 2018 HOLIDAY Isabella Eklof', interview by Russ Fischer, *Legion M*, uploaded 13 March 2018, video, 1:09, https://www.youtube.com/watch?v=7YJ64SrcS-A.
36. Wendy Ide, '"Holiday": Sundance Review', *Screen Daily*, 20 January 2018, https://www.screendaily.com/reviews/holiday-sundance-review/5125348.article.
37. Kimber Myers, 'Unflinching Crime Drama "Holiday" Details the Life of a Modern European Moll', *Los Angeles Times*, 7 February 2019, https://

www.latimes.com/entertainment/movies/la-et-mn-mini-holiday-review-20190207-story.html.
38. See Lodge, 'Sundance'; Myers, 'Unflinching'; McGill, 'Holiday'.
39. MacKenzie, 'On Watching', 162.
40. Eklöf, 'In Conversation with Isabella Eklöf', 4:14.
41. Ibid., 3:36.
42. Eklöf and Sonne, 'LEGION M', 1:56.
43. Ana Fazekaš, '(Auto)Biography of Hurt: Representation and Representability of Rape in Feminist Performance Art', *Sic: Journal of Literature, Culture and Literary Translation* 8, no. 1 (2017), 4.
44. Eklöf, 'In Conversation with Isabella Eklöf', 3:12.
45. Robin Pomeroy, 'Australian Director Jennifer Kent Called a "Whore" at Venice Festival', *Sydney Morning Herald*, 8 September 2018, https://www.smh.com.au/entertainment/movies/australian-director-jennifer-kent-called-a-whore-at-venice-festival-20180908-p502iu.html.
46. Thomas, 'Sydney Film Festival Controversy'.
47. Steph Harmon, 'The Nightingale Director Jennifer Kent Defends "Honest" Depiction of Rape and Violence', *Guardian*, 11 June 2019, https://www.theguardian.com/film/2019/jun/11/nightingale-director-jennifer-kent-defends-honest-depiction-of-and-violence.
48. See Anne Billson, 'Does the "Female Gaze" Make Sexual Violence on Film Any Less Repugnant?' *Guardian*, 2 August 2019, https://www.theguardian.com/film/2019/aug/02/the-female-gaze-does-it-make-sexual-violence-on-film-any-less-repugnant; Cara Buckley, 'When Rape Onscreen is Directed by a Woman', *The New York Times*, 6 August 2019, https://www.nytimes.com/2019/08/02/movies/rape-film-nightingale.html; Madeleine Seidel, 'How The Nightingale Subverts the Rape-revenge Genre', *Little White Lies*, 13 August 2019, https://lwlies.com/articles/the-nightingale-jennifer-kent-sexual-violence-against-women/.
49. Alexandra Heller-Nicholas, 'The Road Less Travelled By', in *The Nightingale*, Second Sight (Blu-ray booklet, 2021), 31.
50. Dominic White, 'The Horror of Australian Films: Entertainment', *Australian Financial Review*, 17 January 2015, 4.
51. Stephen King (@StephenKing), 'THE BABBADOOK [sic]: Deeply disturbing and highly recommended. You don't watch it so much as experience it', Tweet, 22 November 2014, https://twitter.com/StephenKing/status/535984981219479552.
52. William Friedkin (@WilliamFriedkin), 'Psycho, Alien, Diabolique [sic] and now THE BABADOOK', Tweet, 1 December 2014, https://twitter.com/williamfriedkin/status/539244895236390912?lang=en.
53. Thomas, 'Sydney Film Festival Controversy'; Harmon, 'The Nightingale Director Jennifer Kent Defends "Honest" Depiction of Rape and Violence'; Sam Langford, '"The Nightingale" Is Disturbing And Extremely Violent, And It Needs To Be', *Junkee*, 13 June 2019, https://junkee.com/nightingale-

review-sydney-film-festival/209216; Ben Graham, 'Director Hits Back after Cinemagoers Walk Out and Yell Criticism during The Nightingale Screening in Sydney', *News.com.au*, 11 June 2019, https://www.news.com.au/entertainment/movies/new-movies/cinemagoers-walk-out-and-yell-criticism-during-the-nightingale-premiere-in-sydney/news-story/caff28ba212a573619fe1ed29bc98b2e.
54. Thomas, 'Sydney Film Festival Controversy'.
55. Sarah Ward, 'Film Review: The Nightingale is Furious and Grueling', *Screen Hub*, 29 August 2019, https://www.screenhub.com.au/news/reviews/film-review-the-nightingale-is-furious-and-gruelling-257155-1426023/.
56. Sandra Hall, 'A Powerful Portrayal of Our Nation's Brutal History', *Sydney Morning Herald*, 28 August 2019, https://www.smh.com.au/entertainment/movies/a-powerful-portrayal-of-our-nation-s-brutal-history-20190827-p52l6c.html.
57. Keva York, 'The Nightingale Roots Horror in Tasmania's Colonial History with a Tale of Revenge', Australian Broadcasting Corporation, 29 August 2019, https://www.abc.net.au/news/2019-08-29/the-nightingale-review-jennifer-kent-tasmanian-history-colonial/11450322.
58. Harmon, 'The Nightingale Director Jennifer Kent Defends "Honest" Depiction of Rape and Violence'.
59. Heller-Nicholas, 'The Road Less Travelled By', 21.
60. Graham Fuller and Jennifer Kent, 'Once Upon a Time in Van Diemen's Land: An Interview with Jennifer Kent', *Cinéaste* 44, no. 4 (2019), 25.
61. In an essay on the film included with the film's 2021 Blu-ray release, Elena Lazic suggests that Clare cannot be identified with by the spectator insofar as she is a racist and also a historically distant subject, removed from the spectator's own context. For example, Clare initially harbours the racist belief that Billy is a cannibal. She is also highly distrustful of him at first, keeping him constantly at gunpoint. Yet I would argue that empathy with Clare in spite of her historical distance and (initially) racist ignorance is precisely what the film does accomplish: it is only through showing rape as an experience recognisable to a contemporary audience as rape that the film locates us within Clare's experience. (Elena Lazic, 'Empathy and Sympathy in *The Nightingale*', in *The Nightingale*, Second Sight [Blu-ray booklet], 2021.)
62. Devika Girish, 'Interview: Jennifer Kent', interview, *Film Comment Blog*, 30 January 2019, https://www.filmcomment.com/blog/interview-jennifer-kent/.
63. Angelique Szymanek, 'Bloody Pleasures: Ana Mendieta's Violent Tableaux', *Signs: Journal of Women in Culture and Society* 41, no. 4 (2016), 910, 918.
64. The sequence in *The Accused* that depicts the sexual assault takes place in flashback during the court trial of the accused rapists. The entire flashback runs for approximately fourteen minutes. The sequence begins as Jodi Foster's character, Sarah Tobias, arrives at The Mill, the bar where she is attacked. It shows Sarah drinking, flirting and dancing with the men in The

Mill prior to the assault. The scene of sexual assault itself, which I measure from the moment Sarah says she wants to leave and is prevented from doing so, runs for six minutes.

65. Richard Corliss, '"Bad" Women and Brutal Men', *Time*, 24 June 2001, http://content.time.com/time/magazine/article/0,9171,148064,00.html.
66. Windsor, 'Tasmanian Torments'.
67. Sheila O'Malley, 'The Nightingale', *RogerEbert.com*, 2 August 2019, https://www.rogerebert.com/reviews/the-nightingale-2019.
68. Heller-Nicholas, 'The Road Less Travelled By', 31.
69. Rape is one of the experiences that Catherine Breillat addresses in her films (Chapter 1), and it appears also in the works of French director Claire Denis (Chapter 4) and those of American director Anna Biller (Chapter 5).
70. Russell, 'Introduction: Why Rape?' 4–5.

CHAPTER 3

The Provocations of the Pretty: The Films of Lucile Hadžihalilović

An investigation into how contemporary women filmmakers take up the provocative tradition finds an important object in the work of French filmmaker Lucile Hadžihalilović. Since the release of her breakthrough feature *Innocence* in 2004, critics have lauded Hadžihalilović as a talented and exciting auteur of beautiful, evocative art cinema. Fabien Lemercier describes her as 'talented and highly original';[1] Vivian Sobchack praises Hadžihalilović as an 'assured' and promising director;[2] and Jonathan Romney deems her 'an audacious talent'.[3] Compliments also flowed following the release of her follow-up *Évolution* (2015), with Laura Kern naming Hadžihalilović a 'virtuoso'.[4] The film also won the Special Jury Prize at the 2015 San Sebastián International Film Festival. Hadžihalilović's oeuvre so far consists of several visually impressive and distinctive works. She has four shorts: a student film, *La première mort de Nono* (1987), an educational short for television *Good Boys Use Condoms* (1998), and two woodland fantasies, *Nectar* (2014) and *De Natura* (2018). She has also written and directed four features: *Mimi* (*La bouche de Jean-Pierre*, 1996), *Innocence*, *Évolution* and *Earwig* (2021). She works frequently with screenwriters Geoff Cox and Alantė Kavaitė, and has herself collaborated regularly on Gaspar Noé's projects, contributing to the screenplay for *Enter the Void* (2009) and editing his films *Carne* (1991) and *I Stand Alone* (*Seul contre tous*, 1998). Acclaimed for her lush and painterly visual style and the uncanny, fairytale-like tone of her storytelling, Hadžihalilović is an auteur of importance in contemporary art cinema.

Hadžihalilović's films also bear an aura of transgression. Without exception, her features centre on child protagonists between the ages of six and twelve. These characters all find themselves in unsettling situations, overseen by shadowy adult caretakers with ambiguous motives. *Mimi* is a story about an eleven-year-old girl, Mimi (Sandra Sammartino), whose mother attempts suicide. When Mimi goes to live with her aunt and her aunt's sleazy boyfriend, the older man takes a predatory interest in the young girl. *Innocence* concerns a mysterious boarding school secreted in a lush forest. It is attended by girls between six and twelve years of age, and the only lessons provided by their mistresses are ballet and natural history. *Évolution* is set on a remote island within a community of prepubescent boys and their mothers. The story begins as Nicolas (Max Brebant) discovers the corpse of another boy while swimming in the ocean, leading him to become suspicious of his mother and the mysterious surgeries he is forced to undergo in hospital. *Earwig* is about Mia (Romane Hemelaers), a young girl with teeth made of ice. Every day, her caretaker, Albert (Paul Hilton), inserts new frozen dentures to replace the ones that melted away. Although bad things do sometimes befall Hadžihalilović's protagonists, her films are not explicit, depending instead on an underlying tone of ambiguity that mirrors the children's ignorance of (or suspicion about) their own situation. Some critics condemn Hadžihalilović's work for this reason, or at least express a concern that her films are exploitative and unethical due to the intensity with which they centre on imperilled children. Hadžihalilović herself regularly refutes suggestions that her films are deliberatively or even inadvertently provocative, insisting that anything disturbing is in the eye of the onlooker. As she wryly notes, 'It's only when I have finished a film and ... when I hear what the audience feel or see in my film that I realise fully what I have done, what "crime" I have committed'.[5] Atmospheric and occasionally nightmarish, Hadžihalilović's films are intriguing and complex case studies. As an auteur, her relationship to provocation, taboo and controversy is therefore not straightforward.

Complicating matters further is the fact that Hadžihalilović's films do not look like the typical provocations of avant-garde visual culture. Her films consistently win acclaim due to the beauty of their *mise en scène*. Superlatives such as 'painterly', 'beautiful' and 'stunning' arise often in descriptions of her work: after a screening of *Earwig* at the 2021 Toronto International Film Festival, for instance, Cameron Bailey declares it to be 'a beautiful film' and 'very haunting'.[6] At a screening of *Évolution* at New Directors/New Films, the host declared: 'It's a beautiful film. Visually, it's stunning.'[7] Whereas much post-millennium art cinema adopts discordant or explicit aesthetics, Hadžihalilović has instead made a career of directing meticulously composed films that extend visual pleasure to the spectator, whether through images of lush woodlands in *Innocence*, *Nectar* and *De Natura*, the fecund oceans in *Évolution* or the luminous parklands in *Earwig*. Her films are also characterised by pretty objects that adorn the production design: coloured ribbons and starfish, dolls, butterflies and rainbow-patterned crystal glasses. What is at stake in Hadžihalilović's work, then, is the relationship between film aesthetics and the provocativeness of her subject matter.

This chapter investigates Hadžihalilović's work to determine how she breaks with an established aesthetics of provocation – one that has been installed as a dominant style of cinematic transgression and is also highly gendered as masculine. Although this tendency appears across her work, I focus particularly on two of Hadžihalilović's feature films, *Innocence* and *Évolution*, as texts that achieve provocation through visual pleasure rather than displeasure. These films accomplish this manoeuvre via an engagement with what Rosalind Galt calls the feminised aesthetics of 'the pretty' – a complex category understood in terms of its lesser status as a decorative and cosmetic aesthetic. In refuting the typical look of cinematic provocation and opting for a pretty aesthetic, Hadžihalilović draws upon a specifically femininised style. To conduct this discussion, I first examine how discourses of film and aesthetic criticism understand the notion of provocation and authorship in art and cinema more generally. I then explore the shared aesthetic principles in Hadžihalilović's films to consider how they measure up against these notions, particularly in their construction of colourful, fetishistic and pretty *mise en scène*. I also consider the political implications of Hadžihalilović's choice to use pretty aesthetics: first, in her development of a feminised aesthetic of provocation that operates in contradistinction to the masculinised imagery of her peers, and second, one that undertakes political work by giving voice to marginalised child subjects. A close reading of Hadžihalilović's films provides insight into how a contemporary woman director engages with confrontational material on feminised aesthetic terms. Moreover, it facilitates an expanded understanding of provocation as more than simply a masculine author–recipient relationship of aggression, displeasure and scopic offence, but as an approach that can occur on the feminised terms of the pretty.

Provocation and its Aesthetics

Before investigating Hadžihalilović's films in close detail, it is necessary to first establish the way in which they depart from the usual modes of provocation in avant-garde practice – significantly through their use of film aesthetics. Although provocation is foremost an emotional response to film rather than a specific aesthetic property of the text itself, the discourses of art and film criticism regularly focus on aesthetics in their discussions of provocation, identifying certain images as pre-eminently provocative. In other words, these discourses posit an aesthetics of provocation. As I detail in the introduction to this book, this usually consists of scopic offence through gratuitous spectacle or ugly images (and often both simultaneously). As Mattias Frey writes, a characteristic of recent art cinema is a 'recuperation of the prurient, ugly, or disgusting' as part of the trend towards extremist representation.[8] In his germinal essay on extreme French cinema, James Quandt locates the provocation of this mode in its confronting subject matter and gratuitous spectacle:

> Images and subjects once the provenance of splatter films, exploitation flicks, and porn – gang rapes, bashings and slashings and blindings, hard-ons and vulvas, cannibalism, sadomasochism and incest, fucking and fisting, sluices of cum and gore – proliferate in the high-art environs of a national cinema whose provocations have historically been formal, political, or philosophical (Godard, Clouzot, Debord) or, at their most immoderate (Franju, Buñuel, Walerian Borowczyk, Andrzej Zulawski), at least assimilable as emanations of an artistic movement (Surrealism mostly).[9]

This interest in offensive images – whether ugly, startling, explicit or all three – is not new. It extends all the way to foundational works such as *An Andalusian Dog* (*Un chien andalou*, Luis Buñuel, 1929) and its startling images of sliced eyes, as well as the follow-up film *The Golden Age* (*L'Âge d'Or*, 1930) and its comic scene of toe-fellatio. Ugliness and explicitness are not always the same thing – numerous filmmakers have aestheticised explicit sex and violence, such as the baroque *giallo* films of Mario Bava and Dario Argento, and Catherine Breillat's religious obscenities in *Anatomy of Hell* (*Anatomie de l'enfer*, 2004). Yet what matters here is the effect on the spectator, which is an activating absence of pleasure – a negative aesthetic experience that provokes negative emotions.

This film style has important antecedents in the aesthetics of shock and transgression of modernist art of the nineteenth and early twentieth century. As John A. Walker notes, in this period 'harmonious, organic compositions were replaced by fragmented, inconsistent and dissonant compositions. In many instances, the traditional artistic value of beauty was replaced by cults of the primitive and the ugly.'[10] Mechtild Widrich calls this ongoing fascination the 'conquest of ugliness' in the avant-garde.[11] Whereas one of the dominant aims of Western art had been to achieve a pleasing aesthetic experience, or even make contact with the transcendent ideals of beauty itself, the rejection of this pursuit is a hallmark of the avant-garde. The rationales for this rejection are complex and numerous and, indeed, the many books devoted to ugliness suggest that the avant-garde's fascination with the topic is too extensive to completely summarise here.[12] Yet the artistic pursuit of visual ugliness can nonetheless be linked to several goals connected to the experience of negative emotions. The first is novelty both in visual aesthetics and in the experience of the recipient upon viewing them; as Widrich puts it, the goal can be to colonise 'new territories of experience'[13] through new aesthetics that may in turn transform from negative to positive, ugly to beautiful (as she says, the ugly is transformed into beautiful). Ugliness and the negative emotions it elicits can also supposedly put the onlooker in touch with emotions that have been repressed in modernity.[14] This is paradigmatically encapsulated by Antonin Artaud in his second manifesto on the Theatre of Cruelty, which he says 'has been created in order to restore to the theatre a passionate and convulsive conception of life'.[15] Though ultimately perceived by Artaud to be a superior experience that connects the audience to their senses and feelings, the method was not necessarily conducive to pleasure, insofar as it involved presenting the audience with arresting gestures, loud noises, bright lights and other such elements. Lastly, the negative emotions that ugliness elicits can also supposedly facilitate the revelation of difficult truths, particularly those that are characteristic of the modern era: industrialisation, environmental degradation and war. As Widrich states, 'In *existing* society, ugly art allows us to reflect on society's attempt to cover up ugly truths'.[16] The rejection of pleasing aesthetics in favour of ugly, confronting images remains a hallmark of extreme art cinema modes in the late twentieth century and the post-millennium moment. The correlation between ugly aesthetics – or at least the absence of beautification – and the intended outcomes recall those of the earlier avant-garde movements too. Consider Dogme 95, the filmmaking movement started by Danish directors Lars von Trier and Thomas Vinterberg. Their 1995 manifesto advocated for a style of filmmaking that reduced artifice and cosmetics wherever possible, excluding artificial lighting and the use of sets and non-diegetic music. Like their modernist predecessors, adherents to Dogme were required to 'force the truth out of my characters and settings' and 'to do so by all the means available and at the cost of any good taste and any aesthetic considerations'.[17] The resulting Dogme films – with their grainy, poorly lit scenes, muffled sounds and out-of-focus shots – do not conform to conventional definitions of cinematic beauty.

The ugly, avant-garde aesthetic is not gender neutral in philosophy or art criticism. The 'look' of ugliness (and therefore provocation) is regularly conceptualised as intrinsically masculine, both in essence and in its effect on the onlooker. Galt's work on the 'the pretty' is instructive here. Galt extensively maps the gendered, racial and sexual politics of cinema aesthetics, arguing that film theory has consistently valued a supposedly more masculine aesthetic at the expense of the feminine pretty. The exact nature of this 'masculine' aesthetic is heterogeneous (as is 'the pretty'), yet there are some recurrent characteristics that Galt identifies.

In cinema, these include line, monochrome and camera work that gives the impression of indexicality. These, one can infer, are qualities that may appear quite *un*appealing to look at, in some cases even provocatively ugly: dynamic rather than composed images, black and white photography instead of colour, and footage depicting the 'realities' of contemporary life rather than fantasias. Such qualities also stand in symbolic opposition to those found in 'regressive' older media such as oil painting, which is characterised by colour, compositional harmony and tableaux. The manner in which this aesthetics is gendered depends on a set of associations of qualities deemed discursively as masculine as opposed to feminine. One of these has to do with a longstanding devaluation of colour as inferior to line insofar as colour is 'cosmetic' and associated with the excitation of emotion. In the discourse of aesthetics and philosophy, line has a superior semiotic, sense-making and thus rational capacity in comparison to colour, necessarily associating line with the domain of the masculine. Galt notes, 'The hierarchy of line and color attributes masculine reason to line and feminine emotion to color'.[18] This links with Galt's observation that film critics' notion of superior film aesthetics tends to involve qualities that are specific to the medium, such as its supposed indexicality and capacity to capture motion, which are in turn tethered to masculinity. This cinema aesthetics is gendered because of its dynamism and, by extension, its ability to rouse the spectator rather than enervate through pleasure. As Galt explains, 'Activity is masculinizing'.[19] What is more, indexicality implies a connection to truth-telling rather than the deceptions of the cosmetic, a trait associated with feminine duplicity and falsehood.

In contrast, visually appealing images – whether colourful, glittery, floral, curved or luminous – are both feminised and devalued in the discourses of art and the modernist avant-garde. Prettiness, as Galt defines it, is a complex aesthetic with many characteristics that have not always been conceptualised in the same way. One constant, however, is that the pretty is visually appealing in a supposedly superficial, decorative or cosmetic way. Galt lists numerous examples of the pretty in cinema: *Lola Montès* (Max Ophüls, 1955), *Amelie* (*Le fabuleux destin d'Amélie Poulain*, Jean-Pierre Jeunet, 2001), *Moulin Rouge!* (Baz Luhrmann, 2001) and *Hero* (*Ying xiong*, Zhang Yimou, 2002). Individual qualities of the pretty include vivid colour, sparkle, luminosity and features such as arabesques (as opposed to line, monochrome and form). It is, as Galt explains, an overwhelmingly disprized aesthetic. It also happens to be aligned with marginalised identities and groups, such as the feminine, the queer, the infantile, the primitive and the non-Western (including African, Asian and Oriental). The continuum of value between the disprized, enervating pretty and the provocative avant-garde is evident here, with the most aggressive version of the masculine/active aesthetic in cinema appearing in the most notorious provocative films. Images of tongue-pulling in *Salò, or the 120 Days of Sodom* (*Salò o le 120 giornate di Sodoma*, Pier Paolo Pasolini, 1975), the tooth-smashing of *Dogtooth* (*Kynodontas*, Yorgos Lanthimos, 2009) and the genital mutilation in *Antichrist* (Lars von Trier, 2009) all rely on dynamic, violent imagery. They also depend on a horrific, if fleeting and ultimately fanciful, impression of indexicality. Pretty imagery occupies the opposite end of the aesthetic spectrum – the feminine, the placating and the attractive. It is also the composed, carefully placed and staged image.

To understand Hadžihalilović's intervention in the history of provocative cinema, it is important to make sense of her place in the aesthetic traditions that characterise provocation. In contrast to the avant-garde provocation of ugliness, she has made her career producing carefully composed, richly coloured films that are aligned with the cinematic pretty. Her works are both visually appealing and evocative of the highly composed paintings of the surrealists, symbolists and impressionists. Indeed, as I discuss in the sections below, the construction of a painterly visual appeal is an organising goal in the cinematic works of Hadžihalilović. Her works are thus an example of what Galt describes as the radical aesthetics of 'the terrain of the excluded pretty'.[20] She is a contemporary auteur who uses the feminised pretty rather than ugliness precisely to deepen the challenge of her work.

Hadžihalilović's Pretty Provocations

Hadžihalilović uses pretty aesthetics to please and provoke. Most of her films are centred on beautifully rendered images of children in the landscape, which is a defining feature of her *mise en scène*. Children amongst trees, grass, rivers, fruit, insects and sunlight are motifs in *Innocence*, *De Natura* and *Earwig*, while *Évolution* tells a story of young boys who live on a rocky island, surrounded by ocean filled with seagrass and starfish. Each film is strongly coloured: deep forest greens and browns feature in *Innocence* and *De Natura*, sun-bleached white in *Évolution*, honey yellow in *Nectar* and iridescent blues and greens in *Earwig*. Gold and white sunlight illuminates the day scenes all three films, contrasting with the velvety night-time blacks of *Innocence* and *Nectar*, the cool darkness of *Évolution* and the misty outdoor scenes in *Earwig*. For all their attractiveness, however, Hadžihalilović's films routinely deal with provocative themes that could easily arouse negative emotions. The protagonists of *Mimi*, *Innocence*, *Évolution* and *Earwig* are all children who find themselves in peril. When eleven-year-old Mimi goes to live with her aunt Solange and Solange's boyfriend, the older man constantly threatens Mimi with predatory sexual attention. In *Innocence*, the eldest girls at the boarding school are compelled to dance for an unseen adult audience every night. In *Évolution*, the prepubescent hero Nicolas is surgically impregnated by the witch-like women who take care of him and his friends; he escapes death only with the help of the young nurse who pities him. In *Earwig*, the protagonist Mia is either protected or held hostage by her adult caretaker. Hadžihalilović's films therefore allude to one of the most widely condemned taboos of the contemporary era: child abuse. They are, at the same time, works that extend visual pleasure to the viewer through their attractive *mise en scène*. Hadžihalilović's films thus establish a challenging spectatorial situation in which the viewer is invited to take pleasure in scenes that may (or may not) show deeply unethical and taboo scenarios.

The film that mobilises the pretty most consistently and controversially in this way is Hadžihalilović's breakout work, *Innocence*. Indeed, this film not only uses prettiness – and the pleasure that it offers – to complicate the spectator's engagement with the film, it uses its visual appeal to paradoxically intensify the spectators' discomfort. The film is an adaptation of Frank Wedekind's 1903 novella *Mine-Haha, or On the Bodily Education of Young Girls*. Like Wedekind's novella, *Innocence* confirms little about the plot events. The film begins as six-year-old Iris (Zoé Auclair) arrives at the all-girl boarding school in a coffin-like casket. After being shown around by the older girls, she takes a swimming lesson at the river with her new schoolmates – no adults are present. The girls strip down to their underwear and show Iris how to kick and paddle, and they swim and laugh together until dusk settles. In later scenes, the girls wear pleated skirts and coloured ribbons in their hair, and the camera frequently catches their bodies in motion as they dance and play in the forest. The film reveals some aspects of the girls' lives as the story progresses, but not many. During the day the girls take ballet lessons and classes in natural history, which they enjoy without concern or questioning why these are the only subjects offered. In the evening the eldest go to a secret theatre to dance for an unseen audience. When they graduate, these older girls depart by underground train to be released into society. In the final scene, Bianca (Bérangère Haubruge), the eldest of Iris's roommates, emerges from the train into a sun-drenched city square. At the centre is a rushing fountain. Young boys, on the brink of adolescence, await her on the other side.

The response to *Innocence* amongst professional film critics and industry bodies was mixed, with many highlighting the film's suggestive material.[21] In his review, Jonathan Romney suggests that the iconography within *Innocence* is deliberately provocative: 'It's beyond question ... that Hadžihalilović deliberately uses images that were once considered innocuous and are now effectively taboo.'[22] Manohla Dargis and Andrew Sarris go further, condemning the film and declaring it outright voyeuristic.[23] Sarris is especially frank:

> I was shocked by the blatant exploitation of little girls for what would seem to amount to a pedophile's panorama – if only there were the slightest intimation of reality involved in the proceedings. It seems to be a part of the filmmaker's strategy to make the spectator ashamed of all the prepubescent female flesh exposed onscreen in the service of some indecipherable ritual.[24]

Dargis expresses a similar sentiment to Sarris, albeit in more muted terms, writing, 'The images that some might find troubling – the shots of the girls' legs, those peek-a-boo moments when the camera all but noses under their skirts – are not motivated by any seen character. The point of view here is that of the filmmaker and, by extension, us.'[25] However, other commentators heaped praise upon *Innocence* and its director. Although acknowledging the film's provocative material, Romney declares Hadžihalilović 'an audacious talent'.[26] Ginette Vincendeau states that the work is 'testimony to the vitality and diversity of female film-making in France',[27] and the film won the Bronze Horse Award for best film at the Stockholm International Film Festival, the FIPRESCI (International Federation of Film Critics) Prize at Istanbul and the Best New Director award at the San Sebastián International Film Festival. Critics in this latter camp singled out for commendation the film's composed and painterly *mise en scène*, its production design and its cinematography (Figure 3.1). As Sobchack notes, *Innocence* has a 'still, and distilled, mise-en-scène';[28] Romney writes that it has a 'classical, painterly look' and that

Figure 3.1 A painterly landscape in *Innocence*.

'particularly beautiful are the nature shots, the still views of the empty park';[29] Vincendeau says it is filled with 'striking compositions';[30] and Laura Kern describes the film as 'meticulously framed, [and] painterly'.[31]

These differing responses to *Innocence* are equally illuminating, even though they disagree on the film's merit, because they invite us to consider how the beauty of Hadžihalilović's *mise en scène* interacts with the controversial nature of her material. Painterliness is indeed a recurring aspect of Hadžihalilović's style. Locked-down cameras in each film frequently arrest the narrative progression, freezing the movement of the image to capture the subjects interacting in the landscape. Though not *tableaux vivants* per se, Hadžihalilović meticulously arranges the figures in the frame, connecting the image to the visual arts. The *mises en scène* in *Innocence* and Hadžihalilović's later works *Évolution* and *Earwig* are also steeped in references to painting, particularly symbolist and surrealist art. The day-for-night photography of *Innocence* closely recalls René Magritte's evocative paintings *The Empire of Light* (*L'Empire des lumières*, 1949–54), *God's Room* (*Le salon de Dieu*, 1948), and *The Voice of Blood* (*La voix du sang*, 1948).[32] The sun-bleached landscapes of *Évolution* resemble the surrealist works of Giorgio de Chirico, Yves Tanguy and Salvador Dalí, whom Hadžihalilović cites as influences.[33] The gloomy, yellowed interiors of *Earwig* recall the works of Belgian Symbolists such as Léon Spilliaert and Fernand Khnopff; the outdoor scenes with their misty iridescence resemble the impressionism of Claude Monet and Alfred Sisley.

Much historical film discourse characterises the kind of painterly aesthetic that Hadžihalilović employs as conservative, pleasing and, indeed, feminine, as opposed to masculine, avant-garde and shocking. As Galt has explained, film theorists have long displayed suspicion of images that too closely resemble the static compositions of oil painting, aligning them with the denigrated aesthetics of the pretty.[34] As cinema's supposed indexicality and realism became its prized ontological qualities, film theorists criticised painterly films and deemed them too attractive, passive or pretty to embody the uniqueness of the medium and its specific mode of beauty.[35] As Galt explains, the 'scenographic image lacks the dynamism that patriarchal language gives to the modern form of visual making'.[36] Painterly images are also codified as both feminine and belonging to a regressive aesthetic from an outdated medium. Hadžihalilović's *mise en scène* from *Innocence* onwards very much resembles European oil painting. It also contains the same subject matter: natural environments, deep green, yellow and brown hues and attractive human subjects. Even *Évolution*, which draws upon the unsettling surrealist uncanny in its other-worldly beachside landscapes, enlists the pretty imagery of the Renaissance and pre-Raphaelites in its stylisation of the monstrous women who populate the film, all of whom are young and strikingly beautiful. Their pale faces are angular and shapely, their skin translucent and their long hair falls in romantic waves of copper and titian. Hadžihalilović's films therefore correspond more closely with the pretty than with the masculinised offensiveness of post-millennium art cinema. They reject what Walker calls the 'fragmented', 'dissonant' and 'ugly' aesthetics of modernist painting,[37] and avoid what Galt rhetorically describes as 'the sharp and pointy avant-garde'.[38]

The instrument of provocation in *Innocence* is precisely this painterly prettiness. By placing children in a prettified *mise en scène*, *Innocence* draws the viewer in rather than prompting them to look away.[39] It therefore raises questions as to whether it is acceptable to aestheticise young girls and peer voyeuristically into their private world. The discomfort of viewing *Innocence* is the oscillation between the visual pleasure of its images and the creeping worry that such images are morally unacceptable. Scott MacKenzie suggests that this oscillation is a characteristic of much of the New Extremity and *cinéma brut* films of post-millennium art cinema. Hadžihalilović's work differs, however, because it relies on prettiness rather than scopic offence to enact this phenomenon. For instance, MacKenzie refers to Noé's *Irréversible* to make his point, arguing that the film positions the viewer to switch viewing modes repeatedly 'between profound distanciation and voyeuristic scopophilia'.[40] This effect is key to the film's infamous nine-minute-long sexual assault sequence, which positions the spectator to feel self-conscious, even ashamed, about witnessing the onscreen rape. This self-consciousness amounts to distanciation, heightening the spectator's awareness that they are engaging with a film artefact and prompting them to reflect on the ethics of their viewership. *Innocence* accomplishes a similar ethical questioning. The difference, however, is that Hadžihalilović's aesthetics seduce through the pleasing, feminised pretty rather than ugly, violent spectacle. Her work demonstrates that it is possible to activate viewer alienation – to arouse and unsettle the spectator – through pretty landscapes rather than rapes or eye-slices. Moreover, *Innocence* is ambiguous in a way that other New Extremity films are not – the plot never confirms whether the girls' story is indeed a sinister one.

Hadžihalilović's achievement in *Innocence* is that she uses the aesthetic of the pretty in direct departure from the entrenched masculine imagery of provocation favoured by her contemporaries. Although *Évolution* and *Earwig* draw more regularly on the startling modernist imagery of surrealist and symbolist painting than *Innocence* does, these films also draw on the aesthetics of the pretty, incorporating pretty landscapes and aesthetics influenced by pre-Raphaelite art and impressionism into the *mise en scène*. This is significant to scholarly conceptualisation of provocation as an aesthetic and mode of authorial address. One question that motivates Galt's work on the pretty is whether the aesthetic can 'be put to critical, even political, use'.[41] Pretty images in Hadžihalilović's work are indeed political. They advance a feminised aesthetics of provocation, showing how the pretty can activate and unsettle the spectator even as it extends visual pleasure. By enacting this so successfully in *Innocence* and in her later work, Hadžihalilović's films give the lie to a long-established symbolic regime that informs cinematic discussions of the avant-garde – one that suggests that distanciation and discomfort are achieved chiefly through visual shock. Hadžihalilović's films upend the linkages between the scopically offensive, active, boundary-breaking masculine provocateur and the pleasing, passive, uncritical feminine pretty. She makes pretty provocations.

The Child

The question of whether the pretty can be put to critical, even political, use finds another answer in Hadžihalilović's focus on child protagonists. With the exception of her short films *Nectar* and *Good Boys Use Condoms*, all of Hadžihalilović's films centre on young children. Hadžihalilović acknowledges her interest in childhood as a persistent fascination, stating, 'It's kind of against my will that I'm attracted to this time period'.[42] Children in Hadžihalilović's films tend to find themselves in ambiguous circumstances. Some, like the eponymous protagonist of *Mimi* and Nicolas in *Évolution*, are truly in danger. Others, like the girls of *Innocence* and Mia in *Earwig*, never seem to come to any physical harm. Yet all these films make for uncomfortable viewing precisely because of Hadžihalilović's unwillingness to reveal much beyond the child's own understanding of their situation. *Mimi*, *Innocence* and *Évolution* each use a highly restricted narration and, as such, the spectator shares the children's ignorance of their circumstances (*Earwig* begins with restricted narration around Mia's subjectivity too, although this film stands out for having more focus on adult characters than Hadžihalilović's earlier films). Moreover, the adult caretakers in Hadžihalilović's films are shadowy figures with unclear motives. In interviews Hadžihalilović suggests that the ambiguous characterisation of adults in her work stems from personal experience. In *Évolution*, for instance, Nicolas and his friends are admitted to a sinister-looking hospital for invasive surgery, a plot development that alludes to an intense memory from Hadžihalilović's childhood in which she was treated for appendicitis. She states, 'It was the first time in my life when my body was [being] touched by adults I didn't know'.[43] A similar scenario occurs briefly in *Innocence* too, in which Iris witnesses a man administering an injection to a girl slumped in bed – the man says, 'Don't resist, my dear', and it is not clear whether he is a benevolent figure or not. As Hadžihalilović observes, 'I have the feeling that maybe as a child you are kind of isolated from the adult world ... you don't really understand what they're doing, what their purpose is, whether they're good or bad'.[44] This focus on imperilled children and their uncertainty about the motives of adults is a salient feature of Hadžihalilović's work.

Hadžihalilović's pretty aesthetics have a political function within her narratives insofar as they are intrinsically connected to children's ways of seeing – the 'infantile', as Galt puts it. Galt lists children amongst the several identities associated with the pretty, and this association is consistent with the denigration of this aesthetic in Western discourse.[45] Philosophies of art link the disprized pretty with a range of marginalised subjectivities and sensibilities, particularly the queer, the feminine and the non-Western. It is also associated with children and their sensorially 'underdeveloped' aesthetic judgement and preference for bright colour. As David Batchelor notes, in the Western aesthetic imagination colour is aligned with 'the feminine, the oriental, the primitive, the infantile, the vulgar, the queer or the pathological'.[46] Johann Wolfgang von Goethe makes a similar observation, writing that 'savage natives, uneducated people, and children have a great predilection for vivid colours',[47] as does the more contemporary aesthetic philosopher Michael J. Parsons, who notes, 'We know that the young child (let us say to about age seven) is heavily influenced by subject-matter and by pleasing colors'.[48] The characteristics of the pretty most commonly associated with children are sparkle and bright colour. Mary Celeste Kearney, for instance, observes a powerful association between glitter and youthful, white and affluent girl femininity in contemporary culture, noting, 'Sparkle is so ubiquitous in mainstream girls' culture – and so absent in boys' – it vies with pink as the primary signifier of youthful femininity'.[49] In Hadžihalilović's more recent film *Earwig*, luminosity and sparkle play an important role for Mia. Though forbidden to touch them, Mia is fascinated by her caretaker's crystal wine glasses, staring at the refracted light and colours within them. In other films, colour rather than luminosity is the key signifier of child aesthetics, appearing frequently and strategically in Hadžihalilović's *mise en scène*: ribbons in shades of red, blue, yellow, orange, green and violet (*Innocence*); a red starfish (*Évolution*); a doll in a lime-green dress (*Mimi*).

That Hadžihalilović should stylise her *mise en scène* upon an aesthetic associated with child sensibility is significant. As Carrie Tarr and Brigitte

Rollet observe, French women directors frequently tell stories about children, especially girls, because of an affinity between women and children as marginalised subjects. Children live in a world dominated by adults, and, as such, their sensibilities and worldview are easily excluded from cinema. Although the erasure of women's subjectivity within film's phallogocentric regimes occurs on different terms, this shared marginalisation is a point of connection for women filmmakers. For Tarr and Rollet, films about girl children are particularly significant in the French context given the centrality of *The 400 Blows* (*Les quatre cents coups*, François Truffaut, 1959) as the definitive coming-of-age narrative in that culture: when stories about children are told, the preferred subject is the boy embodied by Jean-Pierre Léaud's Antoine Doinel. Further, Tarr and Rollet suggest that foregrounding children's point of view is a political act. Girl children are usually objects of the filmic gaze and their subjectivity does not always shape the narrative point of view in stories about them. As such, 'foregrounding of the perceptions of child or adolescent protagonists whose experiences are normally marginal and marginalized has the potential to challenge hegemonic adult modes of seeing and displace the fetishistic male gaze of dominant cinema'.[50] For women directors in particular, childhood perspectives offer an opportunity for both artistic innovation and the subversion of dominant representational schemas that have marginalised both women *and* children: an act that can take place in both the narrative and the *mise en scène*. Hadžihalilović herself has hinted that her interest in children stems from their capacity to convey strong, unspeakable feelings of oppression in a way that adults cannot. For instance, she explains that the eleven-year-old protagonist of *Mimi* is partly modelled on her own experience of moving to Paris as a seventeen-year-old and feeling 'isolation', 'depression', 'xenophobia' and 'oppression'. Rather than casting an adolescent, however, she claims that children communicate such feelings with greater intensity: 'Children resonate stronger emotionally. I need a child to channel the oppression and coldness ... Children amplify things.'[51] Here Hadžihalilović articulates her belief that children have a privileged relationship to feelings of oppression and that they are therefore superior avatars for such emotions onscreen.

Hadžihalilović's interest in children as victimised subjects is enacted through her use of the pretty as an infantile aesthetic. The pretty is how Hadžihalilović articulates child subjectivity and how her work voices their unspoken desires. It is also the source of much of the apparent feelings of provocation that her work inspires. When asked about the unsettling imagery of *Innocence*, Hadžihalilović says that the charged mode of looking in the film is in fact the girls' gaze, not that of a paedophilic adult voyeur: 'There is a certain fetishism in the film, but it's the fetishism of a girl who loves those clothes and hairdos – the fetishism is from the girls' point of view.'[52] These comments provide an important clue about the relationship between the pretty and the child gaze in Hadžihalilović's work. Hadžihalilović's films prettify numerous fetish objects in the *mise en scène*, which become invested with the child characters' desire and longing. In *Mimi*, the titular protagonist develops a fascination with her aunt Solange's doll, which is resplendent in a green Latin American dress. In *Évolution*, Nicolas keeps a red starfish in a bowl of seawater by his bed. *Innocence* is replete with butterfly wings, white school uniforms and pink ballet costumes. The most significant fetish objects in *Innocence* are the ribbons the girls use to indicate their year level. When Iris arrives in the first scene of the film – naked and lying in a wooden casket – her new classmates help dress her for school. They all wear ribbons in their hair. Bianca instructs them to swap and they do, exchanging colours and tying four red bows on Iris's pigtails. Bianca explains, 'See, Iris? We each have our own colour. Red is for the youngest, violet for the eldest.' A decorative object connected to both girlhood and femininity, the ribbons are part of the annual ritual of welcoming the new student, where the ribbons are swapped amongst the girls (Figure 3.2). The ribbons also facilitate the girls' self-understanding in their society and establishes the hierarchy between them: Bianca as the eldest, and Iris as the youngest. Yet the moment is the first of many fetishistic scenes that centres on the girls' interaction with sensual and pretty objects. The ribbons are particularly key given their function as colourful, decorative items designed to prettify. Later scenes in *Innocence* teem with other pretty objects too: the girls play with hula-hoops, gymnastic ribbons and butterfly wings. The prominence of these objects in the

Figure 3.2 The girls exchange coloured hair ribbons in *Innocence*.

mise en scène establish a way of looking and understanding aligned with the girls (indeed, this corresponds with Wedekind's source material, an ambiguous work that presents the setting as a childhood utopia and 'bodily culture of the senses'[53]). In this logic, *Innocence* depicts the school as a place that replicates the sensory immanence of childhood, filled with items of play and pleasure.

Évolution also contains a fetish object – Nicolas's red starfish – which becomes a complex symbol in the narrative of the film. Nicolas first spots the echinoderm while swimming in the ocean near his village, its bright red colour cutting through the underwater darkness. It clings to the naked abdomen of a corpse: a dead boy of Nicolas's age. Nicolas raises the alarm but, by the time he returns to the beach with his mother, the corpse has disappeared. Only the starfish remains. Nicolas keeps it in a bowl of saltwater by his bed, a flash of red in his otherwise bare stone bedroom. He draws the starfish repeatedly in his notebook and, on one occasion, conducts a brutal experiment upon it, maiming one of its limbs with a rock – the starfish slowly regenerates itself as the days pass. The starfish has several symbolic meanings in culture and in *Évolution*, and it is, significantly, an object of intense fascination for Nicolas in his otherwise ascetic world. As the only evidence of the dead boy, the starfish represents Nicolas's lingering suspicion of the island and everything unexplained about his life there. It is also a pretty object connected to Nicolas's undiscovered, and still unspeakable, erotic desires. It shares a name with Stella (Roxane Duran), the young woman who takes pity on Nicolas and helps him escape from the island. Like the other women, she is clearly an amphibious creature of some kind. When she swims Nicolas to a dinghy offshore, in an erotically charged moment she gives him the kiss of life to help him breathe. The starfish is therefore subsequently emblematic of what Romney calls the 'implicit' theme of child sexuality in the film.[54]

As objects, starfish are also connected to the pretty, and this is how the red starfish functions in *Évolution* too. Not only are starfish common as decorative ornaments in and of themselves, they are a motif in rococo art alongside other submarine lifeforms, such as crabs, seahorses and corals. As Killian Quigley explains, 'In eighteenth century Europe, the submarine was made visible via dazzling objects and ornaments, rendered in porcelain, silver, jewels, stucco, and other materials'.[55] For Quigley, the rococo is a 'playful, sensual, and frequently ostentatious mode' that favoured undersea forms, including the curves, curls and textures of oceanic life.[56] However, just like the pretty in Galt's formulation, the discourses of aesthetics and philosophy have denigrated the rococo as ostentatious, excessive, feminine and superficial. The fact that Nicolas should cherish an object so associated with the decorative and pretty positions him as different from the other boys who live on the island. Whereas they occupy themselves by torturing the ugly, gelatinous lifeforms they drag from the ocean, Nicolas's starfish is mostly a silent ornament and talisman of something nascent and unspeakable. Like the ribbons of *Innocence*, the prominence of the starfish in *Évolution* – the lingering images of it silently inhabiting the glass bowl – ushers in a way of looking that fetishises the pretty object and fills it with meaning. It radiates the unspoken child emotions of the film.

Through such objects, Hadžihalilović uses pretty aesthetics to insert the spectator into the children's world and identify the onlooker with their sensibility. The pretty is therefore at the centre of both her provocations and her politics as a filmmaker. By structuring her films from children's point of view, Hadžihalilović continues a trend in women's filmmaking that connects women and children as social and cultural subjects. Pretty objects glimmer in Hadžihalilović's *mise en scène*, filled with longings, sensuality and desires. Her challenge to the spectator therefore consists of what her aestheticised *mise en scène* articulates on behalf of her victimised child subjects. Her works demand the spectator look as the children do, to see pretty objects charged with the feeling and desires of childhood, and the failure to do so amounts to an obstruction of the children's gaze. For example, Dargis damningly entitles her review of *Innocence* 'Young Girls and Their Bodies, All for the Sake of Art'.[57] However, rather than their bodies, it is the girls' uniforms, ribbons and costumes that are fetishistically rendered onscreen. This distinction is important. To feel provoked when watching *Innocence* or *Évolution* amounts to a failure to adopt the child's gaze. Indeed, it is yet another act of adult power. To look as the children do is an act of identification with those who cannot speak their desires, and whose subjectivities are not served by cinema's dominant representational regimes. However, there is a dilemma within Hadžihalilović's films that makes it difficult to wholly dismiss Dargis's claims. In response to the claim that her work is voyeuristic, Hadžihalilović insists that any suggestion of paedophilia in *Innocence* is 'in the eye of the beholder' and not inherent in the film itself.[58] This is true insofar as the narrative never confirms this disturbing interpretation. However, the demand that *Innocence* and *Évolution* make of the spectator – to identify with the children fully and not respond to the films' ambiguity with adult suspicion – is not easy to fulfil. Along with *Mimi* and *Earwig*, these films ask the spectator to relinquish adult knowledge, to avoid interpreting the prettified as the sexualised. Such ways of seeing are not easily overturned. While Hadžihalilović's films do 'challenge hegemonic adult modes of seeing',[59] they can also produce uneasiness, a feeling of voyeuristic complicity and a hyperawareness of one's own sexual understanding. It is here that Hadžihalilović's provocation ultimately lies. She challenges the spectator to assume the gaze of childhood innocence. But, if we cannot, her films become something much darker.

Hadžihalilović's Provocations

Hadžihalilović is clearly a filmmaker willing to risk controversy. Her work repeatedly engages with the victimisation of children, a theme she returns to many times, however obliquely. Yet her films also engage the spectator in ways that diverge from the long-established avant-garde tradition of masculine scopic transgression. Hadžihalilović does not offend or assault the eye with discordant or explicit imagery. Instead, she appeals with pretty *mise en scène*, colour and composition, and attractive scenes and subjects. The provocation of ugliness is thus not an underpinning rationale of Hadžihalilović's work. She cultivates a style that the discourses of cinema aesthetics consistently feminise and infantilise – one that extends visual pleasure in ways that are both breathtaking and troubling. Hadžihalilović thus distinguishes herself as an innovative figure in the provocative post-millennium art cinema. She develops and uses a feminised aesthetic of provocation, a style that operates in symbolic opposition to the active and masculinised ugliness common to many of her contemporaries. It is also an aesthetic that supports her interest in children and their experience of the world.

The implications of Hadžihalilović's aesthetic are significant if we are to devise a more complete account of cinematic provocation – one that transcends inherited gendered concepts of authorship and aesthetics. Hadžihalilović's work reveals that the linking of cinematic provocation to the scopically offensive cannot account for all forms of negative engagement or even capture what provocation fully entails. The Buñuelian tradition of scopic offence is central to Asbjørn Grønstad's illuminating account of confrontational art cinema. Grønstad goes so far as to use the term 'razorblade gestures', in reference to the eye-slice of *An Andalusian Dog*, to describe 'the emotional, psychic, and ethical slicing open of the gaze of the spectator' in provocative film.[60] This means that many accounts of cinematic transgression proceed from the idea that provocation is primarily a kind of unwatchable spectacle. As other chapters in this book examine, women directors can and do participate in this tradition. Yet limiting provocation to this definition relies on an exclusionary and gendered set of aesthetics: the ugly, aggressive, discordant, shocking and violating. It also overlooks filmmakers like Hadžihalilović who seek to challenge their viewers in a different way.

Notes

1. Fabien Lemercier, 'Lucile Hadzihalilovic is Back with *Evolution*', *Cineuropa*, 28 August 2014, https://cineuropa.org/en/newsdetail/262214/.
2. Vivian Sobchack, 'Waking Life', *Film Comment* 41, no. 6 (2005), 49.
3. Jonathan Romney, 'School for Scandal', *Sight & Sound* 15, no. 10 (2005), 36.
4. Laura Kern, 'The Miracle of Life', *Film Comment* 52, no. 3 (2016), 36.
5. Lucile Hadžihalilović, 'EARWIG Q&A | TIFF 2021', filmed September 2021, video, 17:59, https://www.youtube.com/watch?v=kYPtF_6J_D4&ab_channel=TIFFOriginals.
6. Hadžihalilović, 'EARWIG Q&A | TIFF 2021', 0:33.
7. Lucile Hadžihalilović, '"Evolution" Q&A | Lucile Hadžihalilović | New Directors/New Films 2016', filmed March 2016 at Film Society Lincoln Center, New York, NY, video, 0:00, https://www.youtube.com/watch?v=EFZLot0Cj3g.
8. Mattias Frey, *Extreme Cinema: The Transgressive Rhetoric of Today's Art Film Culture* (New Brunswick, NJ: Rutgers University Press, 2016), 22.
9. James Quandt, 'Flesh & Blood: Sex and Violence in Recent French Cinema', *Artforum* 42, no. 6 (2004), 128.
10. John A. Walker, *Art and Outrage: Provocation, Controversy, and the Visual Arts* (London: Pluto, 1999), 1.
11. Mechtild Widrich, 'The "Ugliness" of the Avant-Garde', in *Ugliness: The Non-Beautiful in Art and Theory*, eds Andrei Pop and Mechtild Widrich (London: I. B. Tauris, 2014), 70.
12. Examples include Andrei Pop and Mechtild Widrich's collection *Ugliness: The Non-Beautiful in Art and Theory* (2014), Stephen Bayley's *Ugly: The Aesthetics of Everything* (New York: Overlook Press, 2012) and Karl Rosenkranz's *Aesthetics of Ugliness: A Critical Edition* (London: Bloomsbury, 2015).
13. Widrich, 'The "Ugliness" of the Avant-Garde', 70.
14. In many cases, this is linked to the influential yet problematic turn to 'primitivism' in art. Primitivism broadly describes the trend of European artists adopting and appropriating the aesthetics and subject matter of traditional cultures and their art. These were very frequently the arts of early societies and non-Western peoples.
15. Antonin Artaud, *The Theatre and Its Double*, trans. Mary Caroline Richards (New York: Grove Press, 1958), 122.
16. Widrich, 'The "Ugliness" of the Avant-Garde', 72; emphasis in original.
17. Lars von Trier and Thomas Vinterberg, 'The Dogme '95 Manifesto and Vow of Chastity', in *Film Manifestos and Global Cinema Cultures: A Critical Anthology*, ed. Scott MacKenzie (Berkeley: University of California Press, 2014), 203.
18. Rosalind Galt, *Pretty: Film and the Decorative Image* (New York: Columbia University Press, 2011), 45.
19. Ibid., 65.

20. Ibid., 300.
21. Given the gendering of provocation in critical discourse, it is possible that Hadžihalilović's identity as a female filmmaker discouraged many critics from styling her as a rabble-rouser. Indeed, the critics who do lean towards this characterisation – such as Sarris, Romney and Dargis – make a point of noting that for many years Hadžihalilović's domestic partner and frequent professional collaborator was Gaspar Noé, name-checking his confronting work *Irréversible* (2002) in the process. The choice to make this personal and professional connection explicit associates Hadžihalilović with Noé's oeuvre and image, therefore forging an association between Hadžihalilović and controversy.
22. Jonathan Romney, 'School for Scandal', *Sight & Sound* 15, no. 10 (2005), 34–6.
23. Hadžihalilović herself says that the film embodies the girls' point of view, and that any impression of a paedophilic gaze is in the eye of the adult beholder. (Jonathan Romney, 'Freedom to Obey', *Sight & Sound* 15, no. 10 [2005], 36.)
24. Andrew Sarris, 'Joan Plowright Is Mrs. Palfrey in May–December Buddy Drama', *Observer*, 21 November 2005, https://observer.com/2005/11/joan-plowright-is-mrs-palfrey-in-maydecember-buddy-drama/.
25. Manohla Dargis, 'Young Girls and Their Bodies, All for the Sake of Art', *New York Times*, 21 October 2005, https://www.nytimes.com/2005/10/21/movies/young-girls-and-their-bodies-all-for-the-sake-of-art.html.
26. Romney, 'School for Scandal'.
27. Ginette Vincendeau, '*Innocence*', *Sight & Sound* 15, no. 10 (2005), 69.
28. Sobchack, 'Waking Life', *Film Comment* 41, no. 6 (2005), 48.
29. Romney, 'School for Scandal'.
30. Vincendeau, '*Innocence*', 68–9.
31. Laura Kern, 'The Miracle of Life', *Film Comment* 52, no. 3 (2016), 36.
32. Sobchack, 'Waking Life', 48.
33. Hadžihalilović, '"Evolution"', 29:40.
34. Galt, *Pretty*, 114–15.
35. Ibid., 61.
36. Ibid., 65.
37. Walker, *Art and Outrage*, 1.
38. Galt, *Pretty*, 10.
39. In Noé's *I Stand Alone*, for example, a title card addresses the audiences directly, allowing them thirty seconds to leave the cinema before the disturbing climax. In this confrontational moment the film invites a turning-away from the image.
40. Scott MacKenzie, 'On Watching and Turning Away: Ono's *Rape*, *Cinéma Direct* Aesthetics, and the Genealogy of *Cinéma Brut*', in *Rape in Art Cinema*, ed. Dominique Russell (New York: Continuum, 2010), 162.
41. Galt, *Pretty*, 6.
42. Hadžihalilović, '"Evolution"', 4:16.

43. Tara Brady, 'Lucile Hadihalilovic: "The First Idea was the Male Pregnancy and the Hospital"', *Irish Times*, 5 May 2016, https://www.irishtimes.com/culture/film/lucile-hadihalilovic-the-first-idea-was-the-male-pregnancy-and-the-hospital-1.2636456.
44. Dominic Preston, '"The Adult World Is Something Mysterious"', interview with Lucile Hadžihalilović, *Candid*, 5 May 2016, accessed 7 February 2017, https://candidmagazine.com/lucile-hadzihalilovic-interview/ (site discontinued).
45. Galt, *Pretty*, 46–7.
46. David Batchelor, *Chromophobia* (London: Reaktion Books, 2000), 22.
47. Johann Wolfgang von Goethe, *Theory of Colors*, trans. Charles Eastlake (Cambridge, MA: MIT Press, 1970), 55.
48. Michael J. Parsons, 'A Suggestion Concerning the Development of Aesthetic Experience in Children', *Journal of Aesthetics and Art Criticism* 34, no. 3 (1976), 309.
49. Mary Celeste Kearney, 'Sparkle: Luminosity and Post-Girl Power Media', *Continuum: Journal of Media & Cultural Studies* 29, no. 2 (2015), 263.
50. Carrie Tarr with Brigitte Rollet, *Cinema and the Second Sex: Women's Filmmaking in France in the 1980s and 1990s* (New York: Continuum, 2001), 25.
51. Lucile Hadžihalilović, Interview, in *Mimi*, Pathfinder Home Entertainment (DVD Extra), 2012, 4:41.
52. Romney, 'Freedom to Obey', 36.
53. Elizabeth Boa, *The Sexual Circus: Wedekind's Theatre of Subversion* (Oxford and New York: Basil Blackwell, 1987), 191.
54. Jonathan Romney, 'Evolution Director Lucile Hadžihalilović: "The Starfish Was the One Worry"', *Guardian*, 29 April 2016, https://www.theguardian.com/film/2016/apr/28/evolution-lucile-hadzihalilovic-starfish-worry-boys-mothers.
55. Killian Quigley, 'The Porcellaneous Ocean: Matter and Meaning in the Rococo Undersea', in *The Aesthetics of the Undersea*, eds Margaret Cohen and Killian Quigley (Abingdon: Routledge, 2019), 29.
56. Ibid.
57. Dargis, 'Young Girls and Their Bodies, All for the Sake of Art', https://www.nytimes.com/2005/10/21/movies/young-girls-and-their-bodies-all-for-the-sake-of-art.html.
58. Romney, 'Freedom to Obey', 36.
59. Tarr with Rollet, *Cinema and the Second Sex*, 25.
60. Asbjørn Grønstad, *Screening the Unwatchable: Spaces of Negation in Post-Millennial Art Cinema* (Basingstoke: Palgrave Macmillan, 2012), 6.

CHAPTER 4

Pursuing Transgression: Claire Denis's Taboo Intimacies

Critics regularly name Claire Denis as amongst the most important directors working today. Matt Fagerholm calls her 'one of the most revered auteurs in world cinema';[1] Marjorie Vecchio names Denis 'a leader' in the field;[2] and Erika Balsom describes Denis's films as 'among the most compelling of contemporary cinema'.[3] Having worked as a director for over thirty years, Denis's story is now well known. Born in France and raised in colonial West Africa, she worked as an intern at Télé Niger and pursued filmmaking at the IDHEC[4] after dropping her studies in economics. In the 1980s, she worked with Wim Wenders and Jim Jarmusch as an assistant director; she then went on to impress international audiences at the 1988 Cannes Film Festival with her debut feature, *Chocolat* (1988), a story of a white French family living in colonial Cameroon. Throughout her career, Denis has earned many descriptors: a subtle chronicler of contemporary France, an observer of the postcolonial condition, and a sensitive storyteller of human intimacy and relationships. She is also the creator of provocative works. In 2001, Denis's horror film *Trouble Every Day* surprised audiences at the Cannes Film Festival with its melancholy story of people who murder their lovers. James Quandt included the film in his famous account of the New French Extremity alongside other provocateurs such as Bruno Dumont, Patrice Chéreau and Philippe Grandrieux.[5] Yet Denis's engagement with provocative themes did not end with *Trouble Every Day*. She returned to transgressive material in her film noir *Bastards* (*Les salauds*, 2013), a thriller centring on the rape of a teenage girl co-written with her frequent collaborator, Jean-Pol Fargeau. Five years later, Denis directed the science-fiction film *High Life* (2018) – also co-written with Fargeau – a space odyssey filled with instances of rape, forced impregnation and incestuous eroticism. Respected, celebrated and renowned as a sensitive and empathetic filmmaker, Denis also demonstrates a capacity to shock and disturb.

Given her career as a leading female auteur in global cinema, exactly how Denis's films provoke negative emotional responses warrants further exploration. Although critics broadly acknowledge her transgressive tendencies, Denis's identity as an understated director remains a dominant understanding of her persona.[6] In a wide-ranging account of her career, Darren Hughes observes that Denis's authorial signature in English-speaking contexts is very much informed by her earlier films such as *Chocolat*, *No Fear, No Die* (*S'en fout la mort*, 1990), *I Can't Sleep* (*J'ai pas sommeil*, 1994), *Nénette and Boni* (*Nénette et Boni*, 1996) and *Beau travail* (1999).[7] The commentary surrounding these films does not always emphasise their transgressive elements. Instead, critics repeatedly highlight Denis's stylistic focus on bodies and gestures, the staging of proximity and intimacy in the *mise en scène*, and the thematic interest in subtleties of desire and inherited power structures. Yet there is more to Denis's oeuvre. First, Denis's films regularly mobilise the same qualities identified within this commentary to explore disturbing themes: taboo acts, transgressive fantasies and moments of defilement. Sensitive or otherwise, Denis is a director drawn to the darker aspects of human experience: when desire seeks a forbidden object or expression, such as when a 'kiss becomes a bite' (as she says of *Trouble Every Day*).[8] I argue that Denis's provocativeness as a director can be more closely reconciled with dominant understandings of her oeuvre and illuminated further through comparison to her contemporaries. Moreover, Denis's work can be located within the tradition of women's filmmaking and provocation more broadly. According to Judith Mayne, Denis's filmmaking is 'distinctively and stubbornly original' and often resists neat grouping within broader categories such as 'women's cinema'.[9] Denis herself also often rejects the label of woman filmmaker. Yet as a leading auteur and a director known to confront her audience with human darkness, Denis surely is an example of a female provocateur: one who can illuminate the relationship between women's authorship and filmic provocation in important ways.

This chapter considers three of Denis's films – *Trouble Every Day*, *Bastards* and *High Life* – in order to illuminate how a leading woman auteur enacts provocation, particularly in ways that extend beyond the gendered, masculinised norms of the provocative author and text. Each of these films is characterised by transgression, defilement and taboo. Known as Denis's *film maudit*, *Trouble Every Day* is a gothic and melancholy story set in contemporary Paris. Its protagonists suffer from a mysterious affliction, which the plot elliptically suggests was acquired during a venal scientific expedition to the Guyanese jungle. Tormenting its hosts with violent and erotic visions, the disease compels its unfortunates to wander the streets, murdering anyone they can seduce. *Bastards* is a noir thriller, inspired in part by William Faulkner's novel *Sanctuary* (1931) and the French title of *The Bad Sleep Well* (Akira Kurosawa, 1960), 'Les salauds dorment en paix' – 'bastards sleep in peace'. The film begins with the rape of a young teenager, Justine (Lola Créton), and the suicide of her father, Jacques (Laurent Grevill). Like the young woman of Faulkner's novel, Justine has been grotesquely violated in a barn outside of town, and her injuries are so extensive that she requires surgery. *Bastards* begins when Justine's uncle returns from abroad to investigate how this calamity occurred. Set in the sublime territory of space, *High Life* is Denis's first fully English-language work. Co-written with Nick Laird, Jean-Pol Fargeau and Geoff Cox, it tells the story of a group of former death row prisoners travelling into deep space, tasked with seeking out a black hole as an energy source for Earth. They are also subjects in an experiment to conceive a child in space, which is a challenging mission given that cosmic radiation destroys foetuses in utero. The crew eventually destroy themselves through violence and suicide, leaving only one prisoner, Monte (Robert Pattinson), and his baby daughter, Willow (Scarlett Lindsey), as survivors.

Trouble Every Day, *Bastards* and *High Life* are not the only films of Denis's that cause a sense of disquiet; for instance, the elliptical *The Intruder* (*L'intrus*, 2004) implies that the protagonist has committed an act of filicide, ordering the death of his son for the purposes of an illicit heart transplant, and *I Can't Sleep* is inspired by the true story of a pair of men who murder elderly women. Yet *Trouble Every Day*, *Bastards* and *High Life* centralise transgressive acts to a particularly significant degree and are thus pertinent case studies for exploring this aspect of Denis's oeuvre. Moreover, the premieres of *Trouble Every Day* and *Bastards* also reveal Denis's provocative potential, producing shocked responses from critics and audiences. Viewers reportedly fled the cinema during the screening of *Trouble Every Day* at Cannes,[10] while the closing scene of *Bastards* disturbed one critic so deeply that he named Denis 'one more bastard ... in the film's lineup of victims and abusers' in his review.[11] These films elicit feelings of discomfort by engaging with themes that are evident in Denis's earlier works, such as the taboo intimacies of *Chocolat* and *Beau travail* and the familial eroticism of *Nénette and Boni* and *35 Shots of Rum* (*35 rhums*, 2008). I consider how *Bastards* and *High Life* in particular are locatable within a French cultural fascination with eroticised father–daughter relationships but diverge from the depictions of abusive patriarchs common to Denis's contemporaries like Thomas Vinterberg, Michael Haneke, Yorgos Lanthimos and Gaspar Noé. Denis's well-known and celebrated style of sensuous filmmaking also enacts provocation in ways that differ from the highly gendered conceptualisation of provocation as an aggressive author–recipient relationship. Films like *Trouble Every Day* and *High*

Life implicate the spectator in sensuously rendered taboos. They do so in ways that expand entrenched understanding of how cinema provokes.

Denis as Transgressor

Although media and scholarly accounts regularly position her as a sensitive filmmaker rather than an *enfant terrible* or rabble-rouser, naming Denis as a provocateur is a useful hermeneutic that illuminates her oeuvre, particularly the persistent presence of transgressive desire in her work. Since the beginning of her career, Denis's films have explored how hierarchical power structures shape and foreclose desire. For instance, *Chocolat* and *White Material* (2009) reflect on disfiguring colonial and postcolonial relations, revealing how they complicate the attraction between people and deny the possibility of erotic connection. This scenario is rendered with particular poignancy in Denis's debut *Chocolat*, which concerns the mutual but impossible attraction between a white French woman and her Cameroonian servant. This narrative scenario occurs in Denis's other films too. *Beau travail* tells the story of a soldier's sublimated desire for a charismatic new recruit; his envy of his subordinate transforms into eroticism and, eventually, violence. Penal environments in *High Life* structure sex and desire too: aboard the prison ship, the inmates are coerced into participating in reproductive experiments in an effort to conceive a child while in space. Given this interest in power, laws and eroticism, it is unsurprising that Denis's films should investigate transgression – the moments when such laws are broken. As Martine Beugnet observes, in Denis's films desire 'challenges the taboos and hierarchies erected by social orders that attempt to tame desire by designating its legitimate objects'.[12] The prohibition of desire begets transgression and makes it possible. Accordingly, it follows that Denis's films explore forbidden eroticism in ways that could genuinely disturb an audience.

Denis's films about family relationships are a key site for her explorations of transgression, and for decades her films have examined intimacy in this setting. *Nénette and Boni* concerns a pair of bickering teenage siblings who share a physical intimacy with each other despite their estrangement. When Nénette (Alice Houri) runs away from her father's house to live with her older brother Boni (Grégoire Colin), she surprises him by hiding in his bed. The scene begins with a slow, moving close-up of Boni's naked torso as he lies in bed masturbating – an activity he does often. Suddenly, Nénette speaks: 'C'est moi', she says quietly, her face still hidden in darkness offscreen. Boni is so surprised that he tumbles out of bed. The moment is comic but also undeniably erotic, the slow pan across Boni's body revealed to be Nénette's gaze as well as the spectator's. Such moments suggest a physical intimacy between Nénette and Boni that pushes the conventional boundaries of sibling relationships. *35 Shots of Rum* also contains an ambiguity regarding the connections between family members, underscoring how closely familial intimacy can resemble erotic intimacy. The film centres on the relationship between a widower, Lionel (Alex Descas), and his adult daughter Joséphine (Mati Diop). Their connection is tenderly close but excludes outsiders, particularly those who take a romantic interest in them: Joséphine's admirer, Noé (Grégoire Colin) and Lionel's ex-lover, Gabrielle (Nicole Dogue). However, the opening scene of *35 Shots of Rum* withholds the fact that Lionel and Joséphine are father and daughter. The pair return home after a day at work and study, prepare dinner and eat together: both have purchased a rice cooker for the household, but Joséphine chooses not to mention hers upon realising the coincidence. The scene depicts Lionel and Joséphine's domestic life in a way that leaves open the possibility that they are lovers rather than relatives. It has, as Catherine Wheatley puts it, 'quasi-erotic undertones'.[13] For Dave Kehr, this opening of *35 Shots of Rum* 'continues to cast a spell over the rest of the film, binding Lionel and Joséphine together in a special, undefined intimacy'.[14] These are subtler explorations of family intimacy that never cross over into actual sexuality; however, they find explicit counterparts in Denis's later works *Bastards* and *High Life*, in which taboo and incestuous acts do indeed take place. Provocative potential is therefore intrinsic within Denis's work insofar as taboo desires of different kinds have been an authorial interest of hers from the beginning of her career. Indeed, given Denis's recurring interest in how inherited social structures shape and influence desire, it comes as little surprise that incest should be one expression of this broader concern.

Denis's tendency to hint at transgressive eroticism has not gone unnoticed, with scholars of her work repeatedly noting Denis's interest in taboo. Martine Beugnet, for instance, devotes considerable attention to the director's ongoing engagement with this topic, locating Denis's work within a French art of transgression.[15] Intriguingly, however, in the domain of film criticism, Denis's consistent interest in taboo does not seem to translate into a reputation as a provocateur. Instead, Denis's critical construction in these discourses typically position her as an artful transgressor rather than a rabble-rousing seeker of controversy. This is an important distinction. In most English-speaking contexts, Denis is characterised as a director who represents transgressive acts in ways that do not shock, offend or otherwise elicit a negative emotional response, or, alternatively, as a director who does so in a way that is somehow acceptable. Despite the strong indication of incest at the end of *High Life*, for instance, most critics did not appear to be offended by the film, instead connecting *High Life* to Denis's existing reputation as a director who tells stories in a sensitive manner. Adrian Martin states that *High Life* for the most part 'seems quiet, cool, calm, contemplative, not at all provocative'.[16] Referring to a consensual sex act in the film, Alexandra Heller-Nicholas praises Denis's 'profound and often disturbing representations of erotic desire and sensual pleasure'.[17] Other critics turned to the beauty of *High Life* as a point of emphasis. Critic Thomas Caldwell, for example, says that *High Life* is 'beautiful & confronting'.[18] Mark Jenkins calls it 'beautiful and grim'.[19] Nick Pinkerton says it is 'a vision both carnal and cosmic, sacred and profane'.[20] Though clearly grappling with simultaneous feelings of disquiet and approval, critics seldom accuse Denis of empty provocation. While there are some exceptions,[21] the reception of Denis's more recent films exemplifies an enduring reluctance to strongly identify her as a provocateur. In the discourses of film criticism, Denis remains the trustworthy, tasteful auteur, a guarantor 'of good taste'[22] to use Patricia White's term, rather than the 'hated' artist or scandal-seeking incendiary.

Denis herself mostly resists playing the provocateur, repeatedly saying that her works are not meant to scandalise. At the same time, however, she acknowledges her films' unsettling power. In an interview following the release of *Trouble Every Day*, for example, Denis insists, 'It's weird to measure a film by how much scandal it makes or how much violence it contains; it feels like you're manipulating the audience'. She adds, 'I think it is a very naive and innocent film'. However, she then immediately agrees when the interviewer describes *Trouble Every Day* as 'disturbing and unsettling'.[23] This pattern appears in later interviews during which Denis acknowledges her films' disquieting potential while rejecting characterisations of them as provocations, the implication being that she sees such characterisations as one-dimensional and unable to accommodate the complexity of her objectives. Discussing *Bastards*, for example, Denis admits that the final scene of the film is confronting. The scene consists of a video recording that shows Justine and her father together at a makeshift sex club and reveals that an incestuous encounter has taken place between them. In the video, Justine lies naked on a vinyl couch. Her father approaches her with an ear of corn in his hand, and she embraces him (the corn is a direct reference to the events of *Sanctuary*, in which Temple Drake, the young woman at the centre of the narrative, is also raped with an ear of corn). While acknowledging the confrontational nature of the moment, Denis also insists that the scene is not especially explicit: 'I think the footage I show is not that horrible.'[24] Denis also found herself in a paradoxical position in an interview with *Cahiers du cinéma*, shocking her interviewer by refusing to overtly condemn the sexual abuse in *Bastards* and insisting on the mundanity of incest as part of the spectrum of human behaviour, stating, 'I understand that such things can happen. There is humanity in incest. I acknowledge this.' When the interviewer responds with shock, Denis doubles down by claiming the incest in *Bastards* is consensual: 'She is not locked up in a barn, she consents. After all, you are allowed to love your father, I can't see what's wrong with that.'[25] Nikolaj Lübecker argues that, in this moment, Denis allowed herself to be carried away with the desire 'not to judge' (and also exhibited a 'desire to provoke' the interviewer).[26] However, Denis's answer is also characteristic of her usual response to questions about her films' unsettling attributes and echoes her statements about *Trouble Every Day*. While acknowledging the transgressive quality of the subject matter, her words indicate a desire to reject the characterisation of 'mere' or 'sensationalist' provocation.

Denis's relationship to provocation is thus not as clear as self-declared controversy-seekers like Lars von Trier, Michael Haneke, Catherine Breillat and Gaspar Noé. Interviews and critical reactions to her work suggest that she is best described as a serial transgressor whose power to disturb her audience is both acknowledged and downplayed by critics as well as by Denis herself. Her films demonstrate a continuing interest in transgression and taboo; they also demonstrably position audiences in negative emotional situations, as the reaction to *Trouble Every Day* and *Bastards* attest. It is therefore even more important to highlight Denis's capacity as a provocateur. Doing so does not diminish her work, nor does it undermine the ways in which her films are indeed often sensitive and tender. Reading Denis as a provocateur highlights another facet of an already complex filmmaker; a transgressive tendency that has long been present within even the most celebrated of her films. Investigating this complexity – her interest in taboo combined with her sensual and elliptical style – also exposes a specific aesthetic strategy of provocation.

Family and the First Law

The family is one of the important domains of transgression in Denis's films. It is also a theme that aligns her oeuvre with other contemporary provocateurs in European art cinema as well as distinguishing her from this corpus in important ways. Abusive, dysfunctional families appear with notable frequency in the works of millennial European filmmakers. To name a few examples, Noé's *Carne* (1991) and *I Stand Alone* (*Seul contre tous*,

1998), Vinterberg's *The Celebration* (*Festen*, 1998), Lanthimos's *Dogtooth* (*Kynodontas*, 2009), and Haneke's *The White Ribbon* (*Das weiße Band*, 2009) all tell stories of abuses that occur within a patriarchal and often bourgeois family. In each film, the father is implicated in committing an act of incest or instigating one between siblings. Such narrative events usually have a metaphorical purpose, signifying a profound corruption within the family and, allegorically, within society at large. These films' emphasis on the father as the abusive figure is key to their criticism of social power, and these figures tend to have numerous character flaws: the unnamed protagonist of *Carne* and *I Stand Alone* is both violent and a racist, the father of *Dogtooth* is physically and emotionally abusive, and the father in *The Celebration* is an entitled businessman. In these films, incestuous acts are indicative of a broken society and gesture towards the corruption and perversity of those who hold power. Moreover, the fact that corruption takes place inside the family itself – the very institution that conservative discourses so frequently insist is the foundation of moral decency – deepens these films' criticism of traditional social masters and institutions.[27]

Fathers and the incest taboo also play an important role in Denis's films *Bastards* and *High Life*. Denis herself makes the connection between incest and social dysfunction:

> The first taboo is incest, because it's not good for society. It's the origin of the law, the creation of society. To create a society that is rich and that has protective patrimonium, to protect the health of the people, you have to avoid incest. It's probably the first law that was invented on earth. But if it was the first law …[28]

Denis does not finish the thought, yet the implication here is straightforward. If incest is the first law, then incestuous acts are indicative of a culture that is fundamentally dysfunctional. By looking at *High Life* and *Bastards*, it is possible to see how Denis also uses families and incest as confronting allegories of social corruption. However, an important difference between Denis's films and those of Noé, Haneke, Lanthimos and Vinterberg is in her treatment of the father–daughter pairing, which departs from the depictions of the abusive and tyrannical patriarch in these other films. There are further connections to make too. First, Denis also participates in a common trend in French women's filmmaking of engaging with the family as a theme, which she has done in earlier works such as *Chocolat*, *Nénette and Boni* and *35 Shots of Rum*. According to Carrie Tarr and Brigitte Rollet, French women filmmakers regularly tell stories about the family. Most frequently, they argue, these filmmakers depict the father as 'a problematic figure whose unacceptable behaviour, ranging from absent and neglectful to uncaring, autocratic, violent and cruel, accounts for the child's trauma or propels the adolescent daughter into the arms of a lover', although in some instances, these films offer positive depictions of fathers as 'caring father figures'.[29] Although abuse is hinted at in *Nénette and Boni*, Denis fits this latter trend more closely. Second, Denis engages with what Ginette Vincendeau has called a 'master narrative' in French culture of stories of quasi-incestuous father–daughter relations.[30] Denis's depictions of incest in *Bastard* and *High Life* imply the desire of the daughter for the father. Moreover, in *High Life* the father is also represented as a loving caregiver, complicating the provocative depiction of the father as an unambiguous villain. Denis's films thus offer a slight shift in orientation from these connected tendencies in French and European cinema, downplaying the cruelty and hypermasculinity of the patriarch and, in *High Life* and to a lesser degree in *Bastards*, highlighting the desire of the daughter for the father.

In *Bastards*, transgressive sexuality between father and daughter is quite clearly a consequence of a broader social and cultural rot, particularly one centred upon economics and capital. Like Lanthimos, Vinterberg, Haneke and Noé, Denis uses this provocation allegorically and rhetorically to signify the corruption of contemporary urban Europe and in ways that also align *Bastards* with the settings of American film noir of the 1930s and 1940s. The film begins on a rainy night in Paris. A young woman walks tremulously down the wet streets, wearing nothing but a pair of stilettos. Streaks of blood run down the insides of her legs. The girl is Justine and, for reasons not yet clear, her father Jacques suicides that same night. This startling opening marks the beginning of a complex, twisting series of discoveries. Justine's uncle Marco Silvestri (Vincent Lindon) arrives in Paris to investigate who is responsible for his family's calamity. He learns from his sister Sandra (Julie Bataille) that the family shoe company is deeply in debt to a successful businessman, Edouard Laporte (Michel Subor). Marco suspects Laporte is somehow responsible for Justine's attack and Jacques's suicide. Later, he suspects his sister and brother-in-law may have been procuring their daughter for sex to appease their wealthy creditor. Marco finds a sex club on the outskirts of Paris; a barn housing red vinyl couches, cables for connecting digital video cameras, and bloody ears of corn strewn about the floor. As mentioned above, the final moments of the film reveal the truth of what happened to Jacques and Justine. A discovered video recording shows Laporte, Justine and her father together inside the barn. Laporte looks on as Justine lies naked on the vinyl couches, embracing her father as he approaches her with a corn ear in his hand. *Bastards* is thus a film in which father–daughter contact comes about as the result of a destructive capitalism that destabilises the Silvestri family and causes the financial ruin of the family as well as the moral downfall of both daughter and father. The film situates the relationship between Jacques and Justine as part of a dynastic narrative of a family's demise – a curse that has the power to doom others who come near. Justine's uncle Marco is killed by his lover, Raphaëlle (Chiara Mastroianni), when she is forced to choose between him and her role as the mother of Laporte's son.

Bastards differs from other provocative European art films that contain themes of incest, decentring the patriarch from the position of narrative and allegorical prominence he occupies in works like *The Celebration*, *Carne*, *The White Ribbon*, *I Stand Alone* and *Dogtooth*. Indeed, in *Bastards* the father dies in the opening sequence and his name is rarely spoken. Although he is an important absence, he is not a figure of narrative focus or anthropological curiosity in the way of Noé's Butcher (Philippe Nahon) in *Carne* and *I Stand Alone*, or a central character as in *Dogtooth*. Instead, the provocation of *Bastards* is in the implied desire that Justine has for her own father. Early in the film, while lying in her hospital bed, Justine calls out: 'I love him. I want to see him!' At the time it is unclear who 'he' may be. In later scenes, Justine escapes to reunite with the owners of the sex club where she was abused. Also, as Denis has remarked, Justine places her arms around her father in the final scene of the film. Vincendeau observes that some French women directors engage with the father–daughter master narrative by emphasising the female perspective, for example, by addressing 'ambivalent feelings' of attraction to older men and father-type figures.[31] While Justine's perspective is not exactly foregrounded in *Bastards*, Denis has opted to erase the father and any exploration of his motives from the narrative. All that is left is the unsettling ambiguity of Justine's experience of her own abuse. Whether she truly sought out her father – or developed a traumatised emotional connection to him in order to survive – remains an unanswered question.

Although society is certainly in decay in *High Life*, the film opts for a slightly different message to that of *Bastards*, implying that eroticism between parents and children is a tendency that emerges when human laws are stripped away. The film opens with Monte on a run-down spacecraft, alone except for the company of his infant daughter, Willow. Monte is her sole carer, and the first twenty minutes of the film shows him parenting her in intimate detail. He carries her around, soothes her with cooing words, feeds her by hand and sits her on a makeshift potty-chair (Figure 4.1). Willow returns her father's touch, gripping his arms with her chubby hands and responding to him with affectionate babbling. After this lengthy sequence of child-rearing, an extended flashback reveals how

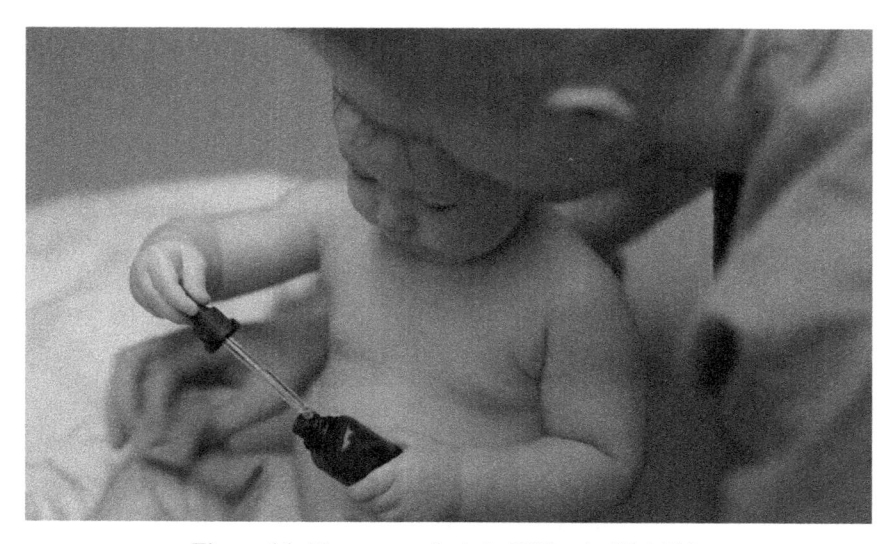

Figure 4.1 Monte cares for baby Willow in *High Life*.

father and daughter came to find themselves together. Monte's earlier life on board the ship with the other death row prisoners was a time of violence and coercion. As an act of resistance against his penal environment, Monte abstains from participating in the reproductive experiments governed by the ship's scientist, Dr Dibs (Juliette Binoche). Eventually, however, Dr Dibs drugs and rapes Monte in his sleep and uses his semen to impregnate another inmate, Boyse (Mia Goth), against her will: Willow is the result. The rest of the crew eventually die through conflict or suicide, leaving Monte and the baby alone together. In the third act of the film, Monte and his now-teenage daughter are the only surviving crew and quite possibly the only humans left in the universe. Monte is anxious to maintain boundaries with his daughter. The first time she is seen onscreen as a teenager (played by Jessie Ross), Willow is asleep in Monte's bed, her head upon his chest. Monte wakes up and insists she sleeps in her own bed across the room – clearly, the father–daughter intimacy in the film's opening scenes between adult and baby is no longer appropriate. As Willow sulkily complies, Monte sees she has stained the mattress with menstrual blood.

Like *Bastards*, it is in the final scene of *High Life* in which the foreshadowed incestuous contact takes place. In this scene, Monte and Willow's spacecraft approaches a massive black hole: the object of their mission. Amber light curves and stretches around the void. They decide to investigate, putting on their protective suits to approach the event horizon. As they draw closer, eerie music rings out. Suddenly, they are somewhere else. Monte stands in the darkness, no longer wearing his suit. The music fades as gold light seeps across the frame from an offscreen sunset (or, perhaps, sunrise). Monte turns towards it: 'Shall we?' he asks. Willow replies: 'Yes.' Her face appears onscreen: she seems older, knowing, and she smiles. The gold light expands, silently, to engulf them both. Although ambiguous, this final sequence implies that a transgressive intimacy takes place between father and daughter upon the completion of their mission as they cross into the unknown.

If Denis's enduring authorial interest is in how laws shape human desires, in *High Life*, the relationship between Monte and Willow emerges in the vacuum of governing power and, indeed, of a recognisable society. As Erika Balsom observes, *High Life* is a 'film of bodies and power' that 'underlines the corrosive brutality of authority'.[32] However, it is also a film about what happens in the absence of authority and the intimacies that emerge when there are no laws left to transgress. The second implication of Denis's unfinished thought quoted above – 'But if it was the first law ...' – is that incest is the most deep-seated of human inclinations, the one requiring prohibition first because it is so common. Her remark aligns with Sigmund Freud's observation that incestuous desire is 'the first and most customary choice' of love object for the human subject.[33] The events between Monte and Willow in the final moments of *High Life* gesture to erotic intimacy as a pre-social state. In this regard, the film's depiction of familial eroticism adheres closely to the tendencies of sensual intimacy established in *35 Shots of Rum* and *Nénette and Boni*. The first twenty-five minutes of *High Life* that show Monte caring for his six-month-old daughter, for example, recall the final scene of *Nénette and Boni* in which Boni tenderly holds his sister's newborn baby in his arms, having stolen it from the hospital. In this earlier film, however, Boni's quasi-paternal love for the baby ends upon this more innocent infatuation. Affectionate domestic intimacy occurs between adult fathers and daughters too in *35 Shots of Rum*, particularly the opening scenes, which depict Lionel and Joséphine returning home and preparing a meal together. In this latter film, the intimacy between father and daughter is disrupted by Joséphine's marriage to their neighbour. In *High Life*, however, there is no society left to redirect such desire, and the transgressive love between father and daughter emerges unimpeded. The film is thus an extension of the themes – the interactions of bodies, laws, eroticism and power – that Denis has long considered in her work.

Provocation and Sensation

So far, I have examined how Denis takes the role of provocateur via the transgressive subject matter of her films. What is also significant is her aesthetic approach. One of the most commented-upon aspects of Denis's work is its sensuality. Her cinema possesses a tactile quality, both in what she depicts – people dancing, touching and living in proximity – as well as in the experience of spectatorship her films generate. This sensuality is a much-admired quality, but it is also vital to her films' power to disturb, unsettle and provoke the onlooker. According to Emma Wilson, Denis's filmmaking offers 'a new reckoning' with 'proximity, touch and contact'.[34] Saige Walton observes that Denis's films initiate a 'sensuous relationship' with the spectator.[35] Adam Nayman and Andrew Tracy claim that Denis creates an 'inner-directed sensual world, a world of immersive sensation'.[36] For many, this sensuality is also the source of spectatorial discomfort in works such as *Trouble Every Day* and *High Life*. Tim Palmer describes *Trouble Every Day* as a film of 'agitation, sensation and provocation'.[37] Andrew Asibong claims the viewing experience effects a sense of 'viral' transmission, making the spectator feel contaminated in the same way the protagonists are rendered abject by their cannibalistic disease.[38] In a discussion of *High Life*, Heller-Nicholas says Denis excels in 'profound and often disturbing representations of erotic desire and sensual pleasure'.[39] Such comments suggest that Denis's films both please and unsettle via their sensuality. In *Trouble Every Day* and *High Life* in particular, arrangements of sound and image sensuously implicate the spectator in the scenarios of taboo erotic contact occurring onscreen, positioning spectators to vividly experience moments of touch and intimacy between forbidden subjects.[40] These incite a negative emotional and affective response in the viewer via the same stylistic tendencies that have won Denis critical acclaim.

Before exploring how this aesthetic operates, however, it is important to note that Denis's sensuous approach to provocation stands in contrast to other dominant strategies of provocation that, as I have argued throughout this book, are conceptualised in aesthetic discourse as hypermasculine. Elsewhere, I and other scholars have suggested that Denis's work is characterised by its haptic visuality, an aesthetic that evokes a physical sense of being touched in the viewing experience.[41] (Laura U. Marks developed this concept in her description of intercultural cinema *The Skin of the Film*, but the term has broad application to many types of films.[42]) Importantly, each of these accounts argues that Denis's works convey a specific modality of touch: caressing, stroking and sensuous rather than piercing, crushing or painful. This sensory quality emerges in part from Denis's direction, which typically limits access to her characters' internal psychology (leaving much unsaid and ambiguous) and redirecting the spectator's attention to the films' 'sensible' qualities: their surfaces, visual aspects and aural dimensions. Denis's sensuousness also depends on what she shows: attentive shots and close-ups of skin, textures and gestures, photographed by Denis's frequent collaborator Agnès Godard (and later Yorick Le Saux); scenes of erotic dough-kneading and carefully placed cream puffs in *Nénette and Boni*; dancing figures in *35 Shots of Rum* and *Beau travail*. This type of sensuality is predominantly gentle, and thus it contrasts profoundly with the painful affects of provocative spectacle in other types of cinemas. As I have explained in earlier chapters of this book, scopic offence depends on the experience of shock and pain. Its imagery includes violence presented in exquisite and graphic detail: the eye-slice in *An Andalusian Dog* (*Un chien andalou*, Luis Buñuel, 1929) is an undeniable urtext, but similarly intense images appear in the tooth-smashing scene of *Dogtooth*, the moment of genital mutilation in *Antichrist* (Lars von Trier, 2009) and the flayed flesh of *In My Skin* (*Dans ma peau*, Marina de Van, 2002). Scopic offence can also consist of prolonged or excessive spectacle such as the kind found in *Irréversible* (Gaspar Noé, 2002), *Holiday* (Isabella Eklöf, 2018) and *The Nightingale* (Jennifer Kent, 2018), or the onscreen visibility of obscene acts like in *Salò, or the 120 Days of Sodom* (*Salò o le 120 giornate di Sodoma*, Pier Paolo Pasolini, 1975). Denis's oeuvre does contain some shocking images of this ilk. *Trouble Every Day* shows two scenes in which Coré and Shane attack their lovers, displaying Coré's fingers toying with the flaps of skin she has torn from her victim's torso. A graphic scene in *High Life* depicts Monte punching Boyse repeatedly in the face. Yet these startling visuals are not at the centre of Denis's films nor the most persistent characteristic of her style. Instead, Denis's author–recipient relation is one of a provocative, frequently transgressive sensuality premised on taboo erotic contact. It thus moves away from the gendered concepts of provocation as aggressive, violent and masculine violation of the spectator.

Despite its scenes of extreme violence, *Trouble Every Day* is a strong example of a film that provokes through the sensuous, tactile viewing experience that it creates. The film tells the story of several people, loosely connected to one another, who are caught up in a mysterious affliction: Shane (Vincent Gallo) and his new wife, June (Tricia Vessey), and Coré (Béatrice Dalle) and her husband, Léo (Alex Descas). Coré and Shane are both suffering from a mysterious illness acquired after a research expedition to Guyana. Coré is in the late stage of the disease's progression, whereas Shane is just beginning to manifest symptoms. He experiences intrusive fantasies where he sees his wife covered in blood, while Coré compulsively escapes from her house to seduce and murder men, killing them with her bare hands. In one particularly excruciating scene, two young men break into the house where Coré is being held prisoner by Léo, and Coré seduces the more adventurous of the two. Although initially a gentle, erotic encounter, Coré bites into the young man as they have sex on the bed. As she does so, the camera cuts to the young man's face in extreme close-up as he screams in agony; shortly after, Coré's fingers, sticky with blood, tease the flaps of skin she has torn from his body. Despite this brutality, however, one of the most distinctive features of *Trouble Every Day* is its moody tonal quality and highly sensory storytelling. Through this, the film invites a sensuous identification with Coré and Shane even before they stalk and then ravenously attack their victims. As Nayman and Tracy put it, the film's sensuous organisation of sound and image makes the viewer complicit in the protagonists' monstrous drives: 'The film's astonishingly sensual charge, even in mundane moments ... forces us inside the dreadful immanence of their desires.'[43] *Trouble Every Day* is also therefore a film concerned with the continuities between different types of touch, from the erotic, pleasure-giving and receiving touch to the violent one. Referring to one such moment in the film, Denis says the scene 'is how a kiss becomes a bite', therefore highlighting the continuum between the two forms of touching.[44]

High Life also constructs an intensely sensuous viewing experience that implicates the spectator in transgressive intimacy. Over the course of the film, familial contact between father and daughter transforms into a taboo desire, specifically Willow's for Monte. This occurs from the opening moments of the film, which initiate spectators into a close and sensual engagement with the diegetic sounds and images onscreen. These first scenes are centred on the spectacle of Monte's parenting: he carries six-month-old Willow in his arms, feeds her, baby-talks to her and puts her down to sleep in his bed. Throughout these scenes Willow returns her father's touch, exploring his face with her hands and responding to him vocally. Denis and cinematographer Yorick Le Saux present these moments in careful detail through close-ups and long takes, emphasising the gentle rhythms and closeness between the two bodies. Once established, however, this tenderness transforms into a different form of sensuality. When *High Life* flashes back to the time before Willow's birth, the film switches its emphasis from Willow and Monte as a parent–child dyad to Monte himself. Through Denis and Le Saux's camerawork and lighting, the *mise en scène* puts a fetishised emphasis on the beauty of Monte's face (Figure 4.2). Scenes inside the ship are flooded with teal, crimson and gold light. Colours bounce off Monte's and the other inmates' skin, the walls and the foliage inside the ship's glittering green garden. This extensive use of coloured lighting aestheticises Monte, accenting the surface of his skin: hairs, pores and the curvature of his brow. Monte is also regularly filmed in close-up. As Manohla Dargis notes, 'Denis doesn't just prettify her actors: She lingers on their forms, their skin, stressing texture that becomes tactile. When her camera pans across a downy arm, you see it but also remember – and feel – the downiness and pleasures of other arms, legs, faces.'[45] The camerawork not only positions the spectator into a tactile appreciation of Monte. This mode of looking is also closely identified with Dr Dibs and her desire for him, which is a prominent plot point in the main part of the narrative. Monte is the only male inmate on board the ship who refuses to donate his sperm to the reproductive experiment, leading Dr Dibs to develop an obsession with him. Her desire for Monte corresponds with the tactile onscreen aesthetic that renders his features so luminous and beautiful. However, after Dr Dibs's death, the eroticism of this aesthetic transfers to Willow, becoming representative of her desire for Monte instead. This transfer takes place via the flash forward to Willow's teenage years. The scene begins with yet another close-up on Monte's face. A cut reveals it is some years in the future – Willow, now a teenager, lies beside Monte in his bed. In this moment, Denis's sensuous

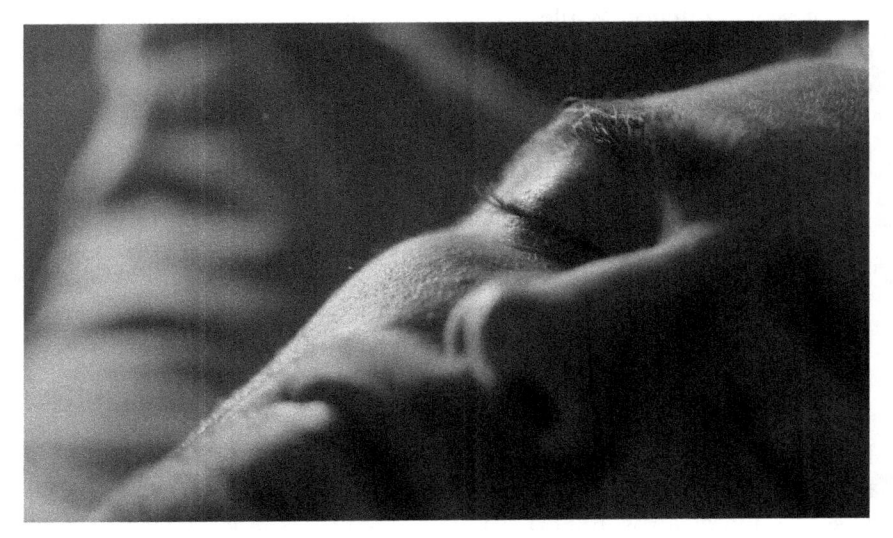

Figure 4.2 Monte's face in sensuous close-up in *High Life*.

visual style articulates Willow's transgressive desire. It also implicates the spectator, positioning them to participate in it too.

The scene where Willow and Monte complete their journey into space is another example of how *High Life* provocatively uses visual style. The scene is the most visually striking sequence in *High Life*. It is also the film's most transgressive moment, in which taboo contact between father and daughter is enacted via a spectacle of breathtaking light and colour. The scene is derived from a short film that Denis created in response to *Contact* (2014), a series of light installations by artist Ólafur Elíasson, who also created the brutalist design for the prison ship in *High Life*. When Monte and Willow approach the event horizon of the black hole, amber light curves and stretches around the void. Willow remarks that it 'looks like a crocodile's eye'. The two approach the horizon and the rich, gold light spills into the heavy darkness. It illuminates Monte and Willow's faces, and they turn toward the horizon – Willow tells her father, 'Yes'. This radiant imagery implicates the spectator in what appears to be an incestuous transgression. The scene not only beautifies the subjects, positioning the onlooker to take visual pleasure in the moment that Monte and Willow seemingly confirm their taboo relationship. It also enacts their desire. Settling on their skin and hair, the gold light performs the erotic contact between Monte and Willow, touching on their behalf.

To acknowledge Denis as a sensory filmmaker is to understand her aesthetic strategies as a provocateur too. Denis's aesthetics show how cinema can elicit provocation in ways that differ from the sharp and violent imagery of scopic offence. While her films do contain some piercing images of brutality, the chief way in which they unsettle is by implicating the onlooker in taboo contact and intimacy with forbidden bodies. Films like *Trouble Every Day* and *High Life* meditate on gentle skin-on-skin contact more often than they reach for Buñuelian knife-on-eyeball. As Nayman and Tracy put it:

> Unlike the iconoclasm and aesthetic-rhetorical gauntlet-dropping of Noé, Grandrieux and Dumont (as well as such transnational provocateurs as Michael Haneke and Lars von Trier), Denis's aesthetic is not built upon and does not necessitate a strident, wilful challenge to the audience's tolerance and sensibilities; she has instead cultivated an authorial gaze that is unmistakable even as it shifts in focus and intensity from film to film.[46]

Denis establishes an organisation of sound and image that is not only characteristic of her directorial signature but is also an aesthetic that provokes, unsettles and disturbs. Importantly, this is not to essentialise Denis's haptic imagery as a style she employs because she happens to be female. As I have shown throughout this book, Denis and other female filmmakers can create assaultive imagery too. In addition, as Wilson writes, it is tempting to 'to understand haptic visuality as a feminine kind of visuality' in an Irigarayan and essentialising sense.[47] Yet it is worth noticing how Denis's sensuous and caressing imagery contrasts with other means of provocation. Denis's work shows us how provocation can take place on aesthetic terms that profoundly differ to those coded as masculine.

The Laws of Intimacy

Investigating Denis as a provocateur provides important nuance to understandings of cinematic provocation and negative author–recipient relations; Denis both participates in existing trends in provocative European art cinema but also demonstrates a unique strategy and aesthetics of provocation. Her work makes allegorical use of incest in a manner similar to many of her contemporaries; however, Denis's engagement with transgressive desire has also long been a part of her oeuvre, paving the way for such investigations in her later work. Denis's films test the laws of intimacy: who is permitted to desire whom, and in what way. Her work offers little in the way of approval or condemnation of the protagonists who break these laws, irrespective of the terrible consequences that may unfold. Even in darker works like *Bastards* or *High Life*, there are few prescriptions for how or which bodies should become erotically entangled. For Kristin Lené Hole, Denis's films create encounters with others and participate in a feminist tradition of questioning regulatory norms that govern bodies: of 'keeping foundational categories such as "the human" fluid and open.'[48] Hole's point is well taken. As I have shown, Denis's pursuit of this project can extend to deeply unsettling territories.

Denis's filmmaking style also illuminates cinematic provocation as a strategy, sensuously involving the spectator in onscreen taboos: incestuous contact, violence and perverse eroticism. Her films position spectators to make a connection with the sound and screen – one that conveys caressing touch, skin-on-skin contact and physical proximity more often than painful, piercing spectacle. In this respect, Denis's oeuvre illuminates the diversity of cinematic provocation and its aesthetic manifestations. Her films disturb spectators in order to help them better perceive the rules that govern desire, deploying her known authorial signature so that the spectator might feel the operation of such laws in their own affective responses. The feeling of provocation experienced upon viewing Denis's work reveals our own investment in taboos that forbid entanglement of certain bodies. It exposes our discomfort at being implicated in moments of transgressive contact, such as when Justine embraces her father, Coré bites her lover or Willow tells her father, 'Yes'.

Notes

1. Matt Fagerholm, 'A Very Deep Place: Claire Denis on High Life', *Roger Ebert.com*, 15 April 2019, https://www.rogerebert.com/interviews/a-very-deep-place-claire-denis-on-high-life.
2. Marjorie Vecchio, 'Preface', in *The Films of Claire Denis: Intimacy on the Border*, ed. Marjorie Vecchio (London: I. B. Tauris, 2014), xiii.
3. Erika Balsom, '*High Life*', *Sight & Sound* 29, no. 6 (2019), 61.
4. L'Institut des hautes études cinématographiques (IDHEC); in English, the Institute for Advanced Cinematographic Studies.
5. James Quandt, 'Flesh & Blood: Sex and Violence in Recent French Cinema', *Artforum* 42, no. 6 (2004), 126–32.
6. For examples of authors who describe Denis in these terms, see: Samantha Dinning, 'Claire Denis', *Senses of Cinema*, April 2009, http://sensesofcinema.com/author/samantha-dinning/; Fiachra Gibbons and Stuart Jeffries, 'Cannes Audience Left Open-Mouthed', *Guardian*, 14 May 2001, https://www.theguardian.com/world/2001/may/14/cannes2001.cannesfilmfestival; and Laura McMahon, 'The Contagious Body of the Film: Claire Denis's *Trouble Every Day*', in *Transmissions: Essays in French Literature, Thought and Cinema*, eds Bradley Stephens and Isabelle McNeill (Bern: Peter Lang, 2007), 77.
7. Darren Hughes, '"High Life" and the Idea of "A Claire Denis Film"', *Mubi Notebook*, 16 April 2019, https://mubi.com/notebook/posts/high-life-and-the-idea-of-a-claire-denis-film.
8. 'Cannes Courts Controversy Even Before Opening', *Guardian*, 8 May 2001, https://www.theguardian.com/film/2001/may/08/cannes2001.cannesfilmfestival1.
9. Judith Mayne, *Claire Denis* (Urbana: University of Illinois Press, 2005), 9.
10. Martine Beugnet, *Cinema and Sensation: French Film and the Art of Transgression* (Edinburgh: Edinburgh University Press, 2007), 37.
11. Max Nelson, 'Bastards', *Film Comment* 49, no. 5 (2013), 65.
12. Martine Beugnet, *Claire Denis* (Manchester: Manchester University Press, 2004), 132.
13. Catherine Wheatley, 'La Famille Denis', in *The Films of Claire Denis: Intimacy on the Border*, ed. Marjorie Vecchio (London: I. B. Tauris, 2014), 71.
14. Dave Kehr, '35 Shots of Rum', *Film Comment* 45, no. 5 (2009), 67.
15. See Beugnet's publication *Cinema and Sensation: French Film and the Art of Transgression* (2007), as well as her earlier monograph *Claire Denis* (2004).
16. Adrian Martin, '*High Life* – Taboo in Space', *ArtsHub*, 12 March 2019, https://www.screenhub.com.au/news/reviews/film-review-high-life-taboo-in-space-257493-1426240.

17. Alexandra Heller-Nicholas, 'TIFF18 Review: *High Life*', *Alliance of Women Film Journalists*, 18 September 2018, https://awfj.org/blog/2018/09/18/tiff18-review-high-life-alexandra-heller-nicholas/.
18. Thomas Caldwell (@cinemaautopsy), 'HIGH LIFE explores the boundaries between what are and aren't acceptable social norms when it comes to sexual desire & procreation, in Claire Denis's bewildering & intoxicating sci-fi fever dream that's as transgressive, ambiguous, beautiful & confronting as her previous films', Tweet, 6 June 2019, https://twitter.com/i/web/status/1136848521271791616.
19. Mark Jenkins, 'Robert Pattinson's Outer-space Drama 'High Life' is Fascinating Yet Frustrating', *Washington Post*, 10 April 2019, https://www.washingtonpost.com/goingoutguide/movies/robert-pattinsons-outer-space-drama-high-life-is-fascinating-yet-frustrating/2019/04/10/9dce-c7a2-5106-11e9-88a1-ed346f0ec94f_story.html.
20. Nick Pinkerton, 'The Point of No Return', *Film Comment* 55, no. 2 (2019), 29.
21. These include James Quandt in his account of the New French Extremity ('Flesh & Blood') and Max Nelson in his review of *Bastards*, wherein he calls Denis a 'bastard' and equates her with the exploitative victimisers of the film itself ('Bastards', 65).
22. Patricia White, *Women's Cinema, World Cinema: Projecting Contemporary Feminisms* (Durham, NC: Duke University Press, 2015), 72.
23. Denis in Neil Smith, 'Trouble Every Day', interview with Claire Denis, *BBC*, archive date 28 October 2014, www.bbc.co.uk/films/2002/12/24/claire_denis_trouble_every_day_interview.shtml.
24. Denis in Sam Adams, 'Claire Denis on *Bastards* and Tough Women', interview, *The Dissolve*, 24 October 2013, https://thedissolve.com/features/interview/235-claire-denis-on-bastards-and-tough-women/.
25. Denis in Jean-Sébastian Chauvin and Stéphane Delorme, 'L'irrémédiable: dialogue avec Claire Denis', interview, *Cahiers du cinéma*, 691 (2013), 83.
26. Nikolaj Lübecker, *The Feel-Bad Film* (Edinburgh: Edinburgh University Press, 2015), 141.
27. I examine how this critique of fathers operates in films of the so-called Greek weird wave – specifically the works of Athina Rachel Tsangari – in Chapter 6. As I discuss, the failings of authoritarian fathers in these Greek films are sometimes interpreted as an allegorical manoeuvre that critiques the Greek ruling class and its failures, particularly in the aftermath of the Greek sovereign debt crisis.
28. Denis in Nick Pinkerton, 'Interview: Claire Denis', interview, *Film Comment Blog*, 10 October 2013, https://www.filmcomment.com/blog/interview-claire-denis/.
29. Carrie Tarr with Brigitte Rollet, *Cinema and the Second Sex: Women's Filmmaking in France in the 1980s and 1990s* (New York: Continuum, 2001), 125.
30. Ginette Vincendeau, 'Family Plots: The Fathers and Daughters of French Cinema', *Sight & Sound* 1, no. 11 (1992), 15.

31. Ibid., 17.
32. Balsom, '*High Life*', 61–2.
33. Sigmund Freud, *A General Introduction to Psychoanalysis*, trans. G. Stanley Hall (New York: Boni and Liveright, 1920), 177.
34. Emma Wilson, 'Contemporary French Women Filmmakers', *French Studies* 59, no. 2 (2005), 222.
35. Saige Walton, 'Gestures of Intimacy: Claire Denis' *I Can't Sleep*', *Senses of Cinema* 63 (2012), https://www.sensesofcinema.com/2012/cteq/gestures-of-intimacy-claire-denis-i-cant-sleep/.
36. Adam Nayman and Andrew Tracy, 'Arthouse/Grindhouse: Claire Denis and the "New French Extremity"' in *The Films of Claire Denis: Intimacy on the Border*, ed. Marjorie Vecchio (London: I. B. Tauris, 2014), 216.
37. Tim Palmer, *Brutal Intimacy: Analyzing Contemporary French Cinema* (Middletown, CT: Wesleyan University Press, 2011), 71.
38. Andrew Asibong, 'Viral Women: Singular, Collective and Progressive Infection in *Hiroshima mon amour*, *Les Yeux sans visage* and *Trouble Every Day*', in *Alienation and Alterity: Otherness in Modern and Contemporary Francophone Contexts*, eds Helen Vassallo and Paul Cooke (Oxford: Peter Lang, 2009), 105.
39. Heller-Nicholas, 'TIFF18 Review: *High Life*'.
40. *Bastards* does not possess the same strong haptic quality as many of Denis's other works. The film does not contain the images of touching and skin that are so characteristic of her oeuvre and crucial to inducing a sensory viewing experience. That said, there are some moments that convey violent and erotic touching. For example, the shot of Justine walking down the street bleeding is an image revealing the brutal contact she has endured. Moreover, Marco's relationship with Raphaëlle begins when he drops a packet of cigarettes wrapped in his unwashed collared shirt to her over a balcony. This sensual manoeuvre, however, is quickly eradicated by the roughness and impersonality of their first sexual encounter.
41. For an extended analysis, see Janice Loreck, *Violent Women in Contemporary Cinema* (Basingstoke: Palgrave Macmillan, 2016), 36–53.
42. Laura U. Marks, *The Skin of the Film: Intercultural Cinema, Embodiment, and the Senses* (Durham, NC: Duke University Press, 2000).
43. Nayman and Tracy, 'Arthouse/Grindhouse', 220.
44. 'Cannes Courts Controversy Even Before Opening', *Guardian*, 8 May 2001, https://www.theguardian.com/film/2001/may/08/cannes2001.cannesfilmfestival1.
45. Manohla Dargis, '"High Life" Review: Robert Pattinson Is Lost in Space', *New York Times*, 4 April 2019, https://www.nytimes.com/2019/04/04/movies/high-life-review.html.
46. Nayman and Tracy, 'Arthouse/Grindhouse', 223.
47. Wilson, 'Contemporary French Women Filmmakers', 222.
48. Kristin Lené Hole, *Towards a Feminist Cinematic Ethics: Claire Denis, Emmanuel Levinas and Jean-Luc Nancy* (Edinburgh: Edinburgh University Press, 2015), 6.

CHAPTER 5

Posing as an Innocent: Irony, Sincerity and Anna Biller

In an interview after the release of her debut feature *Viva* (2007), American writer-director Anna Biller admits there exists a layered co-presence of sincerity and irony in her work:

> As a filmmaker, I like to pose as an innocent, the same way my character poses as innocent in the film. (Although I am always aware that it's a pose, so perhaps this really makes it a form of irony.)[1]

Based in Los Angeles, Biller has made two features so far in her career, *Viva* and *The Love Witch* (2016), as well as four short films: *Three Examples of Myself as Queen* (1994), *Fairy Ballet* (1998), *The Hypnotist* (2001) and *A Visit from the Incubus* (2001). In over twenty-five years of filmmaking, her reputation has grown from that of an underground filmmaker to a noted independent auteur. In 2019, the speciality distributor Criterion released Biller's short films on its streaming service, an act that firmly situated her oeuvre within an art cinema context. In an article accompanying the release, Hillary Weston notes that Biller had 'emerged from the underground' following her second feature *The Love Witch*, achieving widespread recognition.[2] Biller's films are indeed idiosyncratic and immediately recognisable for their retrospective aesthetics. *The Love Witch* and *Viva* meticulously recreate the performance styles, sets, lighting design and costumes of bygone eras and genres, such as melodrama and sexploitation. Biller is also famed for her artisanal approach to production, which lends her films a handmade quality that is apparent in her *mise en scène*. She not only writes, produces and directs her films, she also oversees the art direction and production design, sews costumes, edits, decorates sets, creates and sources props and composes music and lyrics for her films. Alexandra Heller-Nicholas describes Biller as an 'all-round Renaissance woman',[3] while Kim Morgan calls her 'every inch the auteur'.[4]

Though frequently positive, the reception of Biller's work has been varied. Critics are divided over the tone and meaning of her films; specifically, whether she is, to use Biller's terms, a 'poser' or an innocent. Some commentators perceive Biller as an ironic filmmaker who champions a provocative, oppositional and paracinephilic style of cinema, while others frame Biller as a sincere feminist who is decidedly unironic about the style and themes of her work. Following the release of *The Love Witch*, for example, Mark Kermode gave a glowing review that he admitted conflicted with Biller's own account of her movie: 'I thought it was ripe and camp and I thought it was bathed in a nostalgia for horror and sexploitation movies of the late 60s and early 70s.'[5] Biller herself disagreed with this interpretation. In an interview for *Sight & Sound*, she claimed 'about 80 per cent' of critics misunderstand her work.[6] As a director, Biller thus raises an interesting conundrum about the nature of provocation while also providing a case study for the ways in which an individual filmmaker engages her audience on a complex aesthetic level. Her work is layered with different provocations, both superficial and profound. Biller's use of retrospective colour palettes, such as mustard yellows in *Viva* and jewel tones in *The Love Witch*, strong studio lighting and arch dialogue seem to telegraph a knowing sense of homage to the spectator. This homage appears as recognisable only to those who are cineliterate enough to link the bygone aesthetics and conventions to their original decades and genres. Read this way, Biller's films seem playful, even conspiratorial, in their address to the spectator and their provocative willingness to replicate outdated aesthetics. Yet the themes of Biller's films are consistently dark in a manner that complicates this apparent playfulness. *A Visit from the Incubus* is a tale of a woman's recovery following abuse, *Viva* reveals the failures of the sexual revolution, and *The Love Witch* concerns the impossibility of romantic fulfilment for women. The key question at stake is thus whether Biller is a revivalist of disreputable aesthetics and genres – borrowing their residual aura of titillation, scandal and controversy – or whether her intentions extend beyond this into something more ideologically subversive.

This chapter considers the dual interpretations of Biller's work, analysing her films as both ironic and sincere provocations. Determining exactly how Biller's films engage in acts of provocation is not straightforward. I investigate her works as readable in terms of ironic camp and oppositional taste; however, I also interpret them as sincere works that use outmoded genres to make subversive feminist commentary on heterosexual relations. My focus in this chapter is on Biller's films *A Visit from the Incubus*, *Viva* and *The Love Witch*, three works that amply demonstrate the potential for these two interpretations and provocations. *A Visit from the Incubus* is a horror–Western–musical hybrid about a young woman who is tormented by nocturnal visitations from a demon; *Viva* is a recreation of 1970s sexploitation cinema concerning a housewife who goes on a journey of sexual self-discovery; and *The Love Witch* is an occult-themed melodrama about a young witch's search for romantic love. The nudity, mannered acting and garish costumes characteristic of these films cue a camp, ironic reading. A closer analysis, however, also reveals a deeper provocation. The overall experience of watching Biller's work is not simply one of camp joy, but discomfiting seriousness about the impossibility of sexual and romantic realisation for women. These works produce a confrontational account of heteronormative regimes of love and desire, foreclosing any romantic or erotic fulfilment and presenting them as impossible and out of reach.

By investigating the provocative aspects of her work, this chapter frames Anna Biller as an important contemporary auteur who speaks in a unique aesthetic language. Her work is an instructive example of the polysemy of provocation, demonstrating how the same text might inspire different receptions, different perceptions and definitions of provocativeness, and different types of negative author–recipient relations. It is important to acknowledge that Biller's work is marked by complexities that rise up and challenge straightforward readings. Even as her films examine confronting issues, Biller regularly insists they are made to be enjoyed and give visual pleasure. In one interview, Biller makes a direct comparison between herself and Michael Haneke, a director whom critics regularly describe as a provocateur, stating, 'Michael Haneke says he makes movies to make the audience want to turn away – that's the opposite of my project. I want to make movies that make people want to look.'[7] Her films also contain critiques of classed and raced identity that sit alongside her textual investigations of love and sex. For instance, *Viva* reveals the constructed and performative nature of suburban middle-class white identity, a critique made especially sharp given Biller's Japanese-American heritage. In *Viva*, Biller 'poses' as white in her own film, playing the role of a protagonist who says she is part Italian; by inserting herself as a woman of Asian heritage into a 1970s American setting, Biller exposes the racial homogeneity of this milieu of cinema of the era. Her follow-up feature, *The Love Witch*, also turns attention towards sexual abuse in alternative communities such as Wiccans and neo-pagans, showing that the counterculture offers little escape from societal misogyny. Such ideas require further detailing as aspects of Biller's dense body of work. As a provocateur, however, Biller consistently returns to the tumultuous and traumatising experience of love and sex for women. Heterosexuality as it is internalised and performed – and the consequences that this has for women – is a darkness that cuts through the pleasures of her films, challenging the viewer with their irresolvability.

Irony and Sincerity: The Two Provocations

Prior to undertaking close analysis of Biller's individual films, it is necessary to first consider what I call 'the two provocations' of her work. This is the phrase I propose for differentiating between the two spectatorial reactions to and interpretations of Biller's films. The first provocation reads the director's work as ironic camp. In this approach, *A Visit from the Incubus*, *Viva* and *The Love Witch* are viewed as films that scandalise or amuse by declaring allegiance to an oppositional taste regime, a declaration that occurs via Biller's meticulous recreation of denigrated, outmoded genres: the Hollywood musical, sexploitation and occult horror cinema. Kermode, for instance, adopts this first reading. His positive review of *The Love Witch* describes the film as deliberate camp, deeming it 'ripe' and praising what he considers to be its 'very arch, very funny, very knowing conversations'.[8] Another critic, Manohla Dargis, takes the same view in her account of Biller's earlier film *Viva*, although she is less positive in her assessment:

> Depravity never becomes remotely depraved because Ms. Biller, despite her commitment to verisimilitude, maintains an ironic detachment throughout because she's a Brechtian or a bad actress, or perhaps both ... Yet while desperation and a critique lurk under all these garish surfaces, neither emerges because Ms. Biller, finally, adores this milieu too much to tear it apart.[9]

Such a reading understands the provocation of Biller's work to be its insistence on ironic enjoyment; on its celebration of poor-taste genres as 'so bad they're good' (which, as I shall elaborate below, is a limited provocation at best). Other commentators, however, see another provocation in Biller's work, discerning meaning beyond a mere recreation of outmoded genres. This second reading interprets Biller's work as a sincere and rather pessimistic exploration of heterosexual relations. Elena Gorfinkel's detailed analysis of *Viva*, for example, contends that Biller accomplishes her critique via the attentive recreation of genres. For Gorfinkel, *Viva* is an unironic exploration of the inadequacies of the sexual revolution for women: the protagonist's journey of self-discovery results not in liberation but a series of exploitative sexual experiences, including rape and coercive sex. As such, *Viva* is not a spoof or ironic, but '[takes] the terms and conventions of sexploitation seriously, speaking through its political and aesthetic flaws, not in spite of them', an important yet somewhat subtle distinction.[10] The two interpretations of Biller's films apply across her oeuvre, from *A Visit from the Incubus* and *Viva* to *The Love Witch* as well as *Three Examples of Myself as Queen*. In the following paragraphs, I unpack both readings and responses to Biller's work, framing them both as provocations made possible in the text. Although this chapter ultimately adopts the second reading as the more accurate interpretation – that Biller's films are unironic feminist critiques – reading for both provocations yields a fuller appreciation of the complexity of Biller's films and her expressions of a subversive feminist politics via the languages of genre.

There are compelling grounds for reading Biller's work as celebrations of paracinephilic, oppositional taste and as camp recreations of denigrated genres. This is because the films share iconography, narrative structures and aesthetics with musicals, sexploitation and occult horror films of the 1950s, late 1960s and early 1970s respectively. The plots and settings of Biller's films can evoke this connection rather strikingly for some knowledgeable viewers. As a story of a conventional housewife engaging in erotic experimentation, *Viva* echoes the narrative set-ups of soft-core sexploitation films of the 1960s and 1970s. It particularly resembles the plot of *Suburban Roulette* (Herschell Gordon Lewis, 1968), in which bored, white American suburbanites fill their days with backyard barbeques and partner swapping. *Suburban Roulette* begins as a new couple move to the suburbs in search of a calmer lifestyle, only to find their new neighbours want to enlist them in their swinging practices. Like this film, *Viva* takes place in affluent American suburbia. It contains scenes set beside domestic swimming pools, with the women sunning themselves on lawn chairs and sipping cocktails in bikinis while their husbands busy themselves at the grill. At the centre of *Suburban Roulette* is Ilene (Elizabeth Wilkinson), and she is a similar character to the protagonist of *Viva* – a married woman whose affairs with other men lead her into trouble, including constant threats of rape at the hands of presumptuous men as well as the possibility of her marriage dissolving. *The Love Witch* also has narrative parallels with occult horror films of the 1970s, such as *Mark of the Witch* (Tom Moore, 1970), *Jack's Wife* (George A. Romero, 1972), *Daughters of Satan* (Hollingsworth Morse, 1972) and *Blood Orgy of the She-Devils* (Ted V. Mikels, 1973). These films usually centre a respectable woman, such as a housewife or girlfriend, who gets involved with witchcraft or occult practices. Romero's *Jack's Wife* – also known as *Hungry Wives* and *Season of the Witch* – is a key point of reference here. The protagonist Joan (Jan White) is a bored homemaker who decides to take up witchcraft. Her newfound power coincides with the murder – perhaps accidental, perhaps intentional – of a man in her life, which echoes the events of *The Love Witch*. *A Visit from the Incubus* also takes inspiration from Hollywood Western–musical hybrids, such as the Judy Garland film *The Harvey Girls* (George Sidney, 1946) and the Doris Day-starring *Calamity Jane* (David Butler, 1953). While

A Visit from the Incubus does not share a narrative structure with these films, it takes place in a similar universe: an Old West filled with song, dance and rosy-cheeked heroines.

Biller's films also convey a sense of ironic or deliberate camp in their distinctive style, which is key to explaining their common interpretation as provocative oppositional works. As Susan Sontag describes, deliberate camp is 'when one plays at being campy', in contrast to naive or 'pure' camp, which is the result of a failed attempt to create serious art.[11] Deliberate camp corresponds to the French origins of the term *se camper*, meaning to pose in an exaggerated fashion. The term has also been connected to a specifically queer mode of cultural production: an *écriture gaie* or a language of the closet (specifically the gay male closet). At first glance, it is possible to read Biller's films as deliberate camp due to their distinctive style. *A Visit from the Incubus*, *Viva* and *The Love Witch* eschew naturalism and appear to knowingly recreate earlier genres, 'posing' as them. *Viva* evokes this so strongly that Simon Crook declares the film 'so camp the camera's practically winking'.[12] Biller began the process of creating *Viva* by looking at images from old *Playboy* magazines from the 1970s, weaving her story from the associations the magazines evoked for her.[13] She vividly describes this world and its objects:

> A world of saturated Eastmancolor, beautiful women, masculine hairy men, heavily gender-related consumer products, Hammond organ and flute sound tracks, false eyelashes, Male Tan #5, blobby abstract artwork and furniture, flesh-toned non-underwire bras and filmy negligees, liquor and cigarettes, Euro-sexy accents, hair with height at the top, weird psychedelic patterns on everything, ashtrays on every table, olive green with purple, brown, yellow, orange, and flesh-pink as a standard color scheme, natural-breasted women in large panties.[14]

In *Viva*, Biller recreates this world to an extreme degree, filling the visual field and soundscape with precisely these colours, sounds and objects. These are also the aesthetics of the soft-core sexploitation genre of the same era, which Biller calls the 'world of sex culture from 1967 to 1973'.[15] The first glimpse of the protagonist of *Viva*, Barbi (Anna Biller), depicts her in an aqua-tiled bathroom, her nails painted iridescent coral, her eyelids vivid blue as she reads crocheting and soft-core magazines in the bathtub (Figure 5.1). Upbeat brass, flute and xylophone music plays over the soundtrack as a voice-over sonorously declares: 'This is a story about a housewife during the sexual revolution. The time is 1972, the place Los Angeles, and the people ordinary.' Such a beginning immediately announces *Viva* as a recreation – a film that poses as a sexploitation film from the 1970s. The performance styles that follow further suggest

Figure 5.1 Barbi relaxes in her aqua-tiled bathroom in *Viva*.

that the film is deliberate and ironic. The actors each adopt an affected manner of speaking and converse in sentences resembling advertisements or poorly scripted pornography. For example: 'Now that's a professional camera!' exclaims Mark (Jared Sanford), fondling his recently purchased photographic equipment; 'I've always wanted to be a prostitute – it sounds so romantic!' declares Sheila (Bridget Brno) before accepting a job as a call girl.

Such qualities appear in *A Visit from the Incubus* and *The Love Witch* too. Kermode's review of *The Love Witch* describes the dialogue as 'arch', and a similar remark could be made about *A Visit from the Incubus*. In addition to dialogue that seems to evoke cliché – 'You might say I'm addicted to love!' declares the eponymous *Love Witch* – the protagonists of both of Biller's features speak with a melodic, mellifluous intonation. The effect is not dissimilar to the rounded mid-Atlantic accent and elocution of 1930s and 1940s Hollywood, inviting interpretations of the vocal performance as imitation. *A Visit from the Incubus* and *Viva* also facilitate readings as deliberate camp through their intertextual references to camp icons and queer auteurs. *Viva* ends on a song-and-dance routine that a character explicitly declares is inspired by the French director and auteur of camp cinema Jacques Demy.[16] By so closely referencing *The Harvey Girls* and *Calamity Jane*, *A Visit from the Incubus* also aligns itself with queer culture, particularly the icons of Judy Garland and Doris Day, the stars of each film respectively. Biller's films are therefore notably, and often reflexively, connected to queer culture.[17] Writing on *A Visit from the Incubus*, reviewer Robert Firsching recognises the film's *joie de vivre*, calling it 'the ultimate high-camp vision of old Hollywood, infused with a distinct feminist sensibility and an unabashed joy in the art of filmmaking'.[18] All this supports a reading of Biller's work as deliberate, knowing camp.

Reading Biller's films in this way involves interpreting them as provocative declarations of oppositional taste. In such a formulation, *A Visit from the Incubus*, *Viva* and *The Love Witch* are deemed knowing or ironic celebrations of genres that are outmoded, ideologically suspect or otherwise 'bad'. Biller's provocativeness thus consists of her films' recreation of these genres' aesthetics and narratives and, by implication, celebrating them via studied mimicry. In other words, she scandalises through paracinephilic style. Jeffrey Sconce provides a vivid account of this celebration of oppositional taste in his essay on paracinema, a 'counter-aesthetic turned subcultural sensibility devoted to all manner of cultural detritus'.[19] Sconce describes paracinema as the types of films that cultural authorities and gatekeepers, such as professional film critics and festival curators, have deemed illegitimate or in poor taste. It is a category that is defined in opposition to art cinema or mainstream popular film and thus consists of all manner of media: soft-core film, Z-grade cinema, public hygiene films, splatter films and sword and sandal films, to name only a few. Occult horror films, sexploitation cinema and the once-popular Western–musical hybrid can each be categorised as paracinema in contemporary popular culture. Occult horror and sexploitation films in particular were often cheaply made products and are ideologically problematic given the centrality of female nudity, sexuality and otherwise titillating scenarios in the plots. To borrow Sconce's words, interpreting films like *A Visit from the Incubus*, *Viva* and *The Love Witch* as deliberate camp is to infer that Biller worships 'at "the temple of schlock"'.[20] This reading also explains the evident care that has gone into the production design. Biller's films are highly crafted and artisanal and, as such, they can be interpreted as a form of cinephilic appreciation via mimicry. Under this formulation, camp aesthetics provoke by offending legitimate aesthetic sensibilities and challenging taste hegemonies.

This reading, however, ultimately falls short when applied to Biller's work. Sconce makes the point that the paracinematic sensibility is no longer truly subversive, niche or oppositional. It has long been widely embraced by cultural authorities, with film critics, festival curators and cinema academics often appreciating the kind of Z-grade and exploitation cinema that Sconce lists. Paracinephilic sensibility has infiltrated 'the avant-garde, the academy, and even the mass culture on which paracinema's ironic reading strategies originally preyed'.[21] Reading Biller's work as ironic camp thus leads to a limited understanding of her films as a subversion of taste-regimes that are not as hierarchical, strict or exclusionary as perhaps imagined. Second, reading Biller's work as ironic camp does not fully illuminate the feminist subversiveness of her films or the potential for discomfort upon viewing them. *A Visit from the Incubus*, *Viva* and *The Love Witch* all tell stories about the disappointments and dangers of heterosexual relations for women. Biller's oeuvre is marked by the centrality of rape, sexual coercion and abuse that camp readings cannot fully account for or explain. The heroine of *A Visit from the Incubus* is tormented by visits from a demon who rapes her each night; Barbi in *Viva* constantly faces sexual assault in her attempt to escape her suburban life; the titular witch of *The Love Witch* experiences unwanted sex during a pagan initiation ceremony. This leads to the second reading of Biller's work: that her films are sincere critiques of heteronormative relations, exploring the dangers and limitations that they place upon women. As I examine in following sections, *A Visit from the Incubus*, *Viva* and *The Love Witch* each express a sense of impossibility around this issue. Even when they seem to end on happy notes of triumph, none of the protagonists achieves a fulfilling romance or sexual autonomy. This deeper, more subversive implication of Biller's films is available to those who look beyond irony.

Sexual Impossibilities: *A Visit from the Incubus* and *Viva*

Both *A Visit from the Incubus* and *Viva* are stories about women seeking sexual liberation in the face of coercion and rape. *A Visit from the Incubus*, Biller's third short film, takes place in the Old West. Its heroine is Lucy McGee (Anna Biller), a sweet young woman tormented by visitations from an Incubus (Jared Sanford), a demon who sexually assaults her while she sleeps. After a particularly unpleasant night, Lucy decides to banish the Incubus forever by taking a job as a saloon performer – an act that reclaims her sexual self and defeats the demon. *Viva* centres on the sexual journey of Barbi, a housewife trapped in an emotionally dysfunctional marriage with Rick (Chad England). Following an argument with Rick in which he abandons her, Barbi decides to leave her suburban life and embark on a journey of erotic self-discovery: she takes a job as a call girl, visits a nudist colony, moves in with an artist and attends an orgy dressed as 'Viva', her alter-ego. *A Visit from the Incubus* and *Viva* mirror each other in several aspects. Both tell stories of women who want to reclaim their erotic autonomy in response to violation or neglect. Both are also artisanal in their look and production, as is characteristic of all Biller's films. Biller sewed the costumes, wrote the songs and lyrics, designed the sets, created dozens of props from scratch, penned the scripts and performed the lead role in each film.

A Visit from the Incubus and *Viva* concern the difficulty, even impossibility, of women's sexual self-determination. They are feminist provocations that denounce the foreclosing of women's pleasure and autonomy in a heterosexist culture. The two films make this critique in different ways, however. I turn first to *A Visit from the Incubus*, an important precursor to *Viva* that sets the terms for Biller's provocative engagements with genre and women's sexuality. Biller says the film 'has to do with feeling a lack of power in the world, which is how I feel sometimes as a female'.[22] The story begins as Lucy visits her friend Madeleine (Natalia Schroeder) to tell her about the Incubus visitations. Madeleine consoles Lucy but is unable to offer any help, suggesting that the visits will eventually stop of their own accord. After discovering a lurid semen stain on her nightdress the next morning, Lucy decides to take action. Swapping her modest dress for a garish red and white striped outfit, she goes to the town saloon to ask for a job as a performer – a plan that is evidently meant to solve Lucy's Incubus problem, although it is not entirely clear how. Fortunately, Lucy's 'plan' works. Dressed in a red sequined costume and flanked by dancing girls, her debut song-and-dance routine at the saloon is rapturously received by the all-male audience. The Incubus, who follows Lucy and stages his own performance, is booed off the stage and, presumably, banished forever.

A Visit from the Incubus is told with a level of playfulness that lends itself to a reading as camp homage. In interviews, however, Biller explains that the film is about sexual autonomy:

> It's about a woman who wants to go into show business. But it's also about internal female problems. About sex, about a woman's first sexual experience, and about problems around rape and desire and things like that, and trying to combine that with ideas of fantasies about being on the stage and performance.[23]

Biller also states a personal connection to the story, observing that she has 'had incubus problems' all her life.[24] She describes these terrifying episodes where she would wake up feeling smothered and constricted: 'The film came from that place of deep sorrow and tragedy and then I made it funny.'[25] While infused with cinephilic references to Westerns, musicals and folklore, *A Visit from the Incubus* is also about a woman's strategy to resist rape and regain control of her sexuality. This unfolds metaphorically in the narrative. In preparation for her trip to the saloon, Lucy swaps her modest outfit for showy clothing, including a crimson hat festooned with cherries and a white ostrich plume. She changes costume again for her debut performance, wearing a red sequined gown and matching feathered hat. Her outfit looks similar to the one worn by Em (Angela Lansbury), the sexually confident singer in *The Harvey Girls* and rival to Judy Garland's virtuous heroine, Susan. Indeed, the clothes draw associations with many such character types from Hollywood, including Mae West's extravagant outfits and sexually confident persona. The figure of the saloon singer in these texts stands in as a symbol for an independent and assured woman who is in control of her sexuality (or, at least, in control of the performance of her sexuality). Through her proactive transformation, Lucy thus takes back her sexuality too via choreographed stage performance. While her image is still for male enjoyment, she has greater control than she did before, and Lucy is also protected by her fans. Charmed by her routine, the cowboys at the saloon transform from louts into sweet admirers, and at the film's end they lift Lucy up upon their shoulders for a final reprise. Gorfinkel observes that Biller's choice to end her films on a musical number is a strategy that evokes utopian possibility. Drawing on Richard Dyer's observations, musicals create a sense of utopia not in the reality they represent but the feeling they create. Put another way, they convey what utopia would feel like.[26] *A Visit from the Incubus* thus has a hopeful element. The triumphant final musical number conveys the feeling, if not the reality, of Lucy's sexual liberation. Yet at the same time, something is lost in *A Visit from the Incubus* too. Although Lucy escapes the Incubus and his violations, she does not achieve real sex or pleasure in its place. Only the controlled performance of sexuality, channelled through dance and song, is a possibility for her.

While *A Visit from the Incubus* ends with a rapturous image of Lucy's success, Biller's follow-up feature, *Viva*, leaves a darker impression. The film replicates a common sexploitation narrative structure – a 'respectable' woman becomes curious about the sexual revolution and proliferation of alternative lifestyles around her and decides to experiment with them, for example through nudism (*Diary of a Nudist* [Doris Wishman, 1961]), or swinging (*Suburban Roulette*). Bored, curious and abandoned by her husband, Barbi is such a character. She takes the name Viva, which is also the title of one of the glossy magazines she peruses at home. Barbi's life as Viva leads her into many different scenarios: employment as a call girl, a visit to a nudist colony, a lesbian tryst with a woman named Agnes (Robbin Ryan), and a role as live-in muse for Clyde (Marcus DeAnda), an artist. Throughout all of this, Barbi is searching for something. She renames herself Viva because it means 'to live', and that is her aspiration. She wants other things too: a kind and sensitive lover, as well as the new experiences that the sexual revolution promises. Hers is a journey of discovery, both of herself and her desires, and sex is at the centre. Barbi does eventually experience a moment of transformative pleasure, but it is troubling and ambivalent. After living for some time with Clyde (with whom she refuses to have sex), she attends an elaborate orgy with him at a mansion, where he slips a sedative into her drink. Dressed in exotic gold garb, Barbi performs a sensual song-and-dance routine, growing delirious with the drugs and the eroticism of her performance. Clyde catches her as she swoons and has sex with her on a bed nearby, and Barbi experiences an intense orgasm that the film elaborately depicts. It begins with the camera pulling in and out of focus on Barbi's face as she breathes heavily (Figure 5.2), a direct homage to Marguerite's orgasm in *Camille 2000* (Radley Metzger, 1969), and transforms into a psychedelic animated sequence. Later, Barbi awakens surrounded by naked men and women sleeping beside her, and she is haunted by memories of her erotic dance. The incident at the orgy is troubling in its ambivalence: it is both a rape and orgasmic for Barbi. However, she finds the experience unsettling not because she understands it as sexual assault, but because both the dance and the sex seem to have precipitated a shift in identity. As she tells Sheila:

> It's as if I became a different person. I really became this 'Viva', this sex goddess, and they all worshipped me and wanted me. I became, how can I tell you, totally a woman, and I liked it. But it was too much, I saw a side of myself that was probably better kept hidden. A side that frightened me. It was so powerful. I became a female animal, made only for pleasure. Do you know what I mean?

Sheila does not know what Barbi means – at least not precisely. She replies that Barbi's experience sounds 'kind of dark', but the issue of sexual assault does not arise in their conversation. Barbi and Sheila then both decide to cease their sexual adventuring. As such, Barbi never finds liberation or pleasure in the way she imagines, only a coercive encounter that is

Figure 5.2 The depiction of Barbi's orgasm pays direct homage to *Camille 2000*.

too disturbing for her to want or accept. She returns to her suburban life, ending her journey of discovery.

These events hardly seem congruent with descriptions of *Viva* as a joyous camp recreation of sexploitation. As Gorfinkel notes, 'In a world in which Viva/Barbi should gain liberation, she finds instead a series of rapes and forms of sexual coercion'.[27] Jason Klorfein makes the same point: 'The sexual revolution was never meant for women ... [and] the world of sexploitation is inherently rigged against any kind of empowerment for "Barbi/Viva".'[28] As both Klorfein and Gorfinkel observe, it is precisely through the recreation of sexploitation that Biller is able to highlight the inadequacies of the sexual revolution for women. This message can be discerned in some of the original sexploitation films; for example, the housewife at the centre of *Suburban Roulette* is emotionally destroyed by the turmoil of her extramarital affairs, and the film ends as she is transported to hospital after a suicide attempt. Although readable as an ideological warning against women's promiscuity, a feminist interpretation of *Suburban Roulette* can discern another message: that 'alternative' lifestyles come at a higher price for women than for men. Like Ilene in *Suburban Roulette*, the bored housewife at the centre of *Viva* has few positive experiences beyond sexual dissatisfaction and victimisation. Barbi therefore returns to the life she tried to escape and attempts a reconciliation with Rick. This is far from a happy reunion, however: smelling Mark's overpowering aftershave on Barbi's clothing, Rick accuses Barbi of having an affair mere moments after his return to their home. Rick rushes out in indignation without waiting to hear Barbi's explanation (Mark had tried to force himself on Barbi, hence the lingering smell of his cologne). Rick then breaks his leg after running into oncoming traffic and is rendered housebound, effectively forcing a reunion. *Viva* thus withholds even the conformist pleasure of happy heterosexual coupledom, which, despite all its ideological problems, offers at least one form of closure to the sexploitation narrative. Alternative lifestyles do not work out for Barbi, and sexual and emotional reconciliation with Rick is not possible either. Out of options, Barbi has little chance of transcending her circumstances.

Like *A Visit from the Incubus*, *Viva* ends with Barbi going into showbusiness and performing a musical number with Sheila. In a final intertextual allusion, Barbi and Sheila's outfits in the last scene of *Viva* look precisely like the sequined red costumes worn by Catherine Deneuve and Françoise Dorléac in *The Young Girls of Rochefort* (*Les Demoiselles de Rochefort*, Jacques Demy, 1967). Musical performances uphold Biller's drive to provide spectatorial pleasure in her films and, once again, the moment can be interpreted as hopeful and utopian for Barbi herself, as for Lucy in *A Visit from the Incubus*. As Gorfinkel states, 'A return to the form of the musical offers Viva momentary escape through performance'.[29] Yet while Biller offers her protagonist some joy, she does not offer a real solution to Barbi's thwarted longing. The pessimism and provocation of *Viva* remains intact.

Romantic Disappointments: *The Love Witch*

Whereas *A Visit from the Incubus* and *Viva* explore women's sexuality, *The Love Witch* attends to women's experience of love and romantic relationships. The film begins as Elaine (Samantha Robinson) drives along the Californian coast to begin a new life in the city of Arcata. Elaine is a witch and recovering from a marriage that ended, mysteriously, with the violent death of her husband. Once settled in her new home, Elaine quickly sets about finding a new lover. She seduces a college professor named Wayne (Jeffrey Vincent Parise) as well as the husband of her married friend Trish (Laura Waddell), casting love spells upon them. The magic has a disturbing side effect, however, and the men are overwhelmed by an intense love for Elaine. Elaine is repulsed when her lovers transform into weeping, needy wrecks, and eventually both men die: Wayne from heart failure and Richard by suicide. Things become even more complicated when the handsome police officer investigating Wayne's death, Sergeant Griff Meadows (Gian Keys), begins courting Elaine too. Although Elaine likes him better than her previous two lovers, Griff eventually discovers what she has done to Wayne and ends his relationship with her. Elaine is so traumatised by Griff's rejection that she descends into delirium and stabs him to death.

Like Biller's earlier work, *The Love Witch* is best understood as a sincere feminist provocation centred on the dysfunction of male–female relationships. This time, however, the emphasis is on love. The film was generally well received upon its festival run and limited release in 2016. Yet as with *Viva*, some critics saw *The Love Witch* as another declaration of oppositional taste: as a camp, ironic parody of debased genre films, this time the occult film of the 1970s and Euro-horror from the same era, such as the *giallo* films of Mario Bava and Dario Argento or the work of Spanish director Jess Franco. For instance, Dennis Harvey and Nikki Baughan identify *The Love Witch* as a tribute to the witchcraft films of the early 1970s, which tend to centre on a conventional woman, such as a housewife or girlfriend, who dabbles in black magic.[30] *Jack's Wife*, *Daughters of Satan* and *Blood Orgy of the She-Devils* are all examples of this subgenre. As I discuss in the introduction to this chapter, Mark Kermode also characterised *The Love Witch* as a hybrid of 1950s Hollywood melodrama and 1970s Euro-horror, writing, 'The best way of describing this is that it's *All that Heaven Allows* [Douglas

Sirk, 1955] directed by Jess Franco. Or it's Douglas Sirk's *Vampyros Lesbos* [Jess Franco, 1970].'[31] Biller herself challenges such accounts of her movie. Stating that she is uninterested in exploitation cinema, she instead lists a variety of other references: films such as *Bell, Book and Candle* (Richard Quine, 1958), *Gertrud* (Carl Theodor Dreyer, 1964), *Donkey Skin* (*Peau d'âne*, Jacques Demy, 1970)[32] and *The Decameron* (*Il Decameron*, Pier Paolo Pasolini, 1971); books including *Sin Seance* (1968) by Don Bellmore and *How to Become a Sensuous Witch* (1971) by Abragail and Valaria, and 'photographs of real-life witches in the 1960s, such as Anton LaVey and Alex and Maxine Sanders'.[33] Biller's remarks redirect attention away from reference points in occultist horror cinema and towards a heterogeneous collection of visual and narrative influences, including American romantic comedy, European art cinema and popular occultist writings and figures.

For those who read *The Love Witch* as camp and kitsch as well as a cinephilic revival of denigrated 1970s horror cinema, the provocation of the film is its committed reproduction of culturally outmoded films, aesthetics and performance styles – an exercise in unfashionable genres and retrospective aesthetics, much like *Viva*, even if not so intended by Biller herself. It is important to observe that *The Love Witch* does bear some resemblance to the witchcraft films from the 1970s as well as Euro-horror works from the same era. First there are narrative similarities: like *The Love Witch*, *Jack's Wife*, *Daughters of Satan* and *Blood Orgy of the She-Devils* centre on a woman who experiments with witchcraft, usually leading to murder. A key underlying theme (or anxiety) of these films is the promise of power that the occult can offer women, particularly the possibility of escape from dissatisfying domestic lives. This is a theme in *The Love Witch* too, with Elaine declaring that her rebirth as a witch liberated her from dysfunctional relationships with men. There are also aesthetic similarities between *The Love Witch* and occult horror cinema, particularly similar production design stemming from the occult themes. The *mise en scène* of *The Love Witch* makes prominent use of the colours of the Thoth tarot deck, decorating the sets with strong primary colours and jewel tones. The walls of Elaine's house are painted in crimson, royal blue, violet and royal purple. This colour scheme also appears in the costuming in *Blood Orgy of the She-Devils*, with its red satin dresses, crimson velvet and gold trimmings. *Blood Orgy of the She-Devils* also begins with a strikingly similar shot to one repeatedly used in *The Love Witch* – a close-up of the witch's painted eyes as she casts her magic spells. The titular witch of *The Love Witch* also physically resembles Euro-horror stars of yesteryear. With her dark eyes, heart-shaped face and long hair, Samantha Robinson has a similar look to Jess Franco's frequent collaborator, Soledad Miranda, who appeared in cult films like *Vampyros Lesbos* and *She Killed in Ecstasy* (1971). Taken at face value, such resemblances invite readings of *The Love Witch* as both homage and recreation.

Although foundational to many positive reviews from film critics, this reading of *The Love Witch* is once again a limited interpretation that does not illuminate the deeper critiques of the film. *The Love Witch* does not convey any impression of irony, which Wayne C. Booth defines as a 'canker of negation at the heart of every affirmation'.[34] Elaine is clearly emotionally disturbed and, as her friend Trish frequently points out, her ideas about relationships are regressive. At one point, Elaine declares that she knows what men truly desire: 'Just a pretty woman to love and to take care of them, and to make them feel like a man, and to give them total freedom in whatever they want to do or be.' Although Trish immediately challenges her friend and the problematic nature of such a statement, *The Love Witch* treats Elaine's ideas and desires seriously, and the plot never exposes her to ridicule or refutes her statements. Instead, the film reveals that Elaine is a survivor of abuse and suggests that her beliefs are shaped by these prior traumas. Flashbacks show that Elaine was coerced into undergoing a sex ritual with the leader of her coven, Gahan (Jared Sanford), as part of her initiation. This incident in part explains her ongoing struggle to find security and trust in relationships with men. In addition to treating Elaine's desires seriously, *The Love Witch* does not contain the element of sleaze that is definitive of many occult horror films of the 1970s.[35] Sconce defines sleaze as a tone that derives from insinuation. It is a textually generated impression that an untoward exchange, such as a titillation, has taken place between the film and the viewer. Sleaze as a tone 'is a function of attitude as much as content';[36] it is also therefore a feature of coy, soft-core genres rather than hardcore or gratuitous works, which are frank in their address and textual strategies. Many occult horror works adopt this tone and strategy of sleaze. *Blood Orgy of the She-Devils*, for example, is bookended by erotic spectacles in which scantily clad women dance suggestively before sacrificing their male victim. The film is an example of sleaze insofar as it references what Sconce wryly refers to as the 'vaguely titillating horrors of hippiedom'.[37] As adherents of counter-cultural movements, occultists, Satanists and witches can serve as fitting antagonists for horror narratives, but because of the long cultural association between witches and sexual deviance, such figures also promise titillation through spectacles of ritualistic sex. In contrast, *The Love Witch* is instead characterised by declarations of sincerity; not even the occult scenes of nudity seem sleazy or prurient. Representing a variety of body shapes and ages, Biller's performers dance, sky-clad and without reservation, in front of the camera.

Reading *The Love Witch* as ironic camp not only misidentifies the film's sincere tone, it also misses the film's politics. *The Love Witch* is an indictment of heterosexual men's emotional unavailability and its impact on women's wellbeing. Elaine longs for men to love her, casting spells upon them to make this happen. She also believes that men want a woman to 'take care of them' and to love them. Yet the moment Elaine's lovers *do* want such things from her, she is repulsed by how feminised and needy they seem. Her first lover, the self-professed 'libertine' Wayne, has such an intense reaction to Elaine's love spell that he descends into emotional agony, repeatedly calling her name and weeping. Refusing to respond, Elaine sits coldly on the sofa in another room, smoking a cigarette. 'What a pussy', she thinks to herself in voice-over, 'What a baby. I thought I found a real man, but he's just like a little girl.' At the moment of Wayne's romantic attachment, Elaine pulls away, unable to accept the feelings that do not match with her expectations of masculinity. Wayne's reaction is certainly extreme, yet Elaine's actions – as well as the misogynistic language she uses to denigrate Wayne – suggest that Elaine herself has internalised an expectation of men that makes it impossible for her to accept the love that she herself has magically engineered. The implication is that men and women are incapable of romantic reciprocity and connection; at least, not in a culture in which expectations of emotional performance and gender follow prescriptive scripts. Whereas *Viva* and *A Visit from the Incubus* concern the impossibility of sexual self-realisation for women, *The Love Witch* explores the impossibility of romantic fulfilment.

The idea of the fundamental emotional incompatibility of men and women is also keenly articulated during a scene in which Elaine and Griff attend an Italian Renaissance fair together. While attending the fair, the two are invited to participate in a mock wedding in honour of the gods of love. While canoodling happily with each other at the wedding feast, a voice-over reveals Elaine and Griff's thoughts in a moment of deep dramatic irony; Elaine speaks of her increasing attachment through intimacy, whereas Griff's voice-over suggests the opposite:

> ELAINE (V/O): When you really love him, it's like fireworks and nothing else matters. You love all the little quirks about him ... And you realise that you have more love to give than you ever thought was possible. Because the more you know him, the more you love him!
> GRIFF (V/O): The more you get to know a woman, the less you can feel about her. At first she's this incredible object of mystery who fulfils all your wildest fantasies. Then she starts to reveal little flaws. And after a while, it just gets pretty hard to care. The feminine ideal only exists in a man's mind. No woman could ever fulfil it. And sometimes when she tries to love you more, give you more, you feel like you're suffocating, drowning in oestrogen. It's the most awful feeling.

Biller says this scene is her favourite. 'When I watch that fairytale prince and princess, so in love and so innocent, and then I hear their inner monologues where we realize they are star-crossed, my heart goes into my mouth.' Biller also says she has 'absolutely no irony' about the scene.[38] What it reveals instead is that women and men are not only star-crossed, but are also mismatched in how they desire.

This raises an important question regarding how genres interact with Biller's exploration of love and relationships in *The Love Witch*. The connection between occult horror and *The Love Witch* is not the same as the relationship between sexploitation and *Viva*. In *Viva*, Biller uses sexploitation to demonstrate the impossibility of women's sexual empowerment and liberation within the sexploitation genre, which in turns speaks to a broader impossibility of sexual liberation for women in cultures where structures of patriarchy persist (particularly male sexual entitlement). *The Love Witch* does not deploy occult horror in an analogous way. The film *resembles* this genre because it features iconographies and aesthetics from Wiccan and neo-paganist culture in the *mise en scène*, thus drawing from the same set of reference points as the occult horror film. In generic terms, *The Love Witch* instead more closely employs melodrama in the way it centres female victimhood – Elaine is a woman 'ruined' emotionally by men. Biller notes that a key influence for *The Love Witch* is Carl Theodor Dreyer's *Gertrud*, based on Hjalmar Söderberg's 1906 stage play. The heroine of Dreyer's film encounters three men – her husband, her former lover and a new romantic interest – and finds that none of them are able to love her enough. Her only goal is the purest of loves without compromise. Unable to find it, Gertrud (Nina Pens Rode) decides to live her life alone, without any companionship. Although not usually conceptualised as a melodrama, *Gertrud* centres female sacrifice, idealism and even masochism. Yet whereas Gertrud is saintly in her commitment to love and triumphant in her solitude into old age, Elaine uses manipulation and murder to achieve her goal. Her struggle to attain romantic fulfilment is fruitless, however. Just as for Barbi in *Viva*, Elaine's efforts mean little if heterosexual men remain emotionally unavailable.

Normative heterosexual relations in *The Love Witch* foreclose successful romantic attachment – to be star-crossed is to be thwarted by the cultural scripts that come between men and women. Unlike Biller's earlier films, *The Love Witch* does not end in escape to a utopian place via a song-and-dance routine – at least, not in the diegetic reality of the film. It instead has a tragic conclusion: Elaine stabs Griff and descends into a fantasy where she imagines a return to the Renaissance fair. Griff is there and declares his love for Elaine and desire to marry her, leading her away on a white unicorn. The reality of Elaine's violence, however, recalls the conclusions of the occult films from the 1970s (for example, when Joan Mitchell shoots her husband in *Jack's Wife*). Read as ideological messaging, the death of men in occult horror seems to serve an ideological purpose, warning about the perils of women's empowerment through witchcraft. In *The Love Witch*, however, the empowerment of women is not the problem that bedevils the characters. It is the state of romantic relationships between men and women that is disturbed: by men's abuses of women, and the mismatch of male and female expectations.

Coded Poses

Biller has noted that her work has the capacity to prompt negative emotional responses, stating, 'I think my work *is* confrontational but it's very coded'.[39] Coded is a fitting term, given the distinction between critics who interpret Biller's filmmaking as ironic camp as opposed to those who perceive sincere feminist commentary. Appreciating Biller as a provocateur involves fully considering how her films elicit a variety of responses. Yet while it is important to account for the different ways that *A Visit from the Incubus*, *Viva* and *The Love Witch* are received as provocative works, I have argued that the tendency to read Biller's films as camp declarations of oppositional taste mostly overlooks their unsettling power. As Gorfinkel argues of *Viva*, 'Many critics want the film to be intentional camp so as to better make sense of it, or at least to better make sense of their own discomfort and desire for irony in a relatively unironic text'.[40] This observation applies to *A Visit from the Incubus* and *The Love Witch* too – they are films permeated with women's dissatisfaction, offering indirect solutions or none at all. Reading for irony also misses what is deeply felt and sincere in Biller's work. Biller's heroines repeatedly speak their thoughts and declare their desires, and the films treat these declarations seriously. In *Viva*, Barbi says, 'I want to be called "Viva," which in Italy means "to live." Because that's what I want to do now, to live.' In *The Love Witch*, Elaine says, 'You men, you make us work so hard for your love. If you would just love us for ourselves ... But you won't.' The apparent allusions to outmoded genres in Biller's films do not negate the sincerity of these declarations. The thread that binds Biller's films is therefore an exploration of the limitations of heterosexual relationships for women: of everything they foreclose and make impossible. This is as common to her films as Biller's artisanal production methods and retrospective aesthetics.

Biller is thus an auteur and provocateur, one who uses cinema to relay the darker aspects of women's experiences even as she offers complex cinematic pleasures. Frank and ever willing to explain her work, Biller says,

'What I'm doing is transforming female experience and trauma through fairytale and cinema into something fantastic and beautiful'.[41] Indeed, following her films' appearance on the Criterion Channel and the international success of *The Love Witch*, Biller is gathering recognition as an auteur who demands that her work be understood in its complexity. Biller herself insists on this too: 'I'm often still not given credit for understanding what I'm doing.'[42] Understanding what Biller is doing is necessary to appreciating her contribution as a subversive filmmaker.[43]

Notes

1. Biller in Elena Gorfinkel, 'Unlikely Genres: An Interview with Anna Biller', interview, *Camera Obscura: Feminism, Culture, and Media Studies* 26, no. 3 (2011), 139.
2. Hillary Weston, 'Anna Biller's Pleasure Principles', *Criterion*, 29 May 2019, https://www.criterion.com/current/posts/6400-anna-biller-s-pleasure-principles.
3. Alexandra Heller-Nicholas, 'The Love Witch – An Interview with Anna Biller', 4:3, 8 July 2016, https://fourthreefilm.com/2016/07/the-love-witch-an-interview-with-anna-biller/.
4. Kim Morgan, 'Spellbound', *Sight & Sound* 27, no. 4 (2017), 42.
5. Mark Kermode, 'Mark Kermode Reviews The Love Witch', *Kermode and Mayo*, uploaded 11 March 2017, video, 3:36, https://www.youtube.com/watch?v=v4Py76VXK4s.
6. Biller in Morgan, 'Spellbound', 42.
7. Biller also links this project to feminism: 'I do consider myself a feminist in a general sort of way, in that I'm consciously trying to create a subjective and pleasurable space for women on the screen.' Yet the length with which her camera lingers on yolky, yellow devilled eggs in *Viva* yields as much potential for revulsion and exhaustion as it does pleasure, depending on the aesthetic sensibilities of the onlooker. (Biller in Robert Macmanus, 'A Rush on Anna Biller', interview, *Vice*, 23 September 2009, https://www.vice.com/en/article/5gaq88/a-rush-on-anna-biller.)
8. Kermode, 'Mark Kermode Reviews The Love Witch', 1:25, 3:43.
9. Manohla Dargis, 'Swinging Suburbia and the Sensual City', *New York Times*, 2 May 2008, https://www.nytimes.com/2008/05/02/movies/02viva.html.
10. Elena Gorfinkel, '"Dated Sexuality": Anna Biller's *Viva* and the Retrospective Life of Sexploitation Cinema', *Camera Obscura: Feminism, Culture, and Media Studies* 26, no. 3 (2011), 124.
11. Susan Sontag, 'Notes on "Camp"', in *Against Interpretation and Other Essays* (London: Penguin, 2009 [1961]), 283.
12. Simon Crook, 'Viva Review', *Empire*, 24 April 2009, https://www.empireonline.com/movies/reviews/viva-review/.

13. Anna Biller, '"Viva" director Anna Biller interview Part 1', uploaded 16 June 2010, video, 0:10, https://www.youtube.com/watch?v=-aq6WbxuwR4.
14. Gorfinkel, 'Unlikely Genres', 137–8.
15. Ibid., 137.
16. Judging from the costumes, *The Young Girls of Rochefort* is the clear point of reference in the final sequence of *Viva*. Biller also states that Demy's adaptation of the fairytale *Peau d'âne* directly influenced the aesthetics of *The Love Witch*. (Anna Biller, 'Under the Influence: Anna Biller on DONKEY SKIN', *Criterion Collection*, uploaded 15 February 2017, video, 2:10, https://www.youtube.com/watch?v=DD9MrwcE7o8.)
17. That said, Biller's connection to queer culture is limited by the fact that her works focus almost entirely on heterosexual women and their troubled relationships with men. These films do not concern queer sexuality very much at all. One exception is *Viva*, in which Barbi has a tryst with a beautiful African-American woman named Agnes (Robbin Ryan). It is one of the few relationships in the film that is not marked by exploitation of Barbi. It does not last, however, and the narrative treats the relationship as one of several sexual experiments that Barbi undertakes.
18. Robert Firsching, 'The Amazing World of Cult Movies', *Life of a Star*, accessed 10 March 2020, https://www.lifeofastar.com/incubus.html (site discontinued).
19. Jeffrey Sconce, '"Trashing" the Academy: Taste, Excess, and an Emerging Politics of Cinematic Style', *Screen* 36, no. 4 (1995), 371.
20. Ibid., 372.
21. Ibid., 373.
22. Anna Biller, 'Bzzzline talks to Anna Biller about her film 'A Visit from the Incubus' at Bleedfest', *Bzzzline*, video, 0:56, https://www.youtube.com/watch?v=OVC4YF7_wSE.
23. Ibid., 0:09.
24. There have been several explanations for the myth of incubus visitations, which have been reported as phenomena in cultures throughout history. One is that the sensation of being crushed or immobilised can arise when a person regains a level of wakeful consciousness from sleep but is still experiencing sleep paralysis. Hallucinations of an intruder as well as intense emotions of fear or sexual arousal are also common during such episodes. Additionally, real instances of rape and assaults on women while they are sleeping may contribute to the legend of a supernatural entity.
25. Biller, 'Bzzzline', 1:02.
26. Richard Dyer, *Only Entertainment*, 2nd edn (London: Routledge, 2002), 20.
27. Gorfinkel, '"Dated Sexuality"', 128.
28. Jason Klorfein, '"Myself as Queen": A Profile and Interview with Anna Biller', *Bright Lights Film Journal*, 31 January 2010, https://brightlightsfilm.com/myself-as-queen-a-profile-and-interview-with-anna-biller/.
29. Gorfinkel, '"Dated Sexuality"', 128.

30. Dennis Harvey, 'Film Review: "The Love Witch"', *Variety*, 20 July 2016, https://variety.com/2016/film/markets-festivals/the-love-witch-film-review-1201816145/; Nikki Baughan, 'The Love Witch', *Sight & Sound* 27, no. 4 (2017), 85.
31. Kermode, 'Mark Kermode reviews The Love Witch', 0:15.
32. Weston, 'Anna Biller's Pleasure Principles'.
33. Ibid.
34. Wayne C. Booth, *A Rhetoric of Irony* (Chicago: University of Chicago Press, 1974), ix.
35. I say 'many' occult exploitation films because these films are diverse. Although they may otherwise share similar themes or narrative patterns, they do not all possess the same tone of sleaze. For example, as a story of a housewife who searches for something more in her domestic existence, *Jack's Wife* contains little innuendo and limited titillating content. In contrast, *Blood Orgy of the She-Devils* is very different tonally, containing prolonged erotic spectacle through scenes of occult dancing and ritual.
36. Jeffrey Sconce, 'Introduction', in *Sleaze Artists: Cinema at the Margins of Taste, Style, and Politics*, ed. Jeffrey Sconce (Durham, NC: Duke University Press, 2007), 4.
37. Ibid., 4.
38. Biller in Sam Ankenbauer, 'Staging Pleasure: In Conversation with *The Love Witch*'s Anna Biller', interview, *Bright Lights Film Journal*, 1 May 2017, https://brightlightsfilm.com/staging-pleasure-in-conversation-with-the-love-witchs-anna-biller/.
39. Steve Macfarlane, '"I'm Actually Trying to Create a Film for Women": Anna Biller on *The Love Witch*', interview, *Filmmaker Magazine*, 23 June 2016, https://filmmakermagazine.com/98928-im-actually-trying-create-a-film-for-women-anna-biller-on-the-love-witch/; italics in the original.
40. Gorfinkel, '"Dated Sexuality"', 125.
41. Morgan, 'Spellbound', 42–3.
42. Ellen Freeman, '"I'm a Freak, I'm a Witch … I'm Just a Female"', interview with Anna Biller, *Lenny Letter*, 26 January 2018, https://www.lennyletter.com/story/interview-the-love-witch-filmmaker-anna-biller.
43. At the time of writing, Biller's next project is an adaptation of the tale of 'Bluebeard'. Long of interest to feminists, the fairytale is a story about a woman trapped in marriage to a murderer. Biller's career as a provocateur and chronicler of women's experience thus seems set to continue.

CHAPTER 6

Vaguely Disturbing: Humour in the Films of Athina Rachel Tsangari

In an interview for the Sydney Film Festival in 2011, Greek director Athina Rachel Tsangari observed that audiences have a range of responses to her second feature, *Attenberg* (2010):

> *Attenberg* is a kind of film that's very divisive. People have come out crying, have come out really giddy and laughing and thinking they have just watched a comedy. People leave irate, and people [leave] just thinking that it's a bunch of bollocks.[1]

Film critics, for their part, responded positively to Tsangari's film. Almost without exception, however, their praise came with caveats and descriptors that indicate the complex tonal experience of *Attenberg* and the oddly unsettling nature of Tsangari's work. Boyd van Hoeij calls *Attenberg* 'a captivating and vaguely disturbing experience',[2] Peter Bradshaw describes the film as 'almost unwatchably strange',[3] whereas David Stratton calls *Attenberg* 'funny', 'disturbing' and 'wonderfully done'.[4] Tsangari's follow-up short film *The Capsule* (2012) drew similar responses. Following its screening at the Locarno Film Festival, Eric Kohn described the short as a film of 'lively, shocking abstractions',[5] whereas Rod Machen calls *The Capsule* a story 'dealing with absurdity, cruelty, and sometimes joy'.[6] Such write-ups characterise Tsangari's work as an eccentric mix: as weird and off-beat, but also funny, compelling and original.

This tonal complexity demands closer investigation. As I have discussed throughout this book, women's provocations can be unwatchable, beautiful and obscene. *Attenberg* and *The Capsule* demonstrate that they can also be mixed with humour. Existing critical discussions of Tsangari's work persistently associate her with a spate of films that emerged out of Greece in the first decade of the twenty-first century named by critic Steve Rose as the Greek 'weird wave'. These 'brilliantly strange'[7] films are united by their bizarre plot scenarios, absurdist humour, unusual character behaviour, mannered performances and an estranging, non-naturalistic style.

The trend includes works by Dennis Iliadis (*Hardcore* [2004]), Panos H. Koutras (*Strella* [2009]), Yorgos Lanthimos (*Kinetta* [2005], *Dogtooth* [*Kynodontas*, 2009], *Alps* [*Alpeis*, 2011]) and Ektoras Lygizos (*Boy Eating the Bird's Food* [*To agori troei to fagito tou pouliou*, 2012]). Although the term 'weird wave' has not gone uncontested (Rosalind Galt argues that it is orientalising[8] and Tsangari herself says, 'We don't think we're weird, and we don't think we're a wave'[9]), the concept of weirdness is a useful hermeneutic for investigating these films' stylistic strategies and the tonal experience they create. Works by Tsangari – such as *Attenberg*, *The Capsule* and, to a lesser extent, *Chevalier* (2015) – can be further contextualised in relation to both the place of humour and the participation of women in the provocative avant-garde. As 'weird' films that are both startling and amusing, Tsangari's works highlight the subversive potential of humour and its connection to the author–recipient relation of provocation.

This chapter examines the interaction of amusement and discomfort in *Attenberg* and *The Capsule*, investigating how the films align with both provocation in the history of Western avant-garde art and women's critical utilisation of humour. Following the release of *Attenberg*, Tsangari notably said that she does not use 'psychology' in her films: 'I prefer biology or zoology. These are my tools.' She also states her interest in 'observing and deconstructing human behavior, movement, and speech'.[10] Filled with animal impressions, word games and jarring physical performances, *Attenberg* and *The Capsule* use stylistic strategies to denaturalise the characters' speech and behaviours in ways that both discomfit and invite spectatorial amusement. Speaking in Tsangari's preferred 'biological' terms, *Attenberg* and *The Capsule* expose the forces that act upon the human organism, particularly women. *Attenberg* observes the young protagonist's negotiations of gender and social expectations, depicting such norms as strange and difficult to embody; *The Capsule* takes a broader look at femininity as a behaviour that must be learned rather than intuited. Through their particular methods, Tsangari's films also carry the potential to unsettle even as they prompt laughter. Both *Attenberg* and *The Capsule* construct bizarre performances of womanhood that are uncomfortably embodied and denaturalised. Discomfort is an indispensable component in these films' observation of the forces that shape female subjects.

Investigating Tsangari's work not only provides an important account of a significant female auteur's work in global art cinema. Examining *Attenberg* and *The Capsule* also deepens critical appreciation of provocation and its various manifestations as an author–recipient relationship. In addition to shouting, leaving the cinema or looking away, laughter is another sign of spectatorial provocation – another affective response to negative emotion available to the spectator. Tsangari's work both demonstrates this and also shows the continuing application of this strategy as characteristic of her participation in the so-called 'weird wave'. *Attenberg* and *The Capsule* can also be understood as films operating within a history of women's creative practice that uses subversive humour, reminding of the continuing application and power of provocative comedy for women artists. Through their 'vaguely disturbing' humour, these films demonstrate the continuing uses of comedy as a critical strategy for women artists in subverting the social forces that produce the female: as humans, sexual beings and social subjects.

The Humorous-provocative Avant-garde

Tsangari's films are filled with non-naturalistic and performative moments. In her episodic debut feature *The Slow Business of Going* (2000), the protagonist Petra Going (Lizzie Curry Martinez) travels the world collecting memories of people and her encounters with them. In one episode, she befriends a young man in a sequence that turns into ostensive slapstick: he runs obsessive laps of the hotel where they meet, slips on banana peels and collides face first with a cream pie. *Attenberg* returns to such performative moments, albeit in a setting stripped of the signifiers of vaudevillian slapstick: the protagonist and her father play rhyming, associative word games where nouns devolve into nonsense, and they impersonate grebes and apes. *The Capsule* contains animal impersonations too, with the all-female cast hissing at each other like cats as their heads spin 180 degrees on their bodies. Even *Chevalier*, the most naturalistic of Tsangari's features thus far, contains moments that veer into the absurd: for instance, when two of the male protagonists compare their signature recipes in an aggressive, duel-like exchange. Tsangari's films have the capacity to evoke a range of reactions and, in their absurdity, these performative moments carry the potential to be both startling and humorous. Tsangari's films therefore raise broader questions about how humour and provocation go together in mutually reinforcing ways. To understand Tsangari's work involves taking a closer look at the relationship between laughter and the negative emotions of provocation, including in avant-garde art movements, feminist creative practice and the Greek weird wave.

The history of provocative art reveals that laughter can be a response to negative emotion. Reports of laughter appear frequently in accounts of the debuts of shocking artworks. For instance, along with reports of jeers and derisive outbursts, audience laughter apparently erupted at the exhibition of *Olympia* (Édouard Manet, 1863) at the 1865 Paris Salon,[11] the premiere of Igor Stravinsky's *The Rite of Spring* in May 1913,[12] and the screening of Catherine Breillat's *Anatomy of Hell* (*Anatomie de l'enfer*, 2004) at the 2004 International Toronto Film Festival.[13] Whether these audiences laughed out of embarrassment, scorn or genuine amusement is not always clear, yet such reports suggest that laughter can be a response to anxiety, uncertainty or embarrassment. Indeed, psychologists have long observed this phenomenon. Stanley Milgram's famous 'Behavioural Study of Obedience' at Yale University – in which participants were urged to administer intense electric shocks to an unseen (albeit fake) victim – is a paradigmatic example. Believing that they were genuinely administering electric shocks to another person, some participants reportedly laughed in nervous agitation.[14] As Milgram's experiment indicates, laughter can be a product of discomfort, including by extension the discomfort that provocation brings. Moreover, negative emotions can emerge concurrently with amusement in response to provocative art as a mixed response. Alfred Jarry's obscene comic play *Ubu the King* (*Ubu Roi*, 1896), Harold Pinter's 'comedy of menace' *The Birthday Party* (1957)[15] and Luis Buñuel's *The Exterminating Angel* (*El ángel exterminador*, 1962) are examples of such works, noted for their capacity to elicit laughter as well as more negative emotional disturbances. Such artworks can be tonally complex, simultaneously amusing and unsettling.

There is more to say, however, about the connection between humour and provocation. Humour frequently appears in modernist and postmodernist avant-gardes. The theatre of the absurd, dadaism and surrealism all share a rich comic vein, strategically using wordplay, buffoonery, gags, visual puns and absurdist non-sequiturs. Humour is intrinsic to these movements insofar as humour is often a consequence of avant-gardist attempts to break new aesthetic or stylistic ground. Humour is both a means and a by-product of the search for novelty. As Shun-liang Chao explains:

> Modernist arts (including literature) are often tinged or impregnated with humour ... stylistic innovation either intentionally or inadvertently creates a rich loam for the production of humour. Compelled by the pursuit of novelty, modernist artists engage themselves actively in formal experimentation in order to make it new.[16]

The novelty of the avant-garde can amuse, and for Chao, this humorousness emerges from the incongruity that novel aesthetics and representational strategies can produce. According to this 'incongruity theory' of comedy, humour arises from the breaking of spectators' expectations. Laughter emerges following 'the perception of ... something that violates our mental patterns and expectations'.[17] As such, the formal, aesthetic and thematic innovations of the avant-garde that enact incongruity have intrinsic capacity to amuse spectators. There are many examples of such humour in the twentieth-century arts. A well-known case is Marcel Duchamp's graffitied reproduction of the *Mona Lisa*, irreverently titled *L.H.O.O.Q.* (1919).[18] The sight of Da Vinci's famous sitter sporting a moustache not only undermines the onlookers' existing mental image of the famous lady, but it also conflicts with the genteelness of her bearing and expression. Duchamp's example shows that breaking expectation through incongruity can be amusing, but it can also have the effect of offending the onlooker. The elements that generate novelty and humour in dadaism, surrealism or the theatre of the absurd can also provoke.

Humour is also deeply connected to avant-garde art movements because of this subversive function and accordant capacity to promote critical thinking. Humour is a strategy to shock the onlooker – *épater les bourgeois* – that can also contain elements of social critique. Jokes can be intrinsically provocative because they stage a breaking of convention and norms – a breaking that can call into question established values and mores. In her discussion of the gag in Luis Buñuel's oeuvre, for example, Dominique Russell asserts:

> The gag was central to Dadaism, surrealism and other artistic -isms of the twenties and thirties, as a way to 'épater les bourgeois', but also as a liberating incongruity, a shaking out of old categories, an opening up to chance and unpredictability, to the freedom of the unconscious. The sharp edges of the joke are a provocation, a wink to those on the inside, a kick in the pants to those on the outside.[19]

Will Noonan agrees, noting the power of humour as 'a tool for questioning conventional modes of understanding',[20] and Chao observes that 'humour becomes for modernist artists one of the most effective ways of laughing with, at, or away anxiety' in the modern era.[21] Humour, provocation, avant-gardism and social critique are therefore tightly bound together and mutually reinforcing.

Although discussions of humour in the theatre of the absurd, dadaism and surrealism are dominated by male exemplars like Beckett, Duchamp and Buñuel, women artists have a strong place in the tradition of the humorous-provocative avant-garde. Humour and incongruity can serve subversive feminist purposes; instead of taking aim at the ruling classes or *épater les bourgeois*, feminist humour uses incongruities to highlight the hypocrisies of patriarchy and the naturalisation of gender norms. As B. Ruby Rich puts it, humour is 'a weapon of great power' with 'revolutionary potential as a deflator of the patriarchal order and an extraordinary leveler and re-inventor of dramatic structure'.[22] Many films by women accomplish this type of subversion through comedy. Rich cites Jan Oxenberg's *A Comedy in Six Unnatural Acts* (1975) and Věra Chytilová's *Daisies* (*Sedmikrásky*, 1966) as examples – Oxenberg's episodic film derives its humour from repeatedly setting up and then undermining stereotypes of lesbian women, whereas Chytilová's surrealist classic sees two young women swindle sumptuous dinners out of men of the ruling class. Another, earlier example is Germaine Dulac's *The Smiling Madame Beudet* (*La souriante Madame Beudet*, 1922/3), a film about a depressed housewife who fantasises about shooting her idiot husband; the man discovers the gun and foolishly assumes his wife is suicidal. Another film that cleaves closely to the surreal is Margaret Dodd's *This Woman is Not a Car* (1982), an unsettling, wry experimental short in which women's bodies are literally transformed into automobiles: a housewife's breasts become car headlights and a group of men erotically caress the body of a sedan. Like surrealist filmmakers, Dodd's film literalises a metaphor to create an intense incongruity – woman as car – that in turn illuminates men's objectification of women. (And indeed, this incongruity turns out to be not so incongruous after all: some men do treat women as objects.) This utilisation of incongruity operates as feminist critique, making men's behaviour ridiculous and exposing it to laughter. Women creatives have a history of using incongruity in this way, breaking expectations of femininity and the performance of gender.

This history of humorous-provocative art provides a context for *Attenberg* and *The Capsule* and a way of reading their starting humour; as I discuss below, Tsangari's work connects to a lineage of modernist and feminist work. Tsangari herself details this lineage for her self-described distantiated and black comedy style: classical dramatists Euripides, Aeschylus, Aristophanes and Sophocles; vaudevillian and physical screen performers such as the Marx Brothers, Buster Keaton and Monty Python; filmmakers Jean-Luc Godard and Michalis Kakogiannis; and dramatists Samuel Beckett and Harold Pinter.[23] Yet the history of the humorous-provocative art of the twentieth century not only reveals a context for Tsangari's work but also reveals one for post-millennium Greek cinema. Critic Steve Rose reads the films of Tsangari, Lanthimos and Koutras as allegorical critiques of the Greek state, which is also intrinsically linked to the institutions of family and patriarchy. However, the points of reference for the weird wave extend much further than the immediate circumstance of the domestic financial crisis or the contemporary inadequacies of the family. As Galt explains, these Greek films 'are hard to read, characterized by a narrative opacity that is often understood as allegorical'.[24] Christian Lorentzen writes that Lanthimos's works are 'unstable compounds of comedy and horror' and 'absurd'[25] – comments that apply to *The Capsule* and *Attenberg* also. Bradshaw calls *Attenberg* 'obscurely troubling'.[26] Yet such weirdness is not so strange; it is a manifestation of the incongruous, funny and provocative avant-garde in a post-millennium moment.

The Strange Animals of *Attenberg*

The opening scene of *Attenberg* confronts the onlooker with a jarring spectacle. It begins with an empty shot of a white plastered wall. Marina (Ariane Labed) enters from the right and Bella (Evangelia Randou) from the left. Marina hesitantly leans forward; Bella does too, more assertively. The pair begin to kiss, their tongues jutting and thrusting awkwardly (Figure 6.1). After a while, they stop. Marina says it feels disgusting, but Bella urges they try again: this time, their stiff tongues bump rhythmically. Marina pulls away a second time, but Bella insists they continue, asking, 'Do you want to learn or not?' Marina claims she's 'all out of spit'. The pair squabble, playfully begin to spit at each other, fall to the ground snarling and hissing like animals, before walking and crawling out of frame. Rose describes this moment in his article on the Greek weird wave as 'the worst kiss in screen history'.[27] The use of a cold open with tight framing and a presentational *mise en scène* does make for an unerotic and ostensive spectacle. Like many cinematic provocations, the moment seems to address the spectator directly, presenting the act of kissing as revolting and strange. The scene also presages further comic and absurd moments in *Attenberg*.

Figure 6.1 Marina and Bella kiss in the opening scene of *Attenberg*.

Later, during a conversation about the merits of tits and penises, Bella invites Marina to touch her breasts to 'try them out' (Marina says they are beautiful but that they do not arouse her). Several times in the film, Bella and Marina walk arm in arm in matching dresses, skipping and shuffling in choreographed movements down the streets of their town. *Attenberg* is populated with moments that, through their *mise en scène* and non-naturalist performances, seem to offer a direct challenge to the spectator: to amuse, confuse or disgust.

Although critics have characterised *Attenberg* by its disturbing strangeness, the film in fact corresponds to a recognisable narrative structure best described as a coming-of-age story. Marina is twenty-three years old and lives with her father Spyros (Vangelis Mourikis) in the Greek seaside town of Aspra Spitia; an economically depressed company settlement connected to an aluminium mill. Spyros is a retired architect and a widower; he is also dying of cancer. Marina works part time as a driver but spends much of her time looking after her father, watching David Attenborough documentaries or hanging out with Bella. Marina is intense, serious and deeply curious about the world of people and sex. She is clearly uncomfortable in the society of others and is also sexually inexperienced. She admits she finds the thought of intercourse repellent and strange: she describes penetrative sex using a mechanical metaphor, 'the piston'. Her curiosity and inexperience also lead her occasionally to ask questions about sexual taboos. In an early scene at the chemotherapy clinic, Marina asks her father: 'Do you ever imagine me naked?' Spyros replies, 'No, never. A father's mind represses such thoughts about his daughter.' Marina's routines change, however, when an engineer (Yorgos Lanthimos) arrives in town to work at the aluminium mill. Marina is curious about the man and embarks on an awkward journey of sexual discovery with him, all the while caring for her father and making preparations for his death. Importantly, Marina's late coming of age runs in close parallel with her father's decline, which Spyros overtly compares to Greek society and its progression. Looking out at the rooftops of Aspra Spitia – neatly designed but clearly bearing the signs of neglect – Spyros muses:

> It's as if we were designing ruins. As if calculating their eventual collapse with mathematical precision. Bourgeois arrogance, especially for a country that skipped the industrial age altogether. From shepherds to bulldozers, from bulldozers to mines, and from mines, straight to petit-bourgeois hysteria. We built an industrial colony on top of sheep pens, and thought we were making a revolution.

A real location, Aspra Spitia was built in the 1960s, and Tsangari describes it as a place that embodied the promise of Greece's ascendancy to a prosperous, Westernised state – a promise that experienced a 'setback' following the Greek junta and then the sovereign debt crisis.[28] *Attenberg* is thus a story about arrested development. It addresses Marina's difficulty in living alongside people and performing normative heterosexual sexuality; it also observes Greek society's own struggle to prosper according to the grand plans of its twentieth-century patriarchs.

The 'vaguely disturbing' humour of *Attenberg* is crucial to communicating these themes. The laughter that the film invites, as well as the way it connects its comedy to unsettling scenarios, is intrinsically subversive. *Attenberg* takes place within a recognisable social and historical world: a real Greek town in the late twentieth or early twenty-first century, populated with fathers, daughters and friends. Yet the plot is filled with non-naturalistic events, such as unusually frank conversations about sex between friends and family and awkward erotic acts staged directly for the camera. One scene that encapsulates both is when Marina goes to bed with the engineer and ceaselessly voices her inner monologue out loud, observing every detail of their encounter, which is clearly a turn-off for her lover ('I purse my lips slightly, and stick out my tongue', she narrates; 'I beg you, stop describing what you're doing', he replies). These stylistic qualities do not amount to the kind of provocative obscenities or unwatchabilities examined in previous chapters of this book. Rather, *Attenberg* constructs spectacles and performances of incongruity that break with naturalism, diverging from normative speech and behaviour – the fact that these moments usually relate to either sex or death heightens their discomfiting impropriety. In this respect, *Attenberg* corresponds to the type of disarming humour found in absurdism. As Noonan explains, absurdist humour intensifies the degree of incongruity typically found in mainstream comedy, presenting incongruities that are extreme enough that they 'cannot be resolved into any situation compatible with normal experience'.[29] By so clearly deviating from the norms of speech and behaviour (and indeed of film naturalism), Marina's behaviours in *Attenberg* are startling. However, the performance of incongruity in *Attenberg* also has a critical function, alluding to Marina's difficulties in living up to expectations of normative sexual, social and human development. Marios Psaras argues that *Attenberg* is best described as a queer text insofar as Marina repeatedly acts and behaves in non-normative ways.[30] For instance, this queering extends to the way Marina walks through town with Bella, which Tsangari terms 'silly walks' in homage to the Monty Python skit 'The Ministry of Silly Walks'.[31] Much like the surrealists and absurdists who came before Tsangari, the incongruous scenarios of *Attenberg* are provocative because they make normal acts – walking, talking and having sex – strange.

As Spyros's monologues suggest, a primary target of *Attenberg*'s humour is Greek society as it has been established, and mishandled, by older generations. Both Rose and Psaras observe that the Greek weird wave films emerged in close contemporaneity with the Greek financial crisis.[32] Rose notes, 'Attenberg might not speak directly about Greece's financial crisis, but in its own way, it reflects on today's generation of Greeks and the legacy they've been handed'.[33] Tsangari herself rejects this explanation as a 'tidy' and simplistic invention of film critics.[34] Nevertheless, the feeling that pervades throughout *Attenberg* is that the country's elders have left a damaged society to their youth, who feel both infantilised and unable to cope with the weight of their inheritance.[35] This is explicitly stated in one of Spyros's speeches in the days leading to his death: 'I'm an atheist old man, a toxic remnant of modernism, of post-Enlightenment, and I leave you in the hands of a new century without having taught you anything.' Moreover, Marina herself seems poorly equipped to live in the world; her disarmingly frank discussions about genitals and intercourse, her lack of career and her sexual inexperience characterise her as a twenty-three-year-old woman unable (or unwilling) to conform to social norms and unaccustomed to life without her father. When Spyros tells Marina he would like her to 'start living amongst others', she replies, 'That isn't how you taught me to live'. The challenge Marina faces is highlighted by the perverse logistical difficulty she has in arranging Spyros's funeral. Cremation is almost impossible in Greece due to opposition from the Orthodox Church, so Marina is forced to make elaborate arrangements to send Spyros's body to be cremated overseas in accordance with his wishes. This leads to absurd conversations with funeral directors in which Marina insists that Spyros's casket cannot be synthetic because he is allergic to such fabrics. Such a joke elicits so-called 'hollow laughter' – a kind of morbid, black humour premised on the absurdity of life and the inevitability of death. It not only gestures to the problems of a country that goes to such lengths to inhibit cremation; by extension, it also targets the idea of social and historical progress pursued by Greece's planners and patriarchs.

Attenberg includes many other strange moments, and these too can be aligned with the film's investigation (and refusal) of social norms. Another example is the rhyming games that Marina plays with her father, swapping similar-sounding words whose meanings stray, evolve and sometimes devolve into gibberish. The film's title, 'Attenberg', is itself a misspoken version of 'Attenborough', the surname of the British naturalist David Attenborough. Marina and Bella's silly walks through Aspra Spitia also make for confounding interludes as they shuffle, skip and pose their bodies as they walk up and down the footpath. The film gives no explanation for this activity, although their movements resemble the type of contortions performed by John Cleese in the Monty Python skit. Additionally, Marina, Spyros and Bella all imitate animals. Spyros and Marina do this quite regularly, sometimes after watching David Attenborough documentaries on the television in Spyros's bedroom, flapping their arms like birds or beating their chests like gorillas. Galt suggests that these moments of animal impersonation can be read as an attempt to transcend or reject human structures of language, embodiment and meaning. As Galt writes:

> Lawrence and McMahon ask if cinema can nurture identifications with animals or indeed as animals, and *Attenberg* takes seriously such a possibility as a mode of resistance to the lifeworld of austerity ... Being animals is a way to speak, imaginatively at least, outside of power, outside of death, and outside the norms of social relations.[36]

The provocative humour of *Attenberg* also emerges from these breakdowns in language and movement. Much of this comes across as either nonsense[37] or a kind of strange buffoonery. Yet their meaning can be read in terms of the deeper context that Spyros signals in relation to the social – as further refusals of the social requirements of the subject to act and speak in sanctioned ways. Buffoonery, here, is rebellion.

The strange humour of *Attenberg* is also squarely aimed at sex. Both the act of intercourse itself and the cultural requirement to be a sexual subject are made strange via spectacle and dialogue. The plot of *Attenberg* largely centres on Marina's sexual initiation as she rehearses and tries to embody acts of sexuality. However, in accordance with her worldview, the film overwhelmingly depicts sex, and the bodies that have sex, as strange and unerotic phenomena. *Attenberg* begins this process right away with the grotesque kissing scene at the start of the film. Marina complains about Bella's slug-like tongue and 'slobbery' saliva, declaring, 'I'm going to throw up ... How do people do it?' Giving up on the experiment, the two young women instead begin to hiss and snarl at each other like feral cats, a performance they take up far more comfortably and spontaneously than kissing. Following this opening, *Attenberg* repeatedly de-eroticises bodies, genitals and sex acts, likening them to inanimate objects, machines, animals and plants. In one scene, Bella tells Marina about a dream she had featuring a tree covered in penises: 'erect and milky and juicy ones', 'some with foreskins, others without'. Like Marina's earlier description of penetrative sex as 'the piston', Bella's words defamiliarise the body, making the penis plant-like in a way that mirrors Marina's earlier machine analogy.

Attenberg de-eroticises the female body too. Following a visit to the local swimming pool, Marina stares, expressionless, at her naked body in the mirror. The cool light of the changing room and direct camera-angle do little to beautify her naked form, instead inviting the spectator to observe Marina's breasts, face, legs, arms and pubic area in the same frank way that she does. In another scene, Marina performs a strange manipulation of her shoulder blades as Bella watches, jutting her scapulae and retracting them again, her T-shirt pulled up to expose her stretching skin (and, significantly, to conceal her head, rendering her effectively 'headless' in that moment). Such scenes accord with Tsangari's statement that she is more interested in biology and zoology than psychology. They invite the spectator to adopt an observational gaze and perceive the human form as a set of moving parts rather than connected to a psychologised and desiring sexual subject. Through these acts of estrangement, the moments also have the capacity to startle and amuse the onlooker. Indeed, the strange comedy of *Attenberg* depends on such moments. It is both funny and strange when Marina relentlessly narrates foreplay with the engineer ('I'll give you a blowjob … It's moving slightly … On its own, or is it you doing it?'). Yet this scene, like others before it, makes the body strange and denaturalises sex.

Through this estranging weirdness, *Attenberg* mounts a challenge to the social and sexual requirements of the subject, doing so in a way that enlists the incongruous, making for a funny, vaguely disturbing story. Psaras contends that this is an example of the queerness of the Greek weird wave more generally, not in terms of 'queer desire or non-normative sexuality' but as a queer challenge to the normative movements and uses of the body.[38] Certainly, there is a feminist implication to Tsangari's film also. There is no natural or normal model of feminine (hetero)sexuality in *Attenberg*. Even though Marina eventually does come of age – undertaking sexual exploration with the engineer and farewelling her father – the film does not suggest this leads to other types of normativity for Marina, such as marriage, a career or economic prosperity. After scattering Spyros's ashes in the ocean, Marina and Bella leave the seaside carpark separately, exiting the frame as the film concludes. It is not clear what they do next or where they will go. It is not certain if Marina has actually 'come of age', whether she will cease her silly walks, or whether she has changed her mind about 'the piston'. It is possible she has undergone only a sexual initiation and the loss of a much-loved parent, a journey without *telos*. With or without this certainty, however, Tsangari's story stages a disruption, a disturbance, and an eruption of laughter at the absurdities of negotiating life in a young, Greek, female body.

Girl-training in *The Capsule*

Tsangari's short film *The Capsule* pushes strangeness to further limits. Olaf Möller describes the film as 'weird, outrageous, constantly surprising'. He continues:

> Imagine the absurd dance routines from Tsangari's *Attenberg* expanded into a Gothic horror ballet under the sign of Maya Deren, Catherine Binet, and Katt Shea Ruben. A 35-minute piece of sponsored cinema in the form of a lesbian vampire movie featuring radiantly beautiful women and insanely cute animated creatures performing cryptic rituals.[39]

The Capsule is indeed a mysterious, surreal and startling story. The action unfolds in a mansion perched on the cliffs of a rocky island – a nowhere place outside of time. One night, several women come into existence inside the house: one materialises out of a mattress, another emerges from under a stack of chairs, and yet another appears inside the face of a different woman. There are six in total, and they are each welcomed by the mistress of the household (Ariane Labed). She tells them:

> I've been here since always and forever. I wait for you. I welcome you. I instruct you. I am here for you. To teach you anticipation, fear, rage, boredom, desire, thievery, power, jealousy. The last thing I will teach you is to lack.

True to her word, the mistress engages the new arrivals in a series of exercises. The students stand in rows facing each other, their heads twisting 180 degrees on their shoulders as they hiss viciously. They learn to dance in designer lingerie to America's 'A Horse With No Name'. They kneel in front of their mistress and confess their inner impulses. Eventually the mistress chooses one of the women to become immortal and take her place. As a final test, she bites her favourite pupil on the neck, but the young woman dies. 'You lucky little bitch', the mistress says as her would-be successor expires on the floor. The next day, she welcomes a new set of women to the island.

As an experimental short and commissioned artwork, *The Capsule* is a different type of film to *Attenberg*. Lydia Papadimitriou describes it as a 'surrealist-inspired, haute couture-clad fantasy' that is 'firmly placed within an avant-garde experimental tradition'.[40] The film was commissioned by the destefashioncollection of the DESTE Foundation for Contemporary Art. The commission invites an artist to respond to five fashion pieces with the objective to 'create parallels between the actual objects and the interpretations, leading viewers to a deeper understanding of how fashion can be perceived by the experienced eye'.[41] Fashion items therefore feature prominently in *The Capsule*: the mistress wears a gold-plated collar by Marc Jacobs for Louis Vuitton. At various points she dons a coat made of braided human hair by designer Sandra Backlund, a light-sensitive interactive dress made of organza and electronics by Ying Gao, and wooden shoes by Cat Potter. *The Capsule* was first exhibited as part of an installation in the window of Barneys on Madison Avenue, New York City, in June 2012, appearing alongside the work of other artists tasked with the same project: the art and design partnership M/M Paris, photographer Juergen Teller, artist Helmut Lang and poet Patrizia Cavalli. *The Capsule* also toured the festival circuit a few months later, beginning with the Locarno Film Festival and Thessaloniki International Film Festival. Tsangari cites a range of influences for *The Capsule*, describing it as both gothic and a 'horror fantasy vampire' film.[42] She references *A Girl in Black* (*To koritsi me ta mavra*, Michalis Kakogiannis, 1956) as inspiration for the black outfits worn by the women. Tsangari also notes the contribution of Polish artist Aleksandra Waliszewska, who co-wrote the film and provided the film's animations of strange creatures and faceless women.

The Capsule is darkly comic in its scenes of awkward dancing, confessions and animal mimicry. It is also surreal and unsettling in its tone and filled with imagery noted for its capacity to trigger the *unheimlich* or uncanny. Theories of the uncanny are extensive and contested; I define it here as the anxiety produced upon encountering objects and places that are simultaneously strange yet familiar. In his important essay on the concept, Sigmund Freud observes that the uncanny can be triggered by things such as inanimate objects that become animate, life-like replicas, repetitions, déjà vu and corpses – all reminders of the possibility of death.[43] However, critics such as Hal Foster have explored additional aesthetics of the uncanny too, such the obsolete and outmoded.[44] In keeping with such definitions, the women in *The Capsule* often appear puppet- or mannequin-like as they go about their lessons with the mistress. They look like women but at times act like marionettes or morph into animals. During the sequence where they dance to 'A Horse With No Name', for example, they wear bondage-inspired lingerie consisting of multiple satin straps and harnesses (Figure 6.2). The look recalls the images of rope-bound mannequins found in surrealist art works, such as Man Ray's *Vénus restaurée* (1936), a limbless reproduction of the *Venus de' Medici* (c. 101–100 BCE) bound in rope. Costumed thus, the women jerk around with non-naturalistic movements as they dance. The effect is partly that of ungainly creatures still learning to command their limbs, but it also resembles the movements of poorly handled marionettes. In keeping with this imagery, *The Capsule* also depicts the women's heads twisting on bodies like dolls, the favoured objects of artists like Hans Bellmer and Cindy Sherman. Moments of literalising of metaphor follow: the women hiss and snarl at each other in competition. They poke out their tongues and their necks extend. At one point their heads appear on an animated serpentine creature resembling the mythical many-headed Hydra. The film evokes the uncanny in other ways too. *The Capsule* takes place on an unknown rocky island displaced from time and history, recalling the landscapes of Salvador Dalí, Giorgio de Chirico and Yves Tanguy. The setting of *The Capsule* therefore evokes a surreal uncanniness and *dépaysement*, the sense of being in an unfamiliar place that creates a disquieting viewing experience. The uncanniness of this imagery has the capacity to unsettle the onlooker. Yet, like *Attenberg*, the film draws from the comedy of incongruity, where beautiful women in designer clothing fail to pose beautifully or erotically, instead jerking uncomfortably or contorting their faces like animals. As Michael Richardson explains, humour in surrealism 'tends to induce a feeling of discomfort even as it causes us to laugh',[45] and indeed, *The Capsule* draws on uncanny surrealist aesthetics to create its unsettling atmosphere.

Through bizarre imagery and setting, *The Capsule* stages the struggle to emerge as a female entity, and in this respect, it is thematically similar to *Attenberg*. However, the film deals with its topic in a way that frames the process as an uncanny rather than absurd spectacle, making it both comic and unsettling. With its clear mistress–pupil arrangement, *The Capsule* fits into a trend of what So Mayer calls 'girl-training' narratives, which are films that illustrate how girls are socialised in gender and sexual roles.[46]

Figure 6.2 The women dance to 'A Horse With No Name' in *The Capsule*.

Such films suggest that femininity is not a natural instinct but must be taught and learned; in other words, they dramatise Simone de Beauvoir's pronouncement 'One is not born, but rather becomes, a woman'.[47] *The Capsule* is an uncanny retelling of the girl-training narrative. Like in *Attenberg*, the 'girls' in *The Capsule* are adult women;[48] unlike in *Attenberg*, however, the story is abstracted from a historical time and place, lending a mythic and strange quality to its narrative. For example, while singing and dancing to 'A Horse With No Name', the women move awkwardly, jerking and shuffling in an ungainly dance. Their elaborate underwear – designed by bondage-inspired label Bordelle – and stiletto heels intensify the incongruity of the spectacle. There is a discordance between the eroticism of the clothes, lingerie and stilettos and the physical performance. This amounts not only to a making strange of the performance of femininity, but a making of it as uncanny. Some sequences in *The Capsule* also involve the uncanny literalising of metaphor that Russell identifies as characteristic of surrealism. There is a competitive element to the girl-training in *The Capsule*; only one woman will be chosen to take the mistress's place and live eternally. Jealousy is also part of their training, as the mistress declares. The women literally hiss at each other, poking and wiggling red-stained tongues at one another in a rather alarming Medusan display. *The Capsule* is thus provocative because it presents a world where everything is strange, but especially the women.

Girl-training as a narrative and theme also connects with broader traditions in women's creative practice – ones that also gesture to the performativity of femininity. The theorisation of the masquerade is particularly applicable in further understanding *The Capsule* and its uncanny depiction of femininity. Drawing upon Joan Riviere's concept, Mary Ann Doane describes masquerade as a type of performance of femininity by women that reveals its constructedness and 'effects a defamiliarisation of female iconography'.[49] This occurs via the excessive performance or 'hyperbolisation' of femininity and its associated movements, manners, clothing, modes of speech and so forth. Doane herself formulates the concept in response to Freud's argument that women cannot perceive themselves as objects of representation and signification. However, 'flaunting' femininity allows women to objectify it, hold it 'at a distance' and reveal its performativity.[50] Doing so resists the hegemonic and patriarchal naturalisation of gender performance. Masquerade is thus political. As Kathleen Rowe notes, 'masquerade retains the distance necessary for critique, but a distance that is Brechtian and politicized, created by the subject between herself and various forms of representation available to her'.[51] To return to *The Capsule*, the film makes girl-training perceivable through a process of estrangement and uncanniness. It is also made perceivable by the mistress herself, who masquerades and 'demonstrates' how to be a woman to her pupils. As an embodiment of the eternal feminine, the mistress is a figure of essential womanliness. However, her depiction in *The Capsule* paradoxically estranges womanliness too. She is not only unable to train anyone to take her place, she also, in a fitting analogy, wears clothing that is completely impractical to wear. In one scene she appears in shoes by Cat Potter made of wooden blocks; they are so large and inflexible as to be intolerable (or at least extremely difficult) to walk in. The mistress's garments of human hair and electronic lights are similarly fantastical and impractical. This *haute couture* is non-functional for a living, moving human body. *The Capsule* therefore fulfils its remit as a commissioned work by the DESTE Foundation. It incorporates high fashion into its story as DESTE requires, but it also uses these garments symbolically, commenting on the impossibility of embodying an essential, eternal femininity. This gender performance is as unobtainable to actual women as wooden shoes are impossible to walk in.

The Capsule shows Tsangari's provocations are aligned with feminist strategies of denaturalising femininity, making an uncanny spectacle out of girl-training and supporting this through the mistress's female masquerade. In place of a performance of femininity, the women of *The Capsule* jerk their bodies like fleshy marionettes and hiss like animals. As Tsangari says about her directorial approach, the film involves 'observing and deconstructing human behavior, movement, and speech', and doing so to a bizarre extreme.[52] Compared to *Attenberg*, the film takes this approach to a surrealist degree: it is further away from naturalism and stranger than Marina's odd experiments. The stakes of girl-training are higher too, in ways that connect with the provocative black humour of surrealism. The women of *The Capsule* have no other purpose than to learn the ways of womanhood. If they fail, they will die after four days. The absurdity of gender performance and femininity is therefore tied to a broader absurdity of the limited duration of human life. The weird trials and lessons lead to nothing more than a moment of anti-climax in which the mistress's chosen pupil falls to the ground, dead. The mistress calls her 'a lucky little bitch' – the joke is that death is not only an inevitability for mortals, but perhaps also a welcome escape from girl-training.

Female Organisms

Following the release of *Attenberg* and *The Capsule*, Tsangari's work has become less ostensive and performative, and, arguably, less unsettling as a result. In the years since, she has worked on several projects, directing for television series *Borgia* (Canal+; ZDF; ORF; Sky Italia, 2011–14) and the romantic drama *Trigonometry* (BBC Two, 2020), and working as producer on several features.[53] In 2015, she directed her most successful feature to date, the ensemble film *Chevalier*, co-written with Efthymis Filippou. *Chevalier* is a clear satire of Greek masculinity: a group of middle-class, middle-aged men take a boating trip together and engage in small competitions to determine who is 'the best in general'. They assemble IKEA furniture, swap recipes and measure their erections to gauge their relative merits as men. *Chevalier* bears some of the tonal and thematic hallmarks of Tsangari's earlier work. Critics note the bizarreness of the set-up: Stephen A. Russell calls it 'surreal', while Kate Jinx describes it as 'completely absurd by the end of the film'.[54] Tsangari herself describes the film as the male version of *The Capsule* insofar as it is a story about male instead of female competitiveness. Yet *Chevalier* also breaks with *Attenberg* and *The Capsule* because the film is far more naturalistic. It features no performative acts of animal mimicry and no moments of associative wordplay. The competition is certainly ludicrous given that 'the best in general' is an utterly undefinable status, but *Chevalier* does not achieve its humour through startling or uncanny incongruities. In her critique of the film, Ruby Mastrodimos notes that some reviewers seemed disappointed that the film showed restraint and maintained its focus on the amusing banalities of male behaviour.[55] *Chevalier* is thus best thought of as an evolution of Tsangari's style, demonstrating how her strategies can be deployed in ways that gesture to everyday human foibles rather than the strangeness of the human condition.

Nevertheless, *Attenberg* and *The Capsule* reveal Tsangari's power as a provocateur and inheritor of both the humorous-provocative and feminist avant-gardes. This enduring link between comedy and provocation is easily eclipsed by the legacy of the devastating and extreme post-millennium art cinema moment that I have discussed throughout this book, with its masculinised stance of aggression towards the spectator, violence and hyper-explicitness. Tsangari's films also show how vaguely disturbing humour can emerge in the work of a contemporary woman auteur. Surreal uncanniness and absurd incongruities in these films illuminate the awkwardness of embodiment as a human organism, particularly a female one. In *Attenberg*, existence as a young Greek woman is difficult and uncomfortable for Marina; it is also soon to be without guiding authority as Spyros, the deeply loved father and patriarch, speeds towards literal and symbolic expiration. In keeping with the surreal and absurdist avant-gardes, the provocative humour of both *Attenberg* and *The Capsule* is informed by the inevitability of death. Whereas the mistress of *The Capsule* lives eternal, her students have a life cycle of only four days. Their confessions, competitions and awkward dance lessons amount to little, and the mistress is condemned to eternal repetition of the girl-training process. Although *Attenberg* is not so bleak, Spyros's illness signifies the inevitability of Marina's own process of ageing as well as the pressure to 'move forward' and integrate with the adult world before it is too late. *Attenberg* and *The Capsule* are thus provocations that premise their humour on a morbid darkness. As Richardson observes, humour in surrealism

> reminds us that we know nothing of why we are here or what purpose we are really supposed to serve. At the same time, it asserts that those purposes imposed upon us by society (above all as a result of loyalty to family, nation and church) are false and to be opposed.[56]

Noonan makes a similar remark about absurdist humour, which gestures towards the 'apparent meaninglessness of human existence'.[57] In *Attenberg* and *The Capsule*, the demands of normative femininity become even more comedic, strange and unsettling given the inevitability of the subject's death. The struggle of girl-training, of embodying femininity, seems even more facile and futile – funny and strange though it may be along the way.

Importantly, Tsangari's work also demonstrates the continuing value of provocative humour for women who document the enduring absurdity of life as a female – a project that continues into the twenty-first century. As Hélène Cixous declares in her influential essay 'The Laugh of the Medusa', women possess the power 'to blow up the law, to break up the "truth" with laughter'.[58] As Cixous observes, humour is integral to the provocations and agitations of women. From Germaine Dulac to Margaret Dodd, humour has served a subversive purpose to highlight women's experience under patriarchy and its inadequacies. Tsangari forms a link with this trend, and Tsangari's approach is to expose the conditions of gendered life as strange or, indeed, 'weird'. Patriarchy and gender norms are not necessarily devastating or hyper-disfiguring in Tsangari's work; instead, they are absurd, amusing and vaguely disturbing in their effects on the individual. As Mastrodimos summarises in her review of *Chevalier*, Tsangari opts to express ideas that indicate the disfiguring effects of heteronormative gender expectations, but she does so with a focus on the more banal impositions. As Mastrodimos posits: 'Maybe not all men are murderers or rapists or sociopaths; sometimes they really are just a group of bored, rich idiots on a yacht measuring their erections.'[59] Likewise, maybe not all women are anarchic creatures like Chytilová's characters or desperate individuals like Dulac's housewife, challenging the patriarchy with anarchic vandalism or dreams of violence. Maybe they are just awkward products of a strange culture – a world that demands they have piston-like sex, dance in lingerie and kiss with spit.

Notes

1. Athina Rachel Tsangari, 'SFF2011 – Athina Rachel Tsangari – Attenberg', Sydney Film Festival, uploaded 13 June 2011, video, 2:02, https://www.youtube.com/watch?v=YheMJQf9BtI.
2. Boyd van Hoeij, 'Attenberg', *Variety*, 12 September 2010, https://variety.com/2010/film/markets-festivals/attenberg-1117943531/.
3. Peter Bradshaw, 'Attenberg – Review', *Guardian*, 2 September 2011, https://www.theguardian.com/film/2011/sep/01/attenberg-film-review.
4. David Stratton, 'David Stratton Previews Attenberg', Sydney Film Festival, uploaded 23 May 2011, video, 0:39, https://www.youtube.com/watch?v=v5uVmL6PT54.
5. Eric Kohn, 'Why Athena [sic] Rachel Tsangari's "The Capsule" Is More Than a Twisted Fashion Show', *Indiewire*, 4 August 2012, https://www.indiewire.com/2012/08/locarno-review-why-athena-rachel-tsangaris-the-capsule-is-more-than-a-twisted-fashion-show-45788/.
6. Rod Machen, 'FilmStruck Focus: The Short Films of Athina Rachel Tsangari', *Cinapse*, 16 February 2017, https://cinapse.co/filmstruck-focus-the-short-films-of-athina-rachel-tsangari-fa8886108343.
7. Steve Rose, 'Attenberg, Dogtooth and the Weird Wave of Greek Cinema', *Guardian*, 27 August 2011, https://www.theguardian.com/film/2011/aug/27/attenberg-dogtooth-greece-cinema.
8. Rosalind Galt, 'The Animal Logic of Contemporary Greek Cinema', *Framework: The Journal of Cinema and Media* 58, no. 1–2 (2017), 7.
9. Athina Rachel Tsangari, '"Attenberg" Q&A | Athina Rachel Tsangari', uploaded 7 October 2015, filmed at Film Society Lincoln Center, New York, NY, video, 11:57, https://www.youtube.com/watch?v=hlCiOjkCAb8.
10. Anthony Kaufman, 'Athina Rachel Tsangari Studies the Species in Attenberg', *Village Voice*, 23 March 2011, https://www.villagevoice.com/2011/03/23/athina-rachel-tsangari-studies-the-species-in-attenberg/.
11. T. J. Clark, *The Painting of Modern Life: Paris in the Art of Manet and His Followers* (Princeton: Princeton University Press, 1984), 83.
12. Igor Stravinsky, *Stravinsky: An Autobiography* (New York: Simon & Schuster, 1936), 72.
13. Carina Chocano, 'Anatomy of a Film Both Graphic, Abstract', *Los Angeles Times*, 27 September 2004, https://www.latimes.com/archives/la-xpm-2004-sep-27-et-breillat27-story.html.
14. Stanley Milgram, 'Behavioral Study of Obedience', *Journal of Abnormal and Social Psychology* 67, no. 4 (1963), 375.

15. The term 'comedy of menace' was coined by drama critic Irving Wardle, albeit retracted later and rejected by Pinter himself. Tsangari has stated that Pinter is an inspiration in her own work.
16. Shun-liang Chao, '"A Tomato is Also a Child's Balloon": Surrealist Humour as a Moral Attitude', in *Humour in the Arts: New Perspectives*, eds Vivienne Westbrook and Shun-liang Chao (New York: Routledge, 2019), 194.
17. John Morreall, 'Philosophy of Humor', in *The Stanford Encyclopedia of Philosophy*, ed. Edward N. Zalta, 20 August 2020, https://plato.stanford.edu/archives/fall2020/entries/humor.
18. Spoken aloud, the title sounds like the French phrase 'Elle a chaud au cul', meaning 'She is hot in the arse'.
19. Dominique Russell, 'Buñuel: Storytelling, Desire and the Question of Rape', in *Rape in Art Cinema*, ed. Dominique Russell (New York: Continuum, 2010), 47.
20. Will Noonan, 'Absurdist Humor', in *Encyclopedia of Humor Studies*, ed. Salvatore Attardo (Thousand Oaks: Sage, 2014), 3.
21. Chao, '"A Tomato is Also a Child's Balloon"', 195.
22. B. Ruby Rich, 'In the Name of Feminist Film Criticism', *Chick Flicks: Theories and Memories of the Feminist Film Movement* (Durham, NC: Duke University Press, 1998), 77.
23. Athina Rachel Tsangari, 'GFF Live: Athina Rachel Tsangari', Göteborg Film Festival, streamed live on 5 February 2016, video, 40:53, https://www.youtube.com/watch?v=FbV_IsuKJto.
24. Galt, 'The Animal Logic of Contemporary Greek Cinema', 7.
25. Christian Lorentzen, 'Yorgos Lanthimos's Silly Sadism', *New Republic*, 10 November 2017, https://newrepublic.com/article/145440/trope-trap-yorgos-lanthimos-distinctive-absurd-new-film-strangely-familiar.
26. Bradshaw, 'Attenberg'.
27. Rose, 'Attenberg, Dogtooth'.
28. Tsangari, '"Attenberg" Q&A', 27:59.
29. Noonan, 'Absurdist Humor', 1.
30. Marios Psaras, *The Queer Greek Weird Wave: Ethics, Politics and the Crisis of Meaning* (Cham: Palgrave Macmillan, 2016), 126.
31. Athina Rachel Tsangari, 'NYFF Live | Athina Rachel Tsangari | Chevalier', uploaded 23 October 2015, filmed at Film Society Lincoln Center, New York, NY, video, 30:18, https://www.youtube.com/watch?v=x6BQJ_EUB-Q.
32. Psaras notes the contemporaneity of the Greek financial crisis and the so-called 'Greek weird wave' but is cautious not to draw too simplistic a connection between them, acknowledging various historical and cultural factors that, he argues, influence contemporary Greek cinema. In a measured statement, Psaras observes that contemporary Greek cinema has an 'intrinsic (thematic and formal) alignment with its historical moment', including the financial crisis, but also 'draws on a long genealogy of local production that has insistently and self-consciously pitted its oppositional aesthetics against

the nation's official historicity and self-representation'. (Psaras, *The Queer Greek Weird Wave*, 4–5)
33. Rose, 'Attenberg, Dogtooth'.
34. Tsangari, 'NYFF Live', 23:10.
35. Such a reading is particularly applicable to Yorgos Lanthimos's brutal provocation *Dogtooth*, which tells the story of three adult children imprisoned in a family compound by their father. The three are continually lied to and infantilised by their parents, ostensibly to 'protect' them from the corrupting influence of the outside world.
36. Galt, 'The Animal Logic of Contemporary Greek Cinema', 16.
37. Nonsense is a form of humour that breaks down established signification and representational strategies. In its place, a new language or system of meaning is constructed. Lewis Carroll's poem 'Jabberwocky' is a paradigmatic example of literary nonsense; although using invented words, the poem is nonetheless intelligible on its own terms as a story of a hero, a sword and a monster. Although nonsense can be productively compared to absurdism, the absurd tends to communicate the nonsensical using typical signification. As Wim Tigges writes, 'In nonsense, language *creates* a reality, in the absurd, language *represents* a senseless reality'. (Emphasis in original; Wim Tigges, *An Anatomy of Literary Nonsense* [Amsterdam: Rodopi, 1988], 128.)
38. Psaras, *The Queer Greek Weird Wave*, 126.
39. Olaf Möller, 'The Capsule', *Film Comment* 49, no. 1 (2013), 40.
40. Lydia Papadimitriou, 'Straitened Circumstances', *Sight & Sound* 23, no. 1 (2013), 23.
41. DESTE Foundation for Contemporary Art, 'DESTEFASHION COLLECTION', https://deste.gr/destefashioncollection/.
42. Athina Rachel Tsangari, 'Athina Rachel Tsangari Interview – The Seventh Art', uploaded 24 January 2013, filmed at Onsite Gallery at OCAD University, Toronto, ON, video, 6:10, https://www.youtube.com/watch?v=w5ISGKi-NtI.
43. Sigmund Freud, 'The Uncanny', in *The Standard Edition of the Complete Psychological Works of Sigmund Freud*, trans. James Strachey, eds James Strachey, Anna Freud, Alix Strachey and Alan Tyson (London: Hogarth, 1953), 241.
44. Hal Foster, *Compulsive Beauty* (Cambridge, MA: Massachusetts Institute of Technology, 1993), 164.
45. Michael Richardson, 'Black Humour', in *Surrealism: Key Concepts*, eds Krzysztof Fijalkowski and Michael Richardson (Abingdon: Routledge, 2016), 207.
46. So Mayer, *Political Animals: The New Feminist Cinema* (London: Bloomsbury, 2015), 143.
47. Simone de Beauvoir, *The Second Sex*, ed. and trans. H. M. Parshley (London: Vintage, 1997), 295.

48. There is an important clue in interpreting *The Capsule* insofar as Tsangari describes it as a female version of *Chevalier*. The film is quite clearly a story about male competition and masculinity, whereas *The Capsule* concerns female competition and girl-training. Both involve notions of the gender ideal: in *The Capsule* this is framed as the eternal feminine, whereas in *Chevalier* it is understood competitively and relationally as 'the best in general', as termed by the male characters in the film. See: Tsangari, 'NYFF Live | Athina Rachel Tsangari | Chevalier', 20:40.
49. Mary Ann Doane, 'Film and the Masquerade: Theorising the Female Spectator', *Screen* 23, no. 3–4 (1982), 82.
50. Ibid.
51. Kathleen Rowe, *The Unruly Woman: Gender and the Genres of Laughter* (Austin: University of Texas Press, 1995), 6–7.
52. Kaufman, 'Athina Rachel Tsangari Studies the Species'.
53. As of December 2021, Tsangari currently has twenty-six credits as producer, co-producer and executive producer overall (fifteen from 2013 onwards). These include feature films, documentary, short films and television.
54. Stephen A. Russell with Kate Jinx and Kate Fitzpatrick, 'MIFF Selects: The Festival Gems You Need to Revisit and New Ones to Discover', *SBS*, 21 July 2021, https://www.sbs.com.au/movies/article/2021/07/19/miff-selects-festival-gems-you-need-revisit-and-new-ones-discover.
55. Ruby Mastrodimos, 'Six Men, a Yacht, and an Erection: Troubled Masculinities in Athina Rachel Tsangari's *Chevalier*', *Another Gaze* 4 (2020), 64.
56. Richardson, 'Black Humour', 207.
57. Noonan, 'Absurdist Humor', 1.
58. Hélène Cixous, 'The Laugh of the Medusa', trans. Keith Cohen and Paula Cohen, *Signs* 1, no. 4 (1976), 888.
59. Mastrodimos, 'Six Men', 67.

Conclusion

As this book took shape over the months of 2020, two controversies occurred that spoke directly to its themes. In July, the Melbourne International Film Festival (MIFF) caused a stir in the Australian arts community when it announced that it would remove Sandra Wollner's film *The Trouble with Being Born* (2020) from its online festival programme. The film had premiered at the Berlin International Film Festival earlier that year where it won the Special Jury Prize, and it was subsequently selected for MIFF's programme. The film tells the story of an android named Elli (Lena Watson[1]) who has the appearance of a ten-year-old child. In the first half of the film, she appears to be in a sexual relationship with her adult owner, whom she calls 'Papa'.[2] MIFF initially programmed *The Trouble with Being Born* for its in-person event but was forced to pivot online due to a COVID-19 outbreak in the city of Melbourne. Before the festival went live, however, MIFF announced that it would remove Wollner's film:

> The safety and wellbeing of the MIFF community and broader Australian public is of paramount concern to the festival. With this in mind, we have made the decision to withdraw Sandra Wollner's film *The Trouble with Being Born*. While the Australian Classification Board had cleared the film to screen in this year's festival, after receiving specific, expert advice – in relation to both the content within the film and the online context of MIFF 68½ – we have made the decision to remove the film.[3]

MIFF's decision occurred during, and in response to, the writing of an article about the film for the city's daily broadsheet, *The Age*. The piece included the opinion of two psychologists who suggested that *The Trouble with Being Born* could be used as material for paedophiles. These experts also expressed worry about the impact of at-home streaming during lockdown, which meant the film could be watched alone and thus used as pornographic material.[4] (Of the two psychologists, one had only watched part of *The Trouble with Being Born* and the other had not seen it at all.) After being informed of these expert opinions and invited to respond prior to publication, MIFF announced that it would no longer show Wollner's film.[5] This removal of *The Trouble with Being Born* sparked controversy in the Australian film community. Esteemed critic David Stratton called it a 'shameful and unforgivable' act of censorship,[6] while Tom Ryan called it 'a truly shocking scenario'.[7] Wollner herself insisted that no one who had seen her film could accuse it of promoting child sexual abuse, deliberately or otherwise. She also rejected MIFF's assertion that the decision was made in the interests of public safety, claiming it was instead a pre-emptive capitulation to an outrage that had not actually materialised – a response to a 'ghost mob'.[8] Yet this event confirmed a series of broader points. Cinema continues to confront dark and taboo topics, probing the extremes of human experience and behaviour, and women are frequently the authors of such works. The controversy around *The Trouble with Being Born* also confirmed this book's *raison d'être* – to account for provocative works by women.

Less than a month after MIFF's withdrawal of *The Trouble with Being Born*, another incident arose involving a female filmmaker. In August 2020, the international streaming service Netflix released a poster and trailer for an upcoming release, French filmmaker Maïmouna Doucouré's debut feature *Cuties* (*Mignonnes*, 2020). The film tells the story of an eleven-year-old Senegalese girl, Amy (Fathia Youssouf), who lives in France with her mother and siblings. Amy befriends a group of local girls and joins their dance troupe, and they perform manoeuvres that seemingly imitate the sexualised routines of adult women. The film centres upon Amy's desire to belong, as well as the negotiation of her identity as Senegalese and French. Doucouré's film also explores the pleasure of dancing and how it serves as the basis for friendship and creativity between girls. *Cuties* had an auspicious beginning. In 2017, Doucouré's script won a Sundance Institute Global Filmmaking Award, and the completed film was awarded a directing prize at the Sundance Film Festival in 2020.[9] The trouble came when Netflix acquired *Cuties* and promoted the film using a poster that some claimed sexualised the girl characters. The incident achieved global media attention, making international news and producing a response from both Netflix and Doucouré (who is herself French-Senegalese). In some internet forums, the film was also implicated in the #SaveTheChildren and QAnon conspiracy theory, which centres on the unproven claim that a circle of elite individuals are engaged in secretive, organised paedophilic sex abuse.[10] Netflix replaced the poster for *Cuties* and issued an apology, saying the marketing materials were not representative of the film.[11] Doucouré also penned a response in the *Washington Post*, claiming that her film was a condemnation of the sexualisation of children. She also justified the discomfort that some viewers experienced in watching *Cuties*:

> Some people have found certain scenes in my film uncomfortable to watch. But if one really listens to 11-year-old girls, their lives are uncomfortable ... I wanted to open people's eyes to what's truly happening in schools and on social media, forcing them to confront images of young girls made up, dressed up and dancing suggestively to imitate their favorite pop icon.[12]

Like Wollner, Doucouré had many defenders. Notably amongst these, a group of female filmmakers and artists published an open letter in solidarity with the director, saying, 'As filmmakers and writers who have been at times attacked for our approach to sexuality and gender, we extend our passionate support to you and your film'.[13] Signed by Anna Biller, Lizzie Borden, Nan Goldin, Julie Dash, Mary Harron and others, the signatories are precisely who they claim to be: a group of female creators who are unafraid to engage with sexuality and gender to unsettle their audiences.

It is important to note that *The Trouble with Being Born* and *Cuties* are very different films, even though both provoke anxieties about children: Wollner's film is a meditation on artificial intelligence and human loneliness, whereas Doucouré's is a coming-of-age film about contemporary girlhood and identity. Yet these films' difference reinforces the significance of investigating provocation as something that women engage with as part of the strategies, themes and ambitions of their work. *The Trouble with Being Born* and *Cuties* are timely reminders that, whether for good or ill, cinema has the capacity to provoke public debate and censure. It remains a suspicious and suspectable medium, frequently accused, even presumed, of the exploitation and aggravation of social ills. Cinema is capable of generating 'strong negative emotions on the part of specific individuals or groups'.[14] Indeed, film has been doing so since the earliest surrealist works and avant-garde experiments.

Moreover, as Wollner and Doucouré's films demonstrate, cinema will continue to provoke into the future. As I mentioned in the introduction to this book, more confronting films by women emerge each year on the art and festival film circuit. *The Scary of Sixty-First* (Dasha Nekrasova, 2021), a darkly comic denunciation of convicted sex offender Jeffrey Epstein, co-written by Dasha Nekrasova and Madeline Quinn, premiered at the 2021 Berlin International Film Festival. While praised by critics such as Alexandra Heller-Nicholas, David Robb and Guy Lodge,[15] Simon Miraudo worried that *The Scary of Sixty-First* could be defamatory,[16] whereas others criticised it as 'outrage-baiting'[17] and 'shitposting as cinema'.[18] Only months later at the 2021 Cannes Film Festival,

Julia Ducournau's *Titane* (2021) won the Palme d'Or, becoming only the second film directed by a woman to do so. Recounting the travails of a serial-killing young woman with a literal automobile fetish, critical praise for *Titane* universally acknowledged the film as a violent, shocking, transgressive and visceral experience.[19] The appearance of these films is significant. Whereas critics such as James Quandt and Anthony Julius suggest the transgressive impulse in art has been exhausted of its critical potential, this does not mean the public has become immune to shock or offence.[20] Cinema has not lost its power to provoke. The question of how this quality surfaces in women's art cinema remains mostly unaccounted for.

Inspired by the likes of Wollner, Doucouré, Nekrasova, Ducournau and their predecessors, this book has investigated women's participation in film provocation. To do so, I have offered a definition of provocation as a relation between texts and recipients, frequently involving the impression of authorial intentionality. For the spectator, provocation is defined by a negative viewing experience involving an absence of viewing pleasure and the marked presence of displeasure: shock, offense or discomfort. Provocation is a valuable and portable critical concept. It provides a way of exploring negative relations between texts and recipients: of speaking about films that unsettle or challenge the onlooker and highlighting how and why they disturb the spectator. The discourses of cinema and avant-garde art reveal that provocation has been symbolically conceptualised as a masculine activity: aggression towards a spectator, a slap in the face or 'fork in the eye', and a violent arousal from a state of passivity.[21] From nineteenth-century philosophy to post-millennium film criticism, the provocateur as a figure has been similarly gendered. He is a rebel and maverick; an artist unafraid of being disliked; an anti-people-pleaser; a male genius-hero. This way of thinking is not a relic of ossified Western ideas sourced from earlier centuries. It persists in contemporary cinema discourse and culture, evidenced in the foregrounding of male auteurs in the press and the counter-construction of women's art cinema as humanist, accessible and '"artistic" in a middle-brow understanding of the term'.[22] There are, of course, exceptions: critics describe Catherine Breillat as a provocateur to the point of cliché, and the term appears in descriptions of individual films by Isabella Eklöf, Lisa Aschan, Mary Harron, Ana Kokkinos and others. Yet symbolically and discursively, provocation is unmistakably gendered as masculine.

Women's place in this is the conundrum that inspired this study. Female filmmakers are largely omitted from the discourse of provocation, yet they are simultaneously and obviously present throughout cinema history: from Věra Chytilová to Sandra Wollner, from Liliana Cavani to Julia

Ducournau. This book has sought to challenge the gendering of provocation and redress a discourse of transgressive auteurism that still slants towards male auteurs. It is not my goal, however, to respond to women's comparative elision simply and only by providing a list of female provocateurs. While it is important to challenge the discourse that engenders a male-dominated canon and enact what Ivone Margulies and Jeremi Szaniawski call 'feminist correctives to existing and accepted canons', enshrining a counter-canon of women provocateurs has not been my objective.[23] I have instead proposed that analysing how films achieve provocation via a set of case studies offers a novel way of investigating women's filmmaking. Studying provocation provides a point of entry – a critical lens – to uncovering the diverse manifestations of women's creativity. It is a way of discovering and spotlighting filmmakers whose work leans towards confrontational, challenging topics. Studying provocation therefore also offers a productive way of appreciating the diversity of women's work. Patricia White observes that women directors 'continue to be interpellated discursively and positioned industrially' in ways that frame their films as tasteful tales of the human spirit rather than politically subversive, feminist or, indeed, provocative.[24] The story of women's creativity in cinema cannot be complete without acknowledgement and investigation of the practitioners who dare to challenge their audience.

I have approached this task by investigating individual women auteurs and the films of theirs that generate negative reactions. This book is thus a contribution to ongoing scholarship on the work of women filmmakers. Even though 'the female auteur' is a concept that feminist scholars have challenged repeatedly, it remains a fascinating and productive avenue of enquiry. I chose to include directors who align with a Western tradition connected with an avant-garde practice of provocation. As I define it, this provocation is an extension of the avant-garde impulse toward novelty and subversion of the status quo: the aesthetic norms and sensibilities of the ruling classes. My study has drawn from filmmakers based (and trained) within Western film industries, investigating three French filmmakers, Catherine Breillat, Lucile Hadžihalilović and Claire Denis; two Swedes, Lisa Aschan and Isabella Eklöf; and one filmmaker each from Australia, the United States and Greece: Jennifer Kent, Anna Biller and Athina Rachel Tsangari, respectively. As I signalled in the introduction to this book, provocative films by women from other national contexts offer a compelling further avenue for investigation, and their strategies may intersect and diverge from the ones this book identifies in illuminating ways.

Studying these directors is not a way of deriving an essentialised idea of how women provoke; my point throughout has been that women's work is diverse and heterogeneous. However, there are commonalities among the case studies in this book that suggest thematic trends amongst provocative art films by women. I will outline these here. First, the films in this book form groupings around particular stylistic approaches to provocation: aesthetic strategies that work alongside or in support of the subject matter. At various points throughout this book, I have argued that there is an assumed aesthetics of provocation. Usually, this aesthetics is defined as a kind of scopic offense or transgression: obscenity, explicitness, discordant imagery, ugliness or other forms of visual affrontery. This is an aesthetics that film discourses also frequently gender as masculine due to its supposed active, aggressive and assaultive quality. The directors I have considered in this book demonstrate that provocation can be achieved through other stylistic strategies too. A study of women's provocative works reveals that there is no fixed aesthetics of provocation. To be certain, women can provoke by engaging with the kind of visual transgressions typically associated with provocative cinema, such as obscenity in Catherine Breillat's *Anatomy of Hell* (*Anatomie de l'enfer*, 2004) and the graphic depiction of sexual violence in Isabella Eklöf's *Holiday* (2018). Yet Lisa Aschan's tense *She Monkeys* (*Apflickorna*, 2011) and Claire Denis's sensual filmmaking in *Trouble Every Day* (2001) and *High Life* (2018) reveal that filmmakers can also arouse discomfort through the evocation of tone and sensation. Lucile Hadžihalilović's important works *Innocence* (2004) and *Évolution* (2015) demonstrate that the pleasures of the pretty can unsettle an audience even as they extend visual pleasure; these films trouble the onlooker by aestheticising scenarios that may, or may not, show children in peril. Athina Rachel Tsangari's *Attenberg* (2010) and *The Capsule* (2012) show that women provoke by drawing upon traditions of black humour, and Anna Biller demonstrates that provocation can be achieved through the languages of genre in *A Visit from the Incubus* (2001), *Viva* (2007) and *The Love Witch* (2016).

Second, the films in this study all address themes that are relevant to the shared social and cultural experience of being a woman. Sexuality emerges regularly as a topic, from *Anatomy of Hell* and *She Monkeys* to *Viva* and *High Life*. Sexual violence is a central theme too, not just in the films that graphically depict rape onscreen such as *Holiday* and *The Nightingale* but also in Anna Biller's films *A Visit from the Incubus* and *Viva* as well as Claire Denis's *Bastards* (*Les salauds*, 2013) and *High Life*. Childhood and coming of age are central too, particularly in Hadžihalilović's *Innocence* and *Évolution*, and female 'girl-training' as a process of identity formation surfaces in Tsangari's *Attenberg* and *The Capsule* as well. Provocative films by women thus centre on experiences that are formative and widely shared by those who move through the world as women: sexuality and the possibilities of desire, connection and pleasure, the ever-present risk of sexual violence, and the experience of femininity as expressed through coming-of-age narratives. Told as stories and spectacle, these topics have intrinsic potential to provoke negative reactions as well as negative identifications with the shame and abjection of onscreen protagonists. What these films tell us is that women filmmakers provoke to reveal the aspects of women's lives that remain challenging to experience; the 'shit [that] is supposed to stay hidden', as Eklöf puts it.[25] To paraphrase Doucouré: it can be uncomfortable watching films about women's lives because women's lives are uncomfortable.

The question of cinematic provocation – of why a film elicits negative emotions – remains a contentious but important issue for women. In his largely negative account of transgressive avant-gardism, Anthony Julius questions the value of provocation in the contemporary arts, which he argues has now reached the limits of its subversive potential. He concludes that transgressive artworks, which he largely treats as synonymous with provocative works, only alienate onlookers from their deeply held ethics:

> Taboo-breaking art can thus cause acute but unresolvable psychological discomfort, while also challenging us to admit this discomfort into the repertoire of our aesthetic responses. If we lost our taboos we would be unrecognisable to ourselves: this art gives us the vertiginous experience of our own otherness ... the truth is that only rarely do works with this ambition lead us towards any sense of new possibility. More usually, their effect is to induce a momentary anxiety about our grip on given actualities.[26]

Julius's argument is that this anxiety diminishes the onlooker and 'only rarely' leads to progressive ends. Provocation hurts and cannot open the mind, only temporarily disorient. Yet there is a defence of provocation here, one that is vital to keep in view. Not all viewers experience unhappiness with being challenged – some close their eyes, shout at the screen or leave the cinema, whereas others remain with, and within, the darkness. To recall Tania Modleski's insight that I mention at the beginning of this book, some are counterphobic viewers who want to face the film.[27] In addition, what Julius calls 'given actualities' can indeed be an onlooker's ethics, such as their anti-racism, anti-homophobia and feminism. However, they can also be the norms and hegemonies that really are worth subverting: racist ideologies, homophobia or sexist beliefs. They can be norms that foreclose and make possibilities unimaginable, including possibilities for women. An individual who possesses such actualities should, indeed I argue must, vertiginously experience themselves as other. This is the continuing value of provocation; the enduring need to challenge, or at least question, given actualities. Women have an interest in making this challenge.

Notes

1. The name Lena Watson is a pseudonym, assumed to conceal the identity of the young actor and protect her from any unwanted attention that her role might generate. Her face was also obscured throughout the film by a silicone mask – a feature that not only concealed her identity but added to her artificial appearance.
2. In the second half of the film, Elli runs away and is adopted by an elderly woman, who repurposes her as a grandson figure named 'Emil'.
3. Melbourne International Film Festival (@MIFFofficial), 'The safety and wellbeing of the MIFF community and broader Australian public is of paramount concern to the festival. With this in mind, we have made the decision to withdraw Sandra Wollner's film *The Trouble with Being Born*. While the Australian Classification Board had cleared the film to screen in this year's festival, after receiving specific, expert advice – in relation to both the content within the film and the online context of MIFF 68½ – we have made the decision to remove the film. Anyone who has pre-purchased a ticket will be refunded in full', Tweet, 31 July 2020, https://twitter.com/miffofficial/status/1288942442918682625?lang=en.
4. Karl Quinn, 'Melbourne International Film Festival Dumps Android Child Sex Film', *The Age*, 30 July 2020, https://www.theage.com.au/culture/movies/melbourne-international-film-festival-dumps-android-child-sex-film-20200725-p55fdr.html.
5. Karl Quinn, 'Melbourne International Film Festival (online) – Karl Quinn Responds to Tom Ryan and David Stratton about MIFF's Decision to Pull THE TROUBLE WITH BEING BORN from its Program and Reports on His Interview with the Director Sandra Wollner', *Film Alert 101*, 20 August 2020, http://filmalert101.blogspot.com/2020/08/melbourne-international-film-festival_20.html.
6. David Stratton, 'Melbourne International Film Festival (online) – David Stratton Has Some Thoughts About MIFF's Decision to Withdraw THE TROUBLE WITH BEING BORN (Sandra Wollner, Austria, 2020) From its Program', *Film Alert 101*, 12 August 2020, http://filmalert101.blogspot.com/2020/08/melbourne-international-film-festival_12.html.
7. Tom Ryan, 'Melbourne International Film Festival (Online) – Tom Ryan Takes Exception to MIFF Censoring its Selection', *Film Alert 101*, 11 August 2020, https://filmalert101.blogspot.com/2020/08/melbourne-international-film-festival.html.
8. Alison Taylor, '"A Ghost Mob": Interview with Sandra Wollner', interview, *Senses of Cinema* 96 (2020), https://www.sensesofcinema.com/2020/interviews/a-ghost-mob-interview-with-sandra-wollner/.

9. The directing prize was awarded for the category of World Cinema Dramatic.
10. Stephanie McNeal, 'The Netflix Movie "Cuties" Has Become the Latest Target of #SaveTheChildren Conspiracy Theorists', *Buzzfeed News*, 12 September 2020, https://www.buzzfeednews.com/article/stephaniemcneal/netflix-cuties-qanon-target.
11. Netflix (@Netflix), 'We're deeply sorry for the inappropriate artwork that we used for Mignonnes/Cuties. It was not OK, nor was it representative of this French film which won an award at Sundance. We've now updated the pictures and description', Tweet, 21 August 2020, https://twitter.com/netflix/status/1296486375211053057?ref_src=twsrc%5Etfw.
12. Maïmouna Doucouré, 'I Directed "Cuties". This is What you Need to Know About Modern Girlhood', *Washington Post*, 15 September 2020, https://www.washingtonpost.com/opinions/cuties-director-maimouna-doucoure-why-i-made-the-film/2020/09/15/7e0ee406-f78b-11ea-a275-1a2c2d36e1f1_story.html.
13. Chaz Ebert, 'An Open Letter to Cuties Director Maïmouna Doucouré from Female Filmmakers', *RogerEbert.com*, 2 October 2020, https://www.rogerebert.com/features/an-open-letter-to-cuties-director-ma%C3%AFmouna-doucour%C3%A9-from-female-filmmakers.
14. Mette Hjort, 'The Problem with Provocation: On Lars von Trier, Enfant Terrible of Danish Art Film', *Kinema: A Journal for Film and Audiovisual Media* 36 (2011), 6.
15. Alexandra Heller-Nicholas, 'THE SCARY OF SIXTY-FIRST (Berlinale 2021)', *Alliance of Women Film Journalists*, 2 March 2021, https://awfj.org/blog/2021/03/02/the-scary-of-sixty-first-berlinale-2021-review-by-alexandra-heller-nicholas/; David Robb, 'Review: *The Scary of Sixty-First* Gleefully and Defiantly Captures the Zeitgeist', *Slant*, 5 March, 2021, https://www.slantmagazine.com/film/the-scary-of-sixty-first-review-dasha-nekrasova/; Guy Lodge, '"The Scary of Sixty-First" Review: Nothing Is out of Bounds in This Rude, Riotous, Post-Epstein Horror', *Variety*, 2 March 2021, https://variety.com/2021/film/reviews/the-scary-of-sixty-first-review-1234919297/.
16. Simon Miraudo, 'Spider-Man: No Way Home, Licorice Pizza, The French Dispatch, The Scary of Sixty-First, The Worst Person in the World & Ghostbusters: Afterlife (Movie Squad Podcast #56)', *Movie Squad*, RTR FM, podcast audio, 10:30, 17 December 2021, https://rtrfm.com.au/story/spider-man-no-way-home-licorice-pizza-the-french-dispatch-the-scary-of-sixty-first-the-worst-person-in-the-world-ghostbusters-afterlife-movie-squad-podcast-56/.
17. Cath Clarke, 'The Scary of Sixty-First Review – Outrage-Baiting Jeffrey Epstein Conspiracy Chiller', *Guardian*, 2 March 2022, https://www.theguardian.com/film/2022/mar/01/the-scary-of-sixty-first-review-jeffrey-epstein-conspiracy.

18. Cain Noble-Davies, 'The Scary of Sixty-First', *FilmInk*, 16 December 2021, https://www.filmink.com.au/reviews/the-scary-of-sixty-first/.
19. See, for example: John Bleasdale, 'Titane is a Full-Throttle Masterpiece of Road-Rage, Violence and Queerness', *Sight & Sound*, 14 July 2021, https://www.bfi.org.uk/sight-and-sound/reviews/titane-is-a-full-throttle-masterpiece-road-rage-violence-queerness-julia-ducournau; Mark Kermode, 'Titane Review – Agathe Rousselle is Extraordinary in Palme d'Or-Winning Body Horror', *Observer*, 26 December 2021, https://www.theguardian.com/film/2021/dec/26/titane-review-julia-ducournau-palme-dor-cronenberg-agathe-rousselle; Sheila O'Malley, 'Titane', *RogerEbert.com*, 1 October 2021, https://www.rogerebert.com/reviews/titane-movie-review-2021; Isabel Sandoval, 'Interview: Julia Ducournau', *Film Comment*, 12 October 2021, https://www.filmcomment.com/blog/interview-julia-ducournau-titane-isabel-sandoval/.
20. James Quandt, 'Flesh & Blood: Sex and Violence in Recent French Cinema', *Artforum* 42, no. 6 (2004), 128; Anthony Julius, *Transgressions: The Offences of Art* (London: Thames & Hudson, 2002).
21. Roger Ebert used this phrase to describe Lars von Trier's *Antichrist* (2009), writing: 'Its images are a fork in the eye'. (Roger Ebert, 'Cannes #6: A Devil's Advocate for "Antichrist"', *RogerEbert.com*, 19 May 2009, https://www.rogerebert.com/roger-ebert/cannes-6-a-devils-advocate-for-antichrist.)
22. Patricia White, *Women's Cinema, World Cinema: Projecting Contemporary Feminisms* (Durham, NC: Duke University Press, 2015), 68.
23. Ivone Margulies and Jeremi Szaniawski, 'Introduction: On Women's Films: Moving Thought Across Worlds and Generations', in *On Women's Films: Across Worlds and Generations*, eds Ivone Margulies and Jeremi Szaniawski (New York: Bloomsbury, 2019), 2.
24. White, *Women's Cinema, World Cinema*, 69.
25. Isabella Eklöf, 'In Conversation with Isabella Eklof', *Another Gaze*, uploaded 5 August 2019, video, 3:36, https://www. anothergaze.com/conversation-interview-isabella-eklof/.
26. Julius, *Transgressions*, 191.
27. Tania Modleski, 'Women's Cinema as Counterphobic Cinema: Doris Wishman as the Last Auteur', in *Sleaze Artists: Cinema at the Margins of Taste, Style, and Politics*, ed. Jeffrey Sconce (Durham, NC: Duke University Press, 2007), 62.

Filmography

35 Shots of Rum (*35 rhums*), Claire Denis, 2008.
A Clockwork Orange, Stanley Kubrick, 1971.
A Comedy in Six Unnatural Acts, Jan Oxenberg, 1975.
A Girl in Black (*To koritsi me ta mavra*), Michalis Kakogiannis, 1956.
A Real Young Girl (*Une vraie jeune fille*), Catherine Breillat, 1976.
A Visit from the Incubus, Anna Biller, 2001.
All that Heaven Allows, Douglas Sirk, 1955.
Alps (*Alpeis*), Yorgos Lanthimos, 2011.
Amelie (*Le fabuleux destin d'Amélie Poulain*), Jean-Pierre Jeunet, 2001.
American Psycho, Mary Harron, 2000.
An Andalusian Dog (*Un chien andalou*), Luis Buñuel, 1929.
Anatomy of Hell (*Anatomie de l'enfer*), Catherine Breillat, 2004.
And Nothing Happened, Naima Ramos-Chapman, 2016.
Antichrist, Lars von Trier, 2009.
Attenberg, Athina Rachel Tsangari, 2010.
Baise-moi, Coralie Trinh Thi and Virginie Despentes, 2000.
Bastards (*Les salauds*), Claire Denis, 2013.
Beau travail, Claire Denis, 1999.
Bell, Book and Candle, Richard Quine, 1958.
Benny's Video, Michael Haneke, 1992.
Blood Orgy of the She-Devils, Ted V. Mikels, 1973.
Border (*Gräns*), Ali Abbasi, 2018.
Borgia, Canal+; ZDF; ORF; Sky Italia, 2011–14.
Born in Flames, Lizzie Borden, 1983.
Boy Eating the Bird's Food (*To agori troei to fagito tou pouliou*), Ektoras Lygizos, 2012.
Boys Don't Cry, Kimberly Peirce, 1999.
Brief Crossing (*Brève traversée*), Catherine Breillat, 2001.
Calamity Jane, David Butler, 1953.

FILMOGRAPHY

Camille 2000, Radley Metzger, 1969.
Carne, Gaspar Noé, 1991.
Certain Women, Kelly Reichardt, 2016.
Chevalier, Athina Rachel Tsangari, 2015.
Chocolat, Claire Denis, 1988.
Christmas on Earth, Barbara Rubin, 1963.
Circumstance, Maryam Keshavarz, 2011.
Climax, Gaspar Noé, 2018.
Code Blue, Urszula Antoniak, 2011.
Cuties (*Mignonnes*), Maïmouna Doucouré, 2020.
Daisies (*Sedmikrásky*), Věra Chytilová, 1966.
Dancer in the Dark, Lars von Trier, 2000.
Daughters of Satan, Hollingsworth Morse, 1972.
De Natura, Lucile Hadžihalilović, 2018.
Diary of a Nudist, Doris Wishman, 1961.
Dirty Like an Angel (*Sale comme un ange*), Catherine Breillat, 1991.
Dogtooth (*Kynodontas*), Yorgos Lanthimos, 2009.
Dogville, Lars von Trier, 2003.
Donkey Skin (*Peau d'âne*), Jacques Demy, 1970.
Dunia, Jocelyne Saab, 2005.
Dyketactics, Barbara Hammer, 1974.
Earwig, Lucile Hadžihalilović, 2021.
Enter the Void, Gaspar Noé, 2009.
Évolution, Lucile Hadžihalilović, 2015.
Fairy Ballet, Anna Biller, 1998.
Fat Girl (*À ma sœur!*), Catherine Breillat, 2001.
Fire, Deepa Mehta, 1996.
First Cow, Kelly Reichardt, 2019.
Funny Games, Michael Haneke, 1997.
Fuses, Carolee Schneemann, 1964–6.
Gertrud, Carl Theodor Dreyer, 1964.
Girlhood, Céline Sciamma, 2014.
Good Boys Use Condoms, Lucile Hadžihalilović, 1998.
Hardcore, Dennis Iliadis, 2004
Head On, Ana Kokkinos, 1998.
Hero (*Ying xiong*), Zhang Yimou, 2002.
High Life, Claire Denis, 2018.
Holiday, Isabella Eklöf, 2018.
Holy Smoke!, Jane Campion, 1999.
Hypocrites, Lois Weber, 1915.

I Can't Sleep (*J'ai pas sommeil*), Claire Denis, 1994.
I Stand Alone (*Seul contre tous*), Gaspar Noé, 1998.
In My Skin (*Dans ma peau*), Marina de Van, 2002.
In the Cut, Jane Campion, 2003.
Innocence, Lucile Hadžihalilović, 2004.
Irréversible, Gaspar Noé, 2002.
Jack's Wife, George A. Romero, 1972.
Je tu il elle, Chantal Akerman, 1974.
Kinetta, Yorgos Lanthimos, 2005.
La première mort de Nono, Lucile Hadžihalilović, 1987.
Last Tango in Paris, Bernardo Bertolucci, 1972.
Last Year at Marienbad (*L'Année dernière à Marienbad*), Alain Resnais, 1961.
Let the Right One In (*Låt den rätte komma in*), Tomas Alfredson, 2008.
Lola Montès, Max Ophüls, 1955.
Lost in Translation, Sofia Coppola, 2003.
Manderlay, Lars von Trier, 2005.
Marie Antoinette, Sofia Coppola, 2006.
Mark of the Witch, Tom Moore, 1970.
Mimi (*La bouche de Jean-Pierre*), Lucile Hadžihalilović, 1996.
Monster, Patty Jenkins, 2003.
Moulin Rouge!, Baz Luhrmann, 2001.
Multiple Orgasm, Barbara Hammer, 1976.
Mustang, Deniz Gamze Ergüven, 2015.
Nectar, Lucile Hadžihalilović, 2014.
Nénette and Boni (*Nénette et Boni*), Claire Denis, 1996.
Nitrate Kisses, Barbara Hammer, 1992.
No Fear, No Die (*S'en fout la mort*), Claire Denis, 1990.
Nocturnal Uproar (*Tapage nocturne*), Catherine Breillat, 1979.
Nomadland, Chloé Zhao, 2020.
Notes from Underground (*Noter fra kælderen*), Isabella Eklöf, 2011.
On the Silver Globe (*Na srebrnym globie*), Andrzej Żuławski, 1988.
Only the Brave, Ana Kokkinos, 1994.
Perfect Love (*Parfait amour!*), Catherine Breillat, 1996.
Persepolis, Marjane Satrapi and Vincent Paronnaud, 2007.
Portrait of a Lady on Fire (*Portrait de la jeune fille en feu*), Céline Sciamma, 2019.
Rape, John Lennon and Yoko Ono, 1969.
Rashomon, Akira Kurosawa, 1950.
Revenge, Coralie Fargeat, 2017.
Romance, Catherine Breillat, 1999.

Salò, or the 120 Days of Sodom (*Salò o le 120 giornate di Sodoma*), Pier Paolo Pasolini, 1975.
Sex Is Comedy, Catherine Breillat, 2002.
She Killed in Ecstasy, Jess Franco, 1971.
She Monkeys (*Apflickorna*), Lisa Aschan, 2011.
Strella, Panos H. Koutras, 2009.
Suburban Roulette, Herschell Gordon Lewis, 1968.
TERROR NULLIUS: A Political Revenge Fable in 3 Acts, Soda_Jerk, 2018.
The 400 Blows (*Les quatre cents coups*), François Truffaut, 1959.
The Accused, Jonathan Kaplan, 1988.
The Babadook, Jennifer Kent, 2014.
The Bad Sleep Well (*Warui yatsu hodo yoku nemuru*), Akira Kurosawa, 1960.
The Battle of Algiers (*La battaglia di Algeri*), Gillo Pontecorvo, 1966.
The Book of Revelation, Ana Kokkinos, 2006.
The Capsule, Athina Rachel Tsangari, 2012.
The Celebration (*Festen*), Thomas Vinterberg, 1998.
The Decameron (*Il Decameron*), Pier Paolo Pasolini, 1971.
The Exterminating Angel (*El ángel exterminador*), Luis Buñuel, 1962.
The Golden Age (*L'Âge d'Or*), Luis Buñuel, 1930.
The Harvey Girls, George Sidney, 1946.
The Holy Girl (*La niña santa*), Lucrecia Martel, 2004.
The Hypnotist, Anna Biller, 2001.
The Idiots (*Idioterne*), Lars von Trier, 1998.
The Intruder (*L'intrus*), Claire Denis, 2004.
The Love Witch, Anna Biller, 2016.
The Monkey's Mask, Samantha Lang, 2000.
The Night Porter (*Il portiere di note*), Liliana Cavani, 1974.
The Nightingale, Jennifer Kent, 2018.
The Rider, Chloé Zhao, 2017.
The Scary of Sixty-First, Dasha Nekrasova, 2020.
The Searchers, John Ford, 1956.
The Slow Business of Going, Athina Rachel Tsangari, 2000.
The Smiling Madame Beudet (*La souriante Madame Beudet*), Germaine Dulac, 1922/3.
The Trouble with Being Born, Sandra Wollner, 2020.
The Virgin Suicides, Sofia Coppola, 1999.
The Watermelon Woman, Cheryl Dunye, 1996.
The White Ribbon (*Das weiße Band*), Michael Haneke, 2009.
The Young Girls of Rochefort (*Les Desmoiselles de Rochefort*), Jacques Demy, 1967.

This Woman is Not a Car, Margaret Dodd, 1982.
Three Examples of Myself as Queen, Anna Biller, 1994.
Titane, Julia Ducournau, 2021.
Tomboy, Céline Sciamma, 2011.
Traps (*Pasti, pasti, pastičky*), Věra Chytilová, 1998.
Trash Humpers, Harmony Korine, 2009.
Trigonometry, BBC Two, 2020.
Trouble Every Day, Claire Denis, 2001.
Twentynine Palms, Bruno Dumont, 2003.
Vampyros Lesbos, Jess Franco, 1970.
Violation, Madeleine Sims-Fewer and Dusty Mancinelli, 2020.
Virgin (*36 fillette*), Catherine Breillat, 1988.
Viva, Anna Biller, 2007.
Water Lilies (*Naissance des pieuvres*), Céline Sciamma, 2007.
Water, Deepa Mehta, 2005.
We Need to Talk About Kevin, Lynne Ramsay, 2011.
White Material, Claire Denis, 2009.
Willkommen in Barbaristan, Isabella Eklöf, 2009.
Women I Love, Barbara Hammer, 1976.

Bibliography

Adams, Sam. 'Claire Denis on *Bastards* and Tough Women.' *The Dissolve*, 24 October 2013. https://thedissolve.com/features/interview/235-claire-denis-on-bastards-and-tough-women/.

Ankenbauer, Sam. 'Staging Pleasure: In Conversation with *The Love Witch*'s Anna Biller.' *Bright Lights Film Journal*, 1 May 2017. https://brightlightsfilm.com/staging-pleasure-in-conversation-with-the-love-witchs-anna-biller/.

Anton, Saul. 'Catherine Breillat Opens Up About "Romance", Sex and Censorship.' *Indiewire*, 23 September 1999. https://www.indiewire.com/1999/09/interview-catherine-breillat-opens-up-about-romance-sex-and-censorship-82059/.

Artaud, Antonin. *The Theatre and Its Double*. Translated by Mary Caroline Richards. New York: Grove Press, 1958.

Artaud, Antonin. '"The Theatre and Its Double" (1931–7).' In *Artaud on Theatre*, edited by Claude Schumacher and Brian Singleton, 95–156. London: Methuen Drama, 1989.

Asibong, Andrew. 'Viral Women: Singular, Collective and Progressive Infection in *Hiroshima mon amour*, *Les Yeux sans visage* and *Trouble Every Day*.' In *Alienation and Alterity: Otherness in Modern and Contemporary Francophone Contexts*, edited by Helen Vassallo and Paul Cooke, 93–114. Oxford: Peter Lang, 2009.

Aspley, Keith. *Historical Dictionary of Surrealism*. Lanham: Scarecrow Press, 2010.

Astruc, Alexandre. 'The Birth of a New Avant Garde: *La caméra-stylo* (France, 1948).' In *Film Manifestos and Global Cinema Cultures: A Critical Anthology*, edited by Scott MacKenzie, 603–6. Berkeley: University of California Press, 2014.

Balsom, Erika. '*High Life*.' *Sight & Sound* 29, no. 6 (2019): 61–2.

Batchelor, David. *Chromophobia*. London: Reaktion Books, 2000.

Battersby, Christine. *Gender and Genius: Towards a Feminist Aesthetics*. London: The Women's Press, 1989.

Baughan, Nikki. 'The Love Witch.' *Sight & Sound* 27, no. 4 (2017): 85–6.

Bayley, Stephen. *Ugly: The Aesthetics of Everything*. New York: Overlook Press, 2012.
Beauvoir, Simone. *The Second Sex*. Translated and edited by H. M. Parshley. London: Vintage, 1997.
Berger, John. *Ways of Seeing*. London: Penguin, 2008.
Bernheimer, Charles. 'Manet's Olympia: The Figuration of Scandal.' *Poetics Today* 10, no. 2 (1989): 255–77.
Beugnet, Martine. *Cinema and Sensation: French Film and the Art of Transgression*. Edinburgh: Edinburgh University Press, 2007.
Beugnet, Martine. *Claire Denis*. Manchester: Manchester University Press, 2004.
Biller, Anna. '"Viva" director Anna Biller interview Part 1.' YouTube video, 8:50. 16 June 2010. https://www.youtube.com/watch?v=-aq6WbxuwR4.
Biller, Anna. 'Bzzzline talks to Anna Biller about her film "A Visit from the Incubus" at Bleedfest.' *Bzzzline*. YouTube video, 4:53. 3 April 2011. https://www.youtube.com/watch?v=OVC4YF7_wSE.
Biller, Anna. 'Under the Influence: Anna Biller on DONKEY SKIN.' *Criterion Collection*. YouTube video, 4:22. 15 February 2017. https://www.youtube.com/watch?v=DD9MrwcE7o8.
Billson, Anne. 'Does the "Female Gaze" Make Sexual Violence on Film Any Less Repugnant?' *Guardian*, 2 August 2019. https://www.theguardian.com/film/2019/aug/02/the-female-gaze-does-it-make-sexual-violence-on-film-any-less-repugnant.
Blaetz, Robin. 'Introduction.' In *Women's Experimental Cinema: Critical Frameworks*, edited by Robin Blaetz, 1–19. Durham, NC: Duke University Press, 2007.
Bleasdale, John. 'Titane is a Full-Throttle Masterpiece of Road-Rage, Violence and Queerness.' *Sight & Sound*, 14 July 2021. https://www.bfi.org.uk/sight-and-sound/reviews/titane-is-a-full-throttle-masterpiece-road-rage-violence-queerness-julia-ducournau.
Boa, Elizabeth. *The Sexual Circus: Wedekind's Theatre of Subversion*. Oxford and New York: Basil Blackwell, 1987.
Booth, Wayne C. *A Rhetoric of Irony*. Chicago: University of Chicago Press, 1974.
Bordwell, David. 'The Art Cinema as a Mode of Film Practice.' *Film Criticism* 4, no. 1 (1979): 56–64.
Bradbury-Rance, Clara. *Lesbian Cinema after Queer Theory*. Edinburgh: Edinburgh University Press, 2019.
Bradshaw, Peter. 'Attenberg – Review.' *Guardian*, 2 September 2011. https://www.theguardian.com/film/2011/sep/01/attenberg-film-review.
Brady, Tara. 'Lucile Hadihalilovic: "The First Idea was the Male Pregnancy and the Hospital."' *Irish Times*, 5 May 2016. https://www.irishtimes.com/culture/film/lucile-hadihalilovic-the-first-idea-was-the-male-pregnancy-and-the-hospital-1.2636456.
Breillat, Catherine. '*Fat Girl*: About the Title.' *Criterion*, 3 May 2011. https://www.criterion.com/current/posts/1846-fat-girl-about-the-title.

British Board of Film Classification. '*Baise-moi.*' *BBFC*, 26 February 2001. https://www.bbfc.co.uk/AFF165545/.
Brooks, Xan. 'Gaspar Noé: "Six People Walked Out of Climax? No! I Usually Have 25%".' *Guardian*, 22 May 2018. https://www.theguardian.com/film/2018/may/22/gaspar-noe-six-people-walked-out-of-climax-no-i-usually-have-25.
Buckley, Cara. 'When Rape Onscreen is Directed by a Woman.' *New York Times*, 6 August 2019. https://www.nytimes.com/2019/08/02/movies/rape-film-nightingale.html.
Bürger, Peter. *Theory of the Avant-Garde*. Translated by Michael Shaw. Minneapolis: Minnesota University Press, 1984.
Chao, Shun-liang. '"A Tomato is Also a Child's Balloon": Surrealist Humour as a Moral Attitude.' In *Humour in the Arts: New Perspectives*, edited by Vivienne Westbrook and Shun-liang Chao, 194–216. New York: Routledge, 2019.
Chauvin, Jean-Sébastian and Stéphane Delorme. 'L'irrémédiable: dialogue avec Claire Denis.' *Cahiers du cinéma* 691 (2013): 82–8.
Chocano, Carina. 'Anatomy of a Film Both Graphic, Abstract.' *Los Angeles Times*, 27 September 2004. https://www.latimes.om/archives/la-xpm-2004-sep-27-et-breillat27-story.html.
Cixous, Hélène. 'The Laugh of the Medusa.' Translated by Keith Cohen and Paula Cohen. *Signs: Journal of Women in Culture and Society* 1, no. 4 (1976): 875–93.
Clark, T. J. *The Painting of Modern Life: Paris in the Art of Manet and His Followers*. Princeton: Princeton University Press, 1984.
Clarke, Cath. 'Catherine Breillat: "I Love Blood. It's in All My Films".' *Guardian*, 16 July 2010. https://www.theguardian.com/film/2010/jul/15/catherine-breillat-interview.
Clarke, Cath. 'The Scary of Sixty-First Review – Outrage-Baiting Jeffrey Epstein Conspiracy Chiller.' *Guardian*, 2 March 2022. https://www.theguardian.com/film/2022/mar/01/the-scary-of-sixty-first-review-jeffrey-epstein-conspiracy.
Clover, Carol J. *Men, Women and Chainsaws: Gender in the Modern Horror Film*. London: BFI, 1992.
Constable, Liz. 'Unbecoming Sexual Desires for Women Becoming Sexual Subjects: Simone de Beauvoir (1949) and Catherine Breillat (1999).' *MLN* 119, no. 4 (2004): 672–95.
Corliss, Richard. '"Bad" Women and Brutal Men.' *Time*, 24 June 2001. http://content.time.com/time/magazine/article/0,9171,148064,00.html.
Corrigan, Timothy. 'The Commerce of Auteurism: A Voice Without Authority.' *New German Critique* 49 (1990): 43–57.
Crook, Simon. 'Viva Review.' *Empire*, 24 April 2009. https://www.empireonline.com/movies/reviews/viva-review/.
Dargis, Manohla. 'Four Nights of Sex and Zero Nights of Fun.' *New York Times*, 15 October 2004. https://www.nytimes.com/2004/10/15/movies/four-nights-of-sex-and-zero-nights-of-fun.html.

Dargis, Manohla. 'Young Girls and Their Bodies, All for the Sake of Art.' *New York Times*, 21 October 2005. https://www.nytimes.com/2005/10/21/movies/young-girls-and-their-bodies-all-for-the-sake-of-art.html.
Dargis, Manohla. 'Swinging Suburbia and the Sensual City.' *New York Times*, 2 May 2008. https://www.nytimes.com/2008/05/02/movies/02viva.html.
Dargis, Manohla. '"High Life" Review: Robert Pattinson Is Lost in Space.' *New York Times*, 4 April 2019. https://www.nytimes.com/2019/04/04/movies/high-life-review.html.
DESTE Foundation for Contemporary Art. 'DESTEFASHIONCOLLECTION.' https://deste.gr/destefashioncollection/.
Dinning, Samantha. 'Claire Denis.' *Senses of Cinema* 50 (April 2009). https://www.sensesofcinema.com/2009/great-directors/claire-denis/.
Doane, Mary Ann. 'Film and the Masquerade: Theorising the Female Spectator.' *Screen* 23, no. 3–4 (1982): 74–87.
Doucouré, Maïmouna. 'I Directed "Cuties." This is What You Need to Know About Modern Girlhood.' *Washington Post*, 15 September 2020. https://www.washingtonpost.com/opinions/cuties-director-maimouna-doucoure-why-i-made-the-film/2020/09/15/7e0ee406-f78b-11ea-a275-1a2c2d36e1f1_story.html.
Downing, Lisa. 'French Cinema's New "Sexual Revolution": Postmodern Porn and Troubled Genre.' *French Cultural Studies* 15, no. 3 (2004): 265–80.
Dyer, Richard. *Only Entertainment*. 2nd edn. London: Routledge, 2002.
Ebert, Chaz. 'An Open Letter to Cuties Director Maïmouna Doucouré from Female Filmmakers.' *RogerEbert.com*, 2 October 2020. https://www.rogerebert.com/features/an-open-letter-to-cuties-director-ma%C3%AFmouna-doucour%C3%A9-from-female-filmmakers.
Ebert, Roger. 'Audience Reacts with Confusion, Anger to Lars Von Trier Film.' *RogerEbert.com*, 20 May 2003. https://www.rogerebert.com/festivals/audience-reacts-with-confusion-anger-to-lars-von-trier-film.
Ebert, Roger. '"Anatomy of Hell" Just Disgusts.' *RogerEbert.com*, 11 November 2004. https://www.rogerebert.com/reviews/anatomy-of-hell-2004.
Ebert, Roger. 'Cannes #6: A Devil's Advocate for "Antichrist."' *RogerEbert.com*, 19 May 2009. https://www.rogerebert.com/roger-ebert/cannes-6-a-devils-advocate-for-antichrist).
Eklöf, Isabella and Victoria Carmen Sonne. https://www.sensesofcinema.com/2009/great-directors/claire-denis/. 'LEGION M Sundance 2018 HOLIDAY Isabella Eklof.' YouTube video, 13:10. *Legion M*, uploaded 13 March 2018. https://www.youtube.com/watch?v=7YJ64SrcS-A.
Eklöf, Isabella. 'In Conversation with Isabella Eklöf.' *Another Gaze*, uploaded 5 August 2019. https://www.anothergaze.com/conversation-interview-isabella-eklof/.
Eklöf, Isabella. 'On *Holiday*.' In *Holiday*. Anti-Worlds Blu-ray Extra, 2020.
Fagerholm, Matt. 'A Very Deep Place: Claire Denis on High Life.' *RogerEbert.com*, 15 April 2019. https://www.rogerebert.com/interviews/a-very-deep-place-claire-denis-on-high-life.

Fazekaš, Ana. '(Auto)Biography of Hurt: Representation and Representability of Rape in Feminist Performance Art.' *Sic: Journal of Literature, Culture and Literary Translation* 8, no. 1 (2017): 1–20.

Firsching, Robert. 'The Amazing World of Cult Movies.' *Life of a Star*. Accessed 10 March 2020. https://www.lifeofastar.com/incubus.html (site discontinued).

Foster, Gwendolyn Audrey. '*Anatomy of Hell*: A Feminist Fairy Tale.' *Senses of Cinema* 80 (2016). https://www.sensesofcinema.com/2016/cteq/anatomy-hell/.

Foster, Hal. *Compulsive Beauty*. Cambridge, MA: Massachusetts Institute of Technology Press, 1993.

Freeman, Ellen. '"I'm a Freak, I'm a Witch … I'm Just a Female."' *Lenny Letter*, 26 January 2018. https://www.lennyletter.com/story/interview-the-love-witch-filmmaker-anna-biller.

French, Lisa. '*Centring the Female: The Articulation of Female Experience in the Films of Jane Campion*.' PhD thesis. RMIT University, 2007.

Freud, Sigmund. *A General Introduction to Psychoanalysis*. Translated by G. Stanley Hall. New York: Boni and Liveright, 1920.

Freud, Sigmund. 'The Uncanny.' In *The Standard Edition of the Complete Psychological Works of Sigmund Freud*. Translated by James Strachey and edited by James Strachey, Anna Freud, Alix Strachey and Alan Tyson, 217–56. London: Hogarth, 1953.

Frey, Mattias. *Extreme Cinema: The Transgressive Rhetoric of Today's Art Film Culture*. New Brunswick, NJ: Rutgers University Press, 2016.

Fuller, Graham and Jennifer Kent. 'Once Upon a Time in Van Diemen's Land: An Interview with Jennifer Kent.' *Cinéaste* 44, no. 4 (2019): 25–7.

Galt, Rosalind. *Pretty: Film and the Decorative Image*. New York: Columbia University Press, 2011.

Galt, Rosalind. 'The Animal Logic of Contemporary Greek Cinema.' *Framework: The Journal of Cinema and Media* 58, no. 1–2 (2017): 7–29.

Gibbons, Fiachra and Stuart Jeffries. 'Cannes Audience Left Open-Mouthed.' *Guardian*, 14 May 2001. https://www.theguardian.com/world/2001/may/14/cannes2001.cannesfilmfestival.

Girish, Devika. 'Interview: Jennifer Kent.' *Film Comment Blog*, 30 January 2019. https://www.filmcomment.com/blog/interview-jennifer-kent/.

Gorfinkel, Elena. '"Dated Sexuality": Anna Biller's *Viva* and the Retrospective Life of Sexploitation Cinema.' *Camera Obscura: Feminism, Culture, and Media Studies* 26, no. 3 (2011): 95–135.

Gorfinkel, Elena. 'Unlikely Genres: An Interview with Anna Biller.' *Camera Obscura: Feminism, Culture, and Media Studies* 26, no. 3 (2011): 137–45.

Gorfinkel, Elena. 'Against Lists.' *Another Gaze*, 29 November 2019. https://www.anothergaze.com/elena-gorfinkel-manifesto-against-lists/.

Graham, Ben. 'Director Hits Back after Cinemagoers Walk Out and Yell Criticism during The Nightingale Screening in Sydney.' *News.com.au*, 11 June 2019. https://www.news.com.au/entertainment/movies/new-movies/cinemagoers-

walk-out-and-yell-criticism-during-the-nightingale-premiere-in-sydney/news-story/caff28ba212a573619fe1ed29bc98b2e.
Grant, Catherine. 'Secret Agents: Feminist Theories of Women's Film Authorship.' *Feminist Theory* 2, no.1 (2001): 113–30.
Gregg, Ronald. 'The Documentaries of Barbara Hammer: Lesbian Creativity, Kinship, and Erotic Pleasure in the Historical Margins.' *Camera Obscura: Feminism, Culture, and Media Studies* 36, no. 3 (2021): 105–17.
Grønstad, Asbjørn. 'On the Unwatchable.' In *The New Extremism in Cinema: From France to Europe*, edited by Tanya Horeck and Tina Kendall, 192–206. Edinburgh: Edinburgh University Press, 2011.
Grønstad, Asbjørn. *Screening the Unwatchable: Spaces of Negation in Post-Millennial Art Cinema*. (Basingstoke: Palgrave Macmillan, 2012.
Grønstad, Asbjørn. 'The Two Unwatchables.' In *Unwatchable*, edited by Nicholas Baer, Maggie Hennefeld, Laura Horak and Gunnar Iversen, 151–4. New Brunswick, NJ: Rutgers University Press, 2019.
Guardian News & Media Limited. 'Cannes Courts Controversy Even Before Opening.' *Guardian*, 8 May 2001. https://www.theguardian.com/film/2001/may/08/cannes2001.cannesfilmfestival1.
Hadžihalilović, Lucile. 'Interviews: Lucile Hadzihalilovic.' *Mimi*. Pathfinder Home Entertainment (DVD Extra), 2012.
Hadžihalilović, Lucile. '"Evolution" Q&A | Lucile Hadžihalilović | New Directors/New Films 2016.' YouTube video, 31:41. 15 April 2016, filmed at Film Society Lincoln Center, New York, NY. https://www.youtube.com/watch?v=EFZLot0Cj3g.
Hadžihalilović, Lucile. 'EARWIG Q&A | TIFF 2021.' YouTube video, 22:00. 11 September 2021. https://www.youtube.com/watch?v=kYPtF_6J_D4&ab_channel=TIFFOriginals.
Hall, Sandra. 'A Powerful Portrayal of Our Nation's Brutal History.' *Sydney Morning Herald*, 28 August 2019. https://www.smh.com.au/entertainment/movies/a-powerful-portrayal-of-our-nation-s-brutal-history-20190827-p52l6c.html.
Harmon, Steph. 'The Nightingale Director Jennifer Kent Defends "Honest" Depiction of Rape and Violence.' *Guardian*, 11 June 2019. https://www.theguardian.com/film/2019/jun/11/nightingale-director-jennifer-kent-defends-honest-depiction-of-and-violence.
Harrod, Mary and Katarzyna Paszkiewicz (eds). *Women Do Genre in Film and Television*. London: Routledge, 2018.
Hart, Lynda. *Fatal Women: Lesbian Sexuality and the Mark of Aggression*. Princeton: Princeton University Press, 1994.
Harvey, Dennis. 'Film Review: "The Love Witch."' *Variety*, 20 July 2016. https://variety.com/2016/film/markets-festivals/the-love-witch-film-review-1201816145/.
Heller-Nicholas, Alexandra. 'The Love Witch – An Interview with Anna Biller.' *4:3*, 8 July 2016. https://fourthreefilm.com/2016/07/the-love-witch-an-interview-with-anna-biller/.

Heller-Nicholas, Alexandra. 'TIFF18 Review: *High Life*.' *Alliance of Women Film Journalists*, 18 September 2018. https://awfj.org/blog/2018/09/18/tiff18-review-high-life-alexandra-heller-nicholas/.

Heller-Nicholas, Alexandra. 'What's Up Down Under?: HOLIDAY.' *Alliance of Women Film Journalists*, 26 June 2018. https://awfj.org/blog/2018/06/26/holiday-review-by-alexandra-heller-nicholas/.

Heller-Nicholas, Alexandra. 'THE SCARY OF SIXTY-FIRST (Berlinale 2021).' *Alliance of Women Film Journalists*, 2 March 2021. https://awfj.org/blog/2021/03/02/the-scary-of-sixty-first-berlinale-2021-review-by-alexandra-heller-nicholas/.

Heller-Nicholas, Alexandra. 'The Road Less Travelled By.' In *The Nightingale*, 18–31. Second Sight (Blu-ray booklet), 2021.

Higgins, Lynn A. 'Screen/Memory: Rape and Its Alibis in *Last Year at Marienbad*.' In *Rape in Art Cinema*, edited by Dominique Russell, 15–26. New York: Continuum, 2010.

Hjort, Mette. 'The Problem with Provocation: On Lars von Trier, Enfant Terrible of Danish Art Film.' *Kinema: A Journal for Film and Audiovisual Media* 36 (2011): 5–29.

Hoeij, Boyd van. 'Attenberg.' *Variety*, 12 September 2010. https://variety.com/2010/film/markets-festivals/attenberg-1117943531/.

Hole, Kristin Lené. *Towards a Feminist Cinematic Ethics: Claire Denis, Emmanuel Levinas and Jean-Luc Nancy*. Edinburgh: Edinburgh University Press, 2015.

Horeck, Tanya. *Public Rape: Representing Violation in Fiction and Film*. Routledge: Abingdon, 2004.

Horeck, Tanya and Tina Kendall. 'Introduction.' In *The New Extremism in Cinema: From France to Europe*, edited by Tanya Horeck and Tina Kendall, 1–17. Edinburgh: Edinburgh University Press, 2011.

Hughes, Darren. '"High Life" and the Idea of "A Claire Denis Film".' *Mubi Notebook*, 16 April 2019. https://mubi.com/notebook/posts/high-life-and-the-idea-of-a-claire-denis-film.

Huseby, Brooke. 'Claire Denis is in No Rush to Make Films for You – Or Anyone, Besides Herself.' *Interview Magazine*, 16 April 2019. https://www.interviewmagazine.com/film/claire-denis-is-in-no-rush-to-make-films-for-you-high-life.

Huyssen, Andreas. 'Mass Culture as Woman: Modernism's Other.' In *After the Great Divide: Modernism, Mass Culture, Postmodernism*, 44–62. London: Macmillan, 1986.

Ide, Wendy. '"Holiday": Sundance Review.' *Screen Daily*, 20 January 2018. https://www.screendaily.com/reviews/holiday-sundance-review/5125348.article.

Insdorf, Annette. 'The Night Porter.' *Criterion*, 10 January 2000. https://www.criterion.com/current/posts/66-the-night-porter.

Janisse, Kier-La. *House of Psychotic Women: An Autobiographical Topography of Female Neurosis in Horror and Exploitation Film*. Godalming: FAB Press, 2012.

Jenkins, Mark. 'Robert Pattinson's Outer-space Drama "High Life" is Fascinating Yet Frustrating.' *Washington Post*, 10 April 2019. https://www.washingtonpost.com/goingoutguide/movies/robert-pattinsons-outer-space-drama-high-life-is-fascinating-yet-frustrating/2019/04/10/9dcec7a2-5106-11e9-88a1-ed346f0ec94f_story.html.

Julius, Anthony. *Transgressions: The Offences of Art*. London: Thames & Hudson, 2002.

Kaufman, Anthony. 'Athina Rachel Tsangari Studies the Species in Attenberg.' *Village Voice*, 23 March 2011. https://www.villagevoice.com/2011/03/23/athina-rachel-tsangari-studies-the-species-in-attenberg/.

Kearney, Mary Celeste. 'Sparkle: Luminosity and Post-Girl Power Media.' *Continuum: Journal of Media & Cultural Studies* 29, no. 2 (2015): 263–73.

Keesey, Douglas. *Catherine Breillat*. Manchester: Manchester University Press, 2016.

Kehr, Dave. '35 Shots of Rum.' *Film Comment* 45, no. 5 (2009): 67–8.

Kermode, Mark. 'Mark Kermode Reviews The Love Witch.' YouTube video, 4:35. *Kermode and Mayo*, uploaded 11 March 2017. https://www.youtube.com/watch?v=v4Py76VXK4s.

Kermode, Mark. 'Titane Review – Agathe Rousselle is Extraordinary in Palme d'Or-Winning Body Horror.' *Observer*, 26 December 2021. https://www.theguardian.com/film/2021/dec/26/titane-review-julia-ducournau-palme-dor-cronenberg-agathe-rousselle.

Kern, Laura. 'The Miracle of Life.' *Film Comment* 52, no. 3 (2016): 34–9.

Klorfein, Jason. '"Myself as Queen": A Profile and Interview with Anna Biller.' *Bright Lights Film Journal*, 31 January 2010. https://brightlightsfilm.com/myself-as-queen-a-profile-and-interview-with-anna-biller/.

Kohn, Eric. 'Locarno Review: Why Athena [sic] Rachel Tsangari's "The Capsule" Is More Than a Twisted Fashion Show.' *Indiewire*, 4 August 2012. https://www.indiewire.com/2012/08/locarno-review-why-athena-rachel-tsangaris-the-capsule-is-more-than-a-twisted-fashion-show-45788/.

Kohn, Eric. '"Holiday" Review: Devastating Danish Drama Has the Most Unsettling Rape Scene Since "Irreversible" – Sundance 2018.' *Indiewire*, 26 January 2018. https://www.indiewire.com/2018/01/holiday-review-isabella-eklof-rape-sundance-2018-1201921797/.

Koresky, Michael. 'Eclipse Series 19: Chantal Akerman in the Seventies.' *Criterion*, 9 January 2010. https://www.criterion.com/current/posts/1351-eclipse-series-19-chantal-akerman-in-the-seventies.

Langford, Sam. '"The Nightingale" Is Disturbing And Extremely Violent, And It Needs To Be', *Junkee*, 13 June 2019. https://junkee.com/nightingale-review-sydney-film-festival/209216.

Lazic, Elena. 'Empathy and Sympathy in *The Nightingale*.' In *The Nightingale*, 5–17. Second Sight [Blu-ray Booklet], 2021.

Lee, Matthew. 'LIFF 2011: SHE MONKEYS Review.' *Screen Anarchy*, 27 November 2011. https://screenanarchy.com/2011/11/liff-2011-she-monkeys-review.html.

Lee, Nathan. 'Anatomy of Hell.' *Film Comment* 40, no. 5 (2004): 72.

Lemercier, Fabien. 'Lucile Hadzihalilovic is Back With *Evolution*.' *Cineuropa*, 28 August 2014. https://cineuropa.org/en/newsdetail/262214/.

Lim, Dennis. 'Desert Blue.' *Village Voice*, 9 September 2003. https://www.villagevoice.com/2003/09/09/desert-blue-2/.

Lindner, Katharina. 'Queer-ing Texture: Tactility, Spatiality, and Kinesthetic Empathy in *She Monkeys*.' *Camera Obscura: Feminism, Culture, and Media Studies* 32, no. 3 (2017): 121–54.

Lodge, Guy. 'Sundance Film Review: "Holiday".' *Variety*, 30 January 2018. https://variety.com/2018/film/reviews/holiday-review-1202681429/.

Lodge, Guy. '"The Scary of Sixty-First" Review: Nothing Is out of Bounds in This Rude, Riotous, Post-Epstein Horror.' *Variety*, 2 March 2021. https://variety.com/2021/film/reviews/the-scary-of-sixty-first-review-1234919297/.

Loreck, Janice. *Violent Women in Contemporary Cinema*. (Basingstoke: Palgrave, 2016.

Lorentzen, Christian. 'Yorgos Lanthimos's Silly Sadism.' *New Republic*, 10 November 2017. https://newrepublic.com/article/145440/trope-trap-yorgos-lanthimos-distinctive-absurd-new-film-strangely-familiar.

Lübecker, Nikolaj. *The Feel-Bad Film*. Edinburgh: Edinburgh University Press, 2015.

Macfarlane, Steve. '"I'm Actually Trying to Create a Film for Women": Anna Biller on *The Love Witch*.' *Filmmaker Magazine*, 23 June 2016. https://filmmakermagazine.com/98928-im-actually-trying-create-a-film-for-women-anna-biller-on-the-love-witch/.

Machen, Rod. 'FilmStruck Focus: The Short Films of Athina Rachel Tsangari.' *Cinapse*, 16 February 2017. https://cinapse.co/filmstruck-focus-the-short-films-of-athina-rachel-tsangari-fa8886108343.

MacKenzie, Scott. 'On Watching and Turning Away: Ono's *Rape*, *Cinéma Direct* Aesthetics, and the Genealogy of *Cinéma Brut*.' In *Rape in Art Cinema*, edited by Dominique Russell, 159–70. New York: Continuum, 2010.

Macmanus, Robert. 'A Rush on Anna Biller.' *Vice*, 23 September 2009. https://www.vice.com/en/article/5gaq88/a-rush-on-anna-biller.

Macnab, Geoffrey. 'Written on the Body.' *Sight & Sound* 14, no. 12 (2004): 22.

Mahjouri, Shakiel. 'Asia Argento Accuses "Sadistic and Downright Evil" Director Catherine Breillat of Abuse.' *ET Canada*, 30 March 2018. https://etcanada.com/news/314343/asia-argento-accuses-sadistic-and-downright-evil-director-catherine-breillat-of-abuse/.

Margulies, Ivone and Jeremi Szaniawski. 'Introduction: On Women's Films: Moving Thought Across Worlds and Generations.' In *On Women's Films: Across Worlds and Generations*, edited by Ivone Margulies and Jeremi Szaniawski, 1–24. New York: Bloomsbury, 2019.

Marks, Laura U. *The Skin of the Film: Intercultural Cinema, Embodiment, and the Senses*. Durham, NC: Duke University Press, 2000.
Martin, Adrian. 'High Life – Taboo in Space.' *ArtsHub*, 12 March 2019. https://www.screenhub.com.au/news/reviews/film-review-high-life-taboo-in-space-257493-1426240.
Mastrodimos, Ruby. 'Six Men, a Yacht, and an Erection: Troubled Masculinities in Athina Rachel Tsangari's *Chevalier*.' *Another Gaze* 4 (2020): 63–7.
Matthews, J. H. *The Surrealist Mind*. Selinsgrove, PA: Susquehanna University Press, 1991.
Mayer, So. *Political Animals: The New Feminist Cinema*. London: Bloomsbury, 2015.
Mayne, Judith. *Claire Denis*. Urbana: University of Illinois Press, 2005.
McCauley, Anne. 'Beauty or Beast? Manet's Olympia in the Age of Comparative Anatomy.' *Art History* 43, no. 4 (2020): 742–73.
McGill, Hannah. 'Holiday.' *Sight & Sound* 29, no. 9 (2019): 64–5.
McMahon, Laura. 'The Contagious Body of the Film: Claire Denis's *Trouble Every Day*.' In *Transmissions: Essays in French Literature, Thought and Cinema*, edited by Bradley Stephens and Isabelle McNeill, 77–92. Bern: Peter Lang, 2007.
McNeal, Stephanie. 'The Netflix Movie "Cuties" Has Become the Latest Target of #SaveTheChildren Conspiracy Theorists.' *Buzzfeed News*, 12 September 2020. https://www.buzzfeednews.com/article/stephaniemcneal/netflix-cuties-qanon-target.
Milgram, Stanley. 'Behavioral Study of Obedience.' *Journal of Abnormal and Social Psychology* 67, no. 4 (1963): 371–8.
Miraudo, Simon. 'Spider-Man: No Way Home, Licorice Pizza, The French Dispatch, The Scary of Sixty-First, The Worst Person in the World & Ghostbusters: Afterlife (Movie Squad Podcast #56).' *Movie Squad*. RTR FM. Podcast audio, 10:30. 17 December 2021. https://rtrfm.com.au/story/spider-man-no-way-home-licorice-pizza-the-french-dispatch-the-scary-of-sixty-first-the-worst-person-in-the-world-ghostbusters-afterlife-movie-squad-podcast-56/.
Modleski, Tania. 'Women's Cinema as Counterphobic Cinema: Doris Wishman as the Last Auteur.' In *Sleaze Artists: Cinema at the Margins of Taste, Style, and Politics*, edited by Jeffrey Sconce, 47–70. Durham, NC: Duke University Press, 2007.
Möller, Olaf. 'The Capsule.' *Film Comment* 49, no. 1 (2013): 40.
Morgan, Kim. 'Spellbound.' *Sight & Sound* 27, no. 4 (2017): 40–4.
Morreall, John. 'Philosophy of Humor.' In *The Stanford Encyclopedia of Philosophy*, edited by Edward N. Zalta. 20 August 2020. https://plato.stanford.edu/archives/fall2020/entries/humor.
Mulvey, Laura. 'Visual Pleasure and Narrative Cinema.' *Screen* 16, no. 3 (1975): 6–18.
Myers, Kimber. 'Unflinching Crime Drama "Holiday" Details the Life of a Modern European Moll.' *Los Angeles Times*, 7 February 2019. https://

www.latimes.com/entertainment/movies/la-et-mn-mini-holiday-review-20190207-story.html.
Nayman, Adam and Andrew Tracy. 'Arthouse/Grindhouse: Claire Denis and the "New French Extremity".' In *The Films of Claire Denis: Intimacy on the Border*, edited by Marjorie Vecchio, 215–26. London: I. B. Tauris, 2014.
Nelson, Max. 'Bastards.' *Film Comment* 49, no. 5 (2013): 64–5.
Nesselson, Lisa. 'Anatomy of Hell.' *Variety*, 23 January 2004. https://variety.com/2004/film/reviews/anatomy-of-hell-1200536861/.
Noble-Davies, Cain. 'The Scary of Sixty-First.' *FilmInk*, 16 December 2021. https://www.filmink.com.au/reviews/the-scary-of-sixty-first/.
Noé, Gaspar. 'I'm Happy Some People Walk Out During My Film. It Makes the Ones Who Stay Feel Strong.' *Guardian*, 13 March 1999. https://www.theguardian.com/film/1999/mar/12/features3.
Noonan, Will. 'Absurdist Humor.' In *Encyclopedia of Humor Studies*, edited by Salvatore Attardo, 1–4. Thousand Oaks: Sage, 2014.
Nordine, Michael. 'Catherine Breillat Says Asia Argento Is a "Traitor", Harvey Weinstein Isn't That Bad, and She's Against #MeToo.' *IndieWire*, 29 March 2018. https://www.indiewire.com/2018/03/catherine-breillat-asia-argento-harvey-weinstein-jessica-chastain-me-too-1201945040/.
O'Malley, Sheila. 'The Nightingale.' *RogerEbert.com*, 2 August 2019. https://www.rogerebert.com/reviews/the-nightingale-2019.
O'Malley, Sheila. 'Titane.' *RogerEbert.com*, 1 October 2021. https://www.rogerebert.com/reviews/titane-movie-review-2021.
Palmer, Tim. *Brutal Intimacy: Analyzing Contemporary French Cinema*. Middletown, CT: Wesleyan University Press, 2011.
Papadimitriou, Lydia. 'Straitened Circumstances.' *Sight & Sound* 23, no. 1 (2013): 23.
Parsons, Michael J. 'A Suggestion Concerning the Development of Aesthetic Experience in Children.' *Journal of Aesthetics and Art Criticism* 34, no. 3 (1976): 305–14.
Paszkiewicz, Katarzyna. *Genre, Authorship and Contemporary Women Filmmakers*. Edinburgh: Edinburgh University Press, 2019.
Pease, Allison. *Modernism, Mass Culture, and the Aesthetics of Obscenity*. Cambridge: Cambridge University Press, 2000.
Peirse, Alison (ed.). *Women Make Horror: Filmmaking, Feminism, Genre*. New Brunswick, NJ: Rutgers University Press, 2020.
Pinkerton, Nick. 'Interview: Claire Denis.' *Film Comment Blog*, 10 October 2013. https://www.filmcomment.com/blog/interview-claire-denis/.
Pinkerton, Nick. 'The Point of No Return.' *Film Comment* 55, no. 2 (2019): 24–9.
Polan, Dana. 'Auteur Desire.' *Screening the Past*, upload date 1 March 2001. https://www.screeningthepast.com/issue-12-first-release/auteur-desire/.
Pomeroy, Robin. 'Australian Director Jennifer Kent Called a "Whore" at Venice Festival.' *Sydney Morning Herald*, 8 September 2018. https://www.

smh.com.au/entertainment/movies/australian-director-jennifer-kent-called-a-whore-at-venice-festival-20180908-p502iu.html.

Pop, Andrei and Mechtild Widrich, eds. *Ugliness: The Non-Beautiful in Art and Theory*. London: I. B. Tauris, 2014.

Preston, Dominic. '"The Adult World Is Something Mysterious."' *Candid*, 5 May 2016. Accessed 7 February 2017. https://candidmagazine.com/lucile-hadzi-halilovic-interview/ (site discontinued).

Price, Brian. 'Breillat, Catherine.' *Senses of Cinema* 23 (2002). https://www.sensesofcinema.com/2002/great-directors/breillat/.

Projansky, Sarah. *Watching Rape: Film and Television in Postfeminist Culture*. New York: New York University Press, 2001.

Psaras, Marios. *The Queer Greek Weird Wave: Ethics, Politics and the Crisis of Meaning*. Cham: Palgrave Macmillan, 2016.

Pulver, Andrew. 'She Monkeys – Review.' *Guardian*, 18 May 2012. https://www.theguardian.com/film/2012/may/17/she-monkeys-review.

Quandt, James. 'Flesh & Blood: Sex and Violence in Recent French Cinema.' *Artforum* 42, no. 6 (2004): 126–32.

Quigley, Killian. 'The Porcellaneous Ocean: Matter and Meaning in the Rococo Undersea.' In *The Aesthetics of the Undersea*, edited by Margaret Cohen and Killian Quigley, 28–41. Abingdon: Routledge, 2019.

Quinn, Karl. 'Melbourne International Film Festival (online) – Karl Quinn Responds to Tom Ryan and David Stratton about MIFF's Decision to Pull THE TROUBLE WITH BEING BORN from its Program and Reports on His Interview with the Director Sandra Wollner.' *Film Alert 101*, 20 August 2020. http://filmalert101.blogspot.com/2020/08/melbourne-international-film-festival_20.html.

Quinn, Karl. 'Melbourne International Film Festival Dumps Android Child Sex Film.' *The Age*, 30 July 2020. https://www.theage.com.au/culture/movies/melbourne-international-film-festival-dumps-android-child-sex-film-20200725-p55fdr.html.

Rich, B. Ruby. 'Antiporn: Soft Issue, Hard World (*Not a Love Story*) (1982–83).' In *Chick Flicks: Theories and Memories of the Feminist Film Movement*, 261–73. Durham, NC: Duke University Press, 1998.

Rich, B. Ruby. 'In the Name of Feminist Film Criticism.' In *Chick Flicks: Theories and Memories of the Feminist Film Movement*, 62–84. Durham, NC: Duke University Press, 1998.

Rich, B. Ruby. 'Prologue: Sex, Gender, and Consumer Culture.' In *Chick Flicks: Theories and Memories of the Feminist Film Movement*, 253–60. Durham, NC: Duke University Press, 1998.

Richardson, Michael. 'Black Humour.' In *Surrealism: Key Concepts*, edited by Krzysztof Fijalkowski and Michael Richardson, 207–16. Abingdon: Routledge, 2016.

Robb, David. 'Review: *The Scary of Sixty-First* Gleefully and Defiantly Captures the Zeitgeist.' *Slate*, 5 March, 2021. https://www.slantmagazine.com/film/the-scary-of-sixty-first-review-dasha-nekrasova/.

Romney, Jonathan. 'Anatomy Of Hell (Anatomie De L'Enfer).' *Screen Daily*, 27 January 2004. https://www.screendaily.com/anatomy-of-hell-anatomie-de-lenfer/4017050.article.
Romney, Jonathan. 'Freedom to Obey.' *Sight & Sound* 15, no. 10 (2005): 36.
Romney, Jonathan. 'School for Scandal.' *Sight & Sound* 15, no. 10 (2005): 34–6.
Romney, Jonathan. 'Evolution Director Lucile Hadžihalilović: "The Starfish Was the One Worry".' *Guardian*, 29 April 2016. https://www.theguardian.com/film/2016/apr/28/evolution-lucile-hadzihalilovic-starfish-worry-boys-mothers.
Rose, Steve. 'Attenberg, Dogtooth and the Weird Wave of Greek Cinema.' *Guardian*, 27 August 2011. https://www.theguardian.com/film/2011/aug/27/attenberg-dogtooth-greece-cinema.
Rosenkranz, Karl. *Aesthetics of Ugliness: A Critical Edition*. Translated by Andrei Pop and Mechtild Widrich. London: Bloomsbury, 2015.
Rowe, Kathleen. *The Unruly Woman: Gender and the Genres of Laughter*. Austin: University of Texas Press, 1995.
Russell, Dominique. 'Buñuel: Storytelling, Desire and the Question of Rape.' In *Rape in Art Cinema*, edited by Dominique Russell, 41–53. New York: Continuum, 2010.
Russell, Dominique. 'Introduction: Why Rape?' In *Rape in Art Cinema*, edited by Dominique Russell, 1–12. New York: Continuum, 2010.
Russell, Stephen A. with Kate Jinx and Kate Fitzpatrick. 'MIFF Selects: The Festival Gems You Need to Revisit and New Ones to Discover.' *SBS*, 21 July 2021. https://www.sbs.com.au/movies/article/2021/07/19/miff-selects-festival-gems-you-need-revisit-and-new-ones-discover.
Ryan, Tom. 'Melbourne International Film Festival (Online) – Tom Ryan Takes Exception to MIFF Censoring its Selection.' *Film Alert 101*, 11 August 2020. https://filmalert101.blogspot.com/2020/08/melbourne-international-film-festival.html.
San Filippo, Maria. *Provocauteurs and Provocations: Screening Sex in 21st Century Media*. Bloomington: Indiana University Press, 2020.
Sandoval, Isabel. 'Interview: Julia Ducournau.' *Film Comment*, 12 October 2021. https://www.filmcomment.com/blog/interview-julia-ducournau-titane-isabel-sandoval/.
Sarris, Andrew. 'Joan Plowright Is Mrs. Palfrey In May–December Buddy Drama.' *Observer*, 21 November 2005. https://observer.com/2005/11/joan-plowright-is-mrs-palfrey-in-maydecember-buddy-drama/.
Scheffler, Karl. *Women and Art: A Study* [*Die Frau und die Kunst: Eine Studie*]. Berlin: Julius Bard, 1908.
Sconce, Jeffrey. '"Trashing" the Academy: Taste, Excess, and an Emerging Politics of Cinematic Style.' *Screen* 36, no. 4 (1995): 371–93.
Sconce, Jeffrey. 'Introduction.' In *Sleaze Artists: Cinema at the Margins of Taste, Style, and Politics*, edited by Jeffrey Sconce, 1–16. Durham, NC: Duke University Press, 2007.

Secher, Benjamin. 'Catherine Breillat: "All True Artists Are Hated".' *Telegraph*, 5 April 2008. https://www.telegraph.co.uk/culture/film/starsandstories/3672302/Catherine-BreillatAll-true-artists-are-hated.html.

Seidel, Madeleine. 'How The Nightingale Subverts the Rape-revenge Genre.' *Little White Lies*, 13 August 2019. https://lwlies.com/articles/the-nightingale-jennifer-kent-sexual-violence-against-women/.

Sharrett, Christopher. 'The World That is Known: Michael Haneke Interviewed.' *Kinoeye: New Perspectives on European Film* 4, no. 1 (2004). https://www.kinoeye.org/04/01/interview01.php.

Shone, Tom. 'Michael Haneke Goes Cruelty-Free With *Amour*.' *Vulture*, 9 December 2012. https://www.vulture.com/2012/12/michael-haneke-amour-at-nyff.html.

Simon, Alissa. 'She Monkeys.' *Variety*, 5 February 2011. https://variety.com/2011/film/reviews/she-monkeys-1117944506/.

Smith, Neil. 'Claire Denis: Trouble Every Day.' *BBC*, archive date 28 October 2014. https://www.bbc.co.uk/films/2002/12/24/claire_denis_trouble_every_day_interview.shtml.

Sobchack, Vivian. 'Waking Life.' *Film Comment* 41, no. 6 (2005): 46–9.

Sontag, Susan. 'Notes on "Camp"'. In *Against Interpretation and Other Essays*, 275–92. London: Penguin, 2009.

Stamp, Shelley. *Lois Weber in Early Hollywood*. Oakland: University of California Press, 2015.

Stratton, David. 'David Stratton Previews Attenberg.' *Sydney Film Festival*. YouTube video, 1:32. 23 May 2011. https://www.youtube.com/watch?v=v5uVmL6PT54.

Stratton, David. 'Melbourne International Film Festival (online) – David Stratton Has Some Thoughts About MIFF's Decision to Withdraw THE TROUBLE WITH BEING BORN (Sandra Wollner, Austria, 2020) From its Program.' *Film Alert 101*, 12 August 2020. http://filmalert101.blogspot.com/2020/08/melbourne-international-film-festival_12.html.

Stravinsky, Igor. *Stravinsky: An Autobiography*. New York: Simon & Schuster, 1936.

Swash, Rosie. 'She Monkeys Director Wanted Coming-of-Age Movie to Be "Like a Western".' *Guardian*, 28 April 2012. https://www.theguardian.com/film/2012/apr/28/she-monkeys-lisa-aschan-interview.

Szymanek, Angelique. 'Bloody Pleasures: Ana Mendieta's Violent Tableaux.' *Signs: Journal of Women in Culture and Society* 41, no. 4 (2016): 895–925.

Tarr, Carrie with Brigitte Rollet. *Cinema and the Second Sex: Women's Filmmaking in France in the 1980s and 1990s*. New York: Continuum, 2001.

Taylor, Alison. '"A Ghost Mob": Interview With Sandra Wollner.' *Senses of Cinema* 96 (2020). https://www.sensesofcinema.com/2020/interviews/a-ghost-mob-interview-with-sandra-wollner/.

Thanouli, Eleftheria. '"Art Cinema" Narration: Breaking Down a Wayward Paradigm.' *Scope: An Online Journal of Film and Television Studies* 14 (2009). https://www.nottingham.ac.uk/scope/documents/2009/june-2009/thanouli.pdf.

BIBLIOGRAPHY

Thomas, Sarah. 'Sydney Film Festival Controversy as Audiences Walk Out of The Nightingale.' *Australian Broadcasting Corporation*, 11 June 2019. https://www.abc.net.au/news/2019-06-11/sydney-film-festival-the-nightingale-premiere-sparks-controversy/11198288.

Thornham, Sue. *What If I Had Been the Hero?: Investigating Women's Cinema*. London: BFI, 2012.

Thornham, Sue. *Spaces of Women's Cinema: Space, Place and Genre in Contemporary Women's Filmmaking*. London: BFI, 2019.

Tigges, Wim. *An Anatomy of Literary Nonsense*. Amsterdam: Rodopi, 1988.

Tracz, Tamara. '*Je tu il elle*.' *Senses of Cinema* 67 (2013). https://www.sensesofcinema.com/2013/cteq/je-tu-il-elle/.

Tsangari, Athina Rachel. 'SFF2011 – Athina Rachel Tsangari – Attenberg.' Sydney Film Festival. YouTube video, 6:08. 13 June 2011. https://www.youtube.com/watch?v=YheMJQf9BtI.

Tsangari, Athina Rachel. 'Athina Rachel Tsangari Interview – The Seventh Art.' YouTube video, 50:47. Uploaded 24 January 2013, filmed at Onsite Gallery at OCAD University, Toronto, ON. https://www.youtube.com/watch?v=w5ISGKi-NtI.

Tsangari, Athina Rachel. '"Attenberg" Q&A | Athina Rachel Tsangari.' YouTube video, 38:03. 7 October 2015, filmed at Film Society Lincoln Center, New York, NY. https://www.youtube.com/watch?v=hlCiOjkCAb8.

Tsangari, Athina Rachel. 'NYFF Live | Athina Rachel Tsangari | Chevalier.' YouTube video, 37:39. 23 October 2015, filmed at Film Society Lincoln Center, New York, NY. https://www.youtube.com/watch?v=x6BQJ_EUB-Q.

Tsangari, Athina Rachel. 'GFF Live: Athina Rachel Tsangari.' Göteborg Film Festival. YouTube video, 1:00:17. Streamed live on 5 February 2016. https://www.youtube.com/watch?v=FbV_IsuKJto.

Vecchio, Marjorie. 'Preface.' In *The Films of Claire Denis: Intimacy on the Border*, edited by Marjorie Vecchio, xiii–xviii. London: I. B. Tauris, 2014.

Vincendeau, Ginette. 'Family Plots: The Fathers and Daughters of French Cinema.' *Sight & Sound* 1, no. 11 (1992): 14–17.

Vincendeau, Ginette. '*Innocence*.' *Sight & Sound* 15, no. 10 (2005): 68–9.

Vincendeau, Ginette. '*Fat Girl*: Sisters, Sex, and Sitcom.' *Criterion*, 3 May 2011. https://www.criterion.com/current/posts/495-fat-girl-sisters-sex-and-sitcom.

Von Goethe, Johann Wolfgang. *Theory of Colors*. Translated by Charles Eastlake. Cambridge, MA: MIT Press, 1970.

Von Trier, Lars and Thomas Vinterberg. 'The Dogme '95 Manifesto and Vow of Chastity.' In *Film Manifestos and Global Cinema Cultures: A Critical Anthology*, edited by Scott MacKenzie, 201–2. Berkeley: University of California Press, 2014.

Walker, John A. *Art and Outrage: Provocation, Controversy, and the Visual Arts*. London: Pluto Press, 1999.

Walton, Saige. 'Gestures of Intimacy: Claire Denis' *I Can't Sleep*.' *Senses of Cinema* 63 (2012). https://www.sensesofcinema.com/2012/cteq/gestures-of-intimacy-claire-denis-i-cant-sleep/.

Ward, Sarah. 'Film Review: The Nightingale is Furious and Grueling.' *Screen Hub*, 29 August 2019. https://www.screenhub.com.au/news/reviews/film-review-the-nightingale-is-furious-and-gruelling-257155-1426023/.

Welkos, Robert W. '"Irreversible" Not For the Faint of Heart.' *Los Angeles Times*, 3 March 2003. https://www.latimes.com/archives/la-xpm-2003-mar-03-et-itkirreversible3-story.html.

Weston, Hillary. 'Anna Biller's Pleasure Principles.' *Criterion*, 29 May 2019. https://www.criterion.com/current/posts/6400-anna-biller-s-pleasure-principles.

Wheatley, Catherine. 'She Monkeys.' *Sight & Sound 22, no. 6 (2012): 76.*

Wheatley, Catherine. 'La Famille Denis.' In *The Films of Claire Denis: Intimacy on the Border*, edited by Marjorie Vecchio, 63–77. London: I. B. Tauris, 2014.

White, Dominic. 'The Horror of Australian Films: Entertainment.' *Australian Financial Review*, 17 January 2015: 4.

White, Patricia. *Women's Cinema, World Cinema: Projecting Contemporary Feminisms*. Durham, NC: Duke University Press, 2015.

Widrich, Mechtild. 'The "Ugliness" of the Avant-Garde.' In *Ugliness: The Non-Beautiful in Art and Theory*, edited by Andrei Pop and Mechtild Widrich, 69–82. London: I. B. Tauris, 2014.

Williams, Linda Ruth. 'The Limits of Sex: Sick Sisters.' *Sight & Sound* 11, no. 7 (2001): 28–9.

Williams, Linda. 'Proliferating Pornographies On/Scene: An Introduction.' In *Porn Studies*, edited by Linda Williams, 1–23. Durham, NC: Duke University Press, 2004.

Williams, Linda. 'Cinema's Sex Acts.' *Film Quarterly* 67, no. 4 (2014): 9–25.

Wilson, Emma. 'Contemporary French Women Filmmakers.' *French Studies* 59, no. 2 (2005): 217–23.

Windsor, Harry. 'Tasmanian Torments: Jennifer Kent's "The Nightingale".' *The Monthly*, 1 September 2019. https://www.themonthly.com.au/issue/2019/september/1567260000/harry-windsor/tasmanian-torments-jennifer-kent-s-nightingale#mtr.

Wray, John. 'Minister of Fear.' *New York Times Magazine*, 23 September 2007. https://nyti.ms/2rZn9VS.

York, Keva. 'The Nightingale Roots Horror in Tasmania's Colonial History with a Tale of Revenge.' Australian Broadcasting Corporation, 29 August 2019. https://www.abc.net.au/news/2019-08-29/the-nightingale-review-jennifer-kent-tasmanian-history-colonial/11450322.

Index

#MeToo, 31, 63
#SaveTheChildren, 167

acting *see* performance
adolescence, 37–40, 41
Adolfsson. Josefine, 37
Akerman, Chantal
　Je tu il elle, 30
Algren, Johanne, 61
alienation *see* estrangement
ambiguity, 38–40, 73, 80, 90–1, 95, 104, 109
animals, 144, 145, 149, 153, 156
Antoniak, Urszula, 12
　Code Blue, 11, 56
Aschan, Lisa
　She Monkeys, 25–6, 37–43
art cinema, 2, 6, 7–9, 14–15, 24, 28–9, 82, 83, 89, 96
Artaud, Antonin *see* Theatre of Cruelty
aspect ratio, 69–70
auteur
　as concept, 2, 6, 8–9
　female, 3, 11–12, 13–14, 169, 170
　male, 10–11
　non-binary, 14
　theory, 13–14, 170
avant-garde, 6–7, 17, 28–9, 81–5, 89, 146–8

Balance Ton Porc, 31
Bataille, Georges
　Story of the Eye, 38, 40
Berlin International Film Festival, 2, 166, 168
Brecht, Bertolt, 58–9

Breckon, Anna
　Thrash-Her, 37
Breillat, Catherine
　A Real Young Girl, 24–5, 33–4
　Anatomy of Hell, 31–6
　Fat Girl, 41–5
　Romance, 25, 31–2, 34
Buñuel, Luis, 82, 147
　An Andalusian Dog, 7–8, 11, 54–5, 82, 96, 113
　The Golden Age, 17, 82
Butler, David
　Calamity Jane, 125, 127

camp, 122, 124–9
Cannes Film Festival, 2, 11, 52, 100, 102, 169
Catholicism, 35–6
Cavani, Liliana, 1, 14, 169
　The Night Porter, 3–4
children, 79–80, 85–7, 90–6; *see also* girlhood
Chytilová, Věra, 1, 14, 169
　Daisies, 3, 148
cinéma brut, 2, 56, 58–9, 62, 89
cinéma direct, 59, 62
cinéma du corps, 2
cinematography, 30, 33, 34, 36, 63–5, 69, 71, 87–8, 103, 113–15, 149
Colette, Sidonie Gabrielle, 37
colour, 84, 91, 93–4, 122, 135
counterphobic viewing, 19, 172–3
Cox, Geoff, 79, 102
Criterion, 47n, 121, 140

dada, 146–7
Demy, Jacques, 127

Donkey Skin, 141n
The Young Girls of Rochefort, 133, 141n
Denis, Claire
　35 Shots of Rum, 104, 107, 111, 113
　Bastards, 105–6, 108–9, 120n
　Beau travail, 103, 113
　Chocolat, 100, 103
　High Life, 100, 102–3, 105, 107–8, 109–12, 114–17
　I Can't Sleep, 102
　Nénette and Boni, 103–4,111
　The Intruder, 102
　Trouble Every Day, 17, 100, 102, 105, 112–14, 116–17
　White Material, 103
dépaysement, 157
Despentes, Virginie
　Baise-moi, 4, 27, 56–8
DESTE Foundation for Contemporary Art, 155–6, 159
Dodd, Margaret
　This Woman is Not a Car, 148
Dogme 95, 83
Doucouré, Maïmouna
　Cuties, 16, 167–8
Dreyer, Carl Theodor
　Gertrud, 138
Duchamp, Marcel
　L.H.O.O.Q., 147
Ducournau, Julia
　Titane, 16, 169
Dulac, Germaine
　The Smiling Madame Beudet, 148
Dumont, Bruno, 20n, 100, 116
　Twentynine Palms, 52, 56
Dunham, Lena, 28

editing, 59, 62–5, 74n
Eklöf, Isabella, 12, 60–1
　Holiday, 53, 60–5
　Notes from Underground, 60–1
　Willkommen in Barbaristan, 60
Elíasson, Ólafur, 116
empathy, 39–40, 43, 45, 69–71, 72, 77n
épater les bourgeois, 7, 9, 147
estrangement, 65, 69, 153–4, 159
experimental film, 15, 26–7, 29–30, 37, 148

family, 103–4, 106–11, 148, 164n
Fargeau, Jean-Pol, 100, 102
fathers, 104, 106, 107–11, 114, 119n, 150–1, 152, 160
Faulkner, William
　Sanctuary, 101, 105
feel-bad film, 8
femininity, 41, 91, 93, 148, 157–60
feminism, 10, 13–14, 19, 24, 28–30, 52, 63, 70–1, 117, 122, 125, 130–40, 140n;
　see also humour, feminist
fetishism, 28, 30, 71–2, 92–5, 114–15, 169; see also gaze, visual pleasure, voyeurism
film festivals, 17
　controversies, 2, 11, 17, 33, 37, 53, 65, 67, 100, 146, 166–7
Ford, John
　The Searchers, 71
French cinema, 9, 82, 31, 59, 82, 91–2, 100, 107–8, 109

gaze
　child, 93–6
　male, 26, 28, 40, 47n, 92
　observational, 32–3, 154
gender performance, 158–9
genre, 15
　film noir, 108
　gothic, 15, 155, 156
　horror, 15, 122–3, 125, 128, 134–6, 138, 156
　musical, 124–8, 128, 130–1, 133–4
　rape-revenge, 15, 72
　science fiction, 15, 100
　sexploitation, 121–3, 124–9, 131–3
　Western, 38, 122, 125–8, 129–31
Gill, E. O.
　Thrash-Her, 37
girlhood, 41–5, 93, 168; see also children
girlshine, 41, 42, 44
girl-training, 157–9, 165n, 171
Greek cinema, 119n, 148, 163n
Greek weird wave, 119n, 143–4, 148–9, 152, 154, 163n

Hadžihalilović, Lucile
　De Natura, 80, 58

Earwig, 85, 86, 88, 89, 90, 91, 95
Évolution, 79–81, 85–96
Innocence, 79–81, 85–96
Mimi, 79–80, 85–6, 90, 91, 92, 93, 95
Nectar, 80, 85, 90
Hall, Radclyffe, 37
Hammer, Barbara, 26, 29–30
Haneke, Michael, 2, 3, 11, 54, 116, 123
   Benny's Video, 11
   Funny Games, 11
   The White Ribbon, 107, 109
haptic visuality, 112–13, 116–17, 120n;
   see also sensation
humour, 143–62
   absurd, 145, 146–7, 151, 152, 154, 159, 160–1, 164n
   black, 152, 159
   feminist, 147–8, 161–2
   incongruity, 146–9, 151, 157–8
   subversive, 147–9
   surrealism, 146–8, 157, 159, 161

identification, 13, 39–40, 43–5, 59, 65, 70–2, 77n, 91–6, 114, 153, 172;
   see also empathy
incest, 104–11, 114–17, 150
Indigenous Australians, 53, 67, 68, 70, 72
irony, 43, 124–6, 136, 138, 139

Kakogiannis, Michalis
   A Girl in Black, 156
Kaplan, Jonathan
   The Accused, 56, 70–1, 77–8n
Kavaitė, Alantė, 79
Kent, Jennifer, 65–7
   The Babadook, 66, 67
   The Nightingale, 15, 17, 53–4, 60, 64, 65–73
Kokkinos, Ana
   The Book of Revelation, 16, 75n
Kurosawa, Akira
   Rashomon, 55, 73
   The Bad Sleep Well, 101

Laird, Nick, 102
Lanthimos, Yorgos, 8, 102, 148–9, 164n
   Dogtooth, 8, 85, 107, 109, 113, 164n

laughter, 33, 34, 144–9, 151, 152, 157, 161;
   see also humour
Lewis, Herschell Gordon
   Suburban Roulette, 125, 131, 133

Manet, Édouard
   Olympia, 17, 34–5, 145
masculinity, 10, 12, 84, 108, 137, 160, 165n
masquerade see gender performance
Mehta, Deepa
   Fire, 15
   Water, 12
Melbourne International Film Festival, 166–7
Melbourne Women in Film Festival, 37
Mendieta, Ana
   Untitled (Rape Scene), 57, 70
Metzger, Radley
   Camille 2000, 132
Milgram, Stanley, 146
misogyny, 56–8, 65, 68, 123

Nekrasova, Dasha
   The Scary of Sixty-First, 16, 168
Netflix, 167
New Extremity, 2, 4, 8, 9, 56, 89, 100
Noé, Gaspar, 2, 11, 20n, 79, 98n, 116
   Carne, 79, 106, 107, 109
   I Stand Alone, 11, 79, 98n, 106–7, 109
   Irréversible, 8, 52, 56, 59, 74n, 89, 113
non-binary filmmakers, 14
nonsense, 145, 164n

obscenity, 2, 7, 25, 26–9, 30, 31–6
Oxenberg, Jan
   A Comedy in Six Unnatural Acts, 148

paedophilia, 42–3, 60–1, 87, 92–3, 95, 98n, 166–8
paracinema, 128–9
Pasolini, Pier Paolo
   Salò, or the 120 Days of Sodom, 52, 85, 113
patriarchs see fathers
patriarchy, 30, 138, 147–9, 161–2
performance, 126–7, 130–1, 132, 133–4, 151–4, 158–9
pornography, 9, 26, 27–30, 36, 57, 127

pretty aesthetics, 81, 83–5, 88–90, 91–5
primitivism, 97n
provocateur
    gendering of, 1, 9–12, 169
    origins of, 10
provocation
    aesthetics of, 81–5, 171
    as aggression, 12, 54–5, 169
    as author-recipient relation, 5–6
    gendering of, 9–12, 171
    history, 6–9

QAnon, 167
queer
    aesthetics, 84, 91
    controversies, 37
    culture, 126, 127–8
    desire, 37–40
    Greek weird wave, 151, 154
    sex scenes, 26, 29–30, 37, 47n, 49n

race, 72, 123
Randall, Nat
    Thrash-Her, 37
rape
    as plot device, 63, 71
    in visual arts, 57, 70, 75n
    male victims, 75n, 110
    non-cisgendered victims, 75n
    non-explicit depictions of, 75n
rape scenes, 8, 27, 52–73
    censorship, 4
    feminist critiques, 56–7, 63
    in art cinema, 52–4, 54–60, 73
Resnais, Alain
    Last Year at Marienbad, 52, 55, 73
rococo, 94
romantic relationships, 134–40
Romero, George
    Jack's Wife, 125, 134, 135, 139, 142n
Rubin, Barbara, 24
    Christmas on Earth, 27

Saab, Jocelyne
    Dunia, 15
Schneemann, Carolee, 24, 26
    Fuses, 27

scopic offence, 7–8, 81–3, 85, 89, 96, 113, 116
scopophilia *see* fetishism, gaze, visual
    pleasure, voyeurism
sensation, 39–40, 71, 94, 112–17; *see also*
    haptic visuality
sex scenes
    art cinema, 28, 29–30, 45–6
    explicit, 25, 27–8, 29–30, 45–6
    queer, 29–30, 37, 47n, 49n
    real, 4, 27
sexual violence, 4, 49n, 171, *see also* rape
shame, 27, 28, 41–6, 64, 89
Sidney, George
    The Harvey Girls, 125, 127, 130
sleaze, 136, 142n
Stravinsky, Igor
    The Rite of Spring, 17, 146
Sundance Film Festival, 52, 66, 167
surrealism, 7, 82, 85, 88, 146–7, 148, 156,
    157, 158, 161
Sydney International Film Festival, 17, 53,
    65–6, 67, 143
symbolists, 85, 88

taboo, 32, 33–4, 38, 43, 86, 101, 103–4,
    107, 112, 114–17, 150, 172
taste, 7, 10, 12, 14–15, 105, 170
    oppositional, 122, 124–5, 128–9, 134–5
teenagers *see* adolescence
Theatre of Cruelty, 7, 58, 83
theatre of the absurd, 146–7
Thi, Coralie Trinh
    Baise-moi, 4, 27, 56–8
Toronto International Film Festival, 33,
    80, 146
transgression, 6
    in art, 9, 28, 82, 172
    in cinema, 8–9, 103–11
Trier, Lars von, 2, 9, 11, 66, 83, 116
    Antichrist, 8, 85, 113
    Dogville, 52, 56, 66, 85
    Manderlay, 9
Tsangari, Athina Rachel
    Attenberg, 143–5, 149–54
    Chevalier, 145, 160, 161, 165n
    The Capsule, 155–62
    The Slow Business of Going, 145

ugliness, 7, 36, 82–3, 89, 96
uncanny, the, 88, 156–9
unwatchable, the, 7, 96

Venice Film Festival, 52, 53, 65, 66
Vinterberg, Thomas, 83
   The Celebration, 107, 109
violence, 5, 37–8, 40, 50n, 71–2, 113, 138–9
visual pleasure, 80–1, 85–90, 123; *see also* fetishism, gaze, voyeurism
visual transgression *see* scopic offence

voyeurism, 5, 57, 59, 64, 69, 71–2, 73, 87, 89, 95; *see also* fetishism, gaze, visual pleasure

Waliszewska, Aleksandra, 156
Weber, Lois
   Hypocrites, 3
Wishman, Doris, 19
   Diary of a Nudist, 131
Wollner, Sandra
   The Trouble with Being Born, 16, 166–7, 168